DOING POLITICAL SCIENCE

DOING POLITICAL SCIENCE

An Introduction to Political Analysis

Alan S. Zuckerman
BROWN UNIVERSITY

Westview Press
BOULDER ■ SAN FRANCISCO ■ OXFORD

All rights reserved. No part of this publication may be reproduced or transmitted in any form or by any means, electronic or mechanical, including photocopy, recording, or any information storage and retrieval system, without permission in writing from the publisher.

Copyright © 1991 by Westview Press, Inc.

Published in 1991 in the United States of America by Westview Press, Inc., 5500 Central Avenue, Boulder, Colorado 80301, and in the United Kingdom by Westview Press, 36 Lonsdale Road, Summertown, Oxford OX2 7EW

Library of Congress Cataloging-in-Publication Data
Zuckerman, Alan S., 1945–
  Doing political science : an introduction to political analysis / Alan S. Zuckerman.
    p. cm.
  Includes bibliographical references and index.
  ISBN 0-8133-1002-4 (cloth). — ISBN 0-8133-1003-2 (paperback)
  1. Political science. 2. Political science—Research. I. Title.
JA71.Z83 1991
320—dc20   91-15809
                                                                           CIP

Printed and bound in the United States of America

The paper used in this publication meets the requirements of the American National Standard for Permanence of Paper for Printed Library Materials Z39.48-1984.

10   9   8   7   6   5   4   3   2   1

For Greg, Ezra, and Shara
with love and pride.
May they receive the blessings of Psalm 128.

CONTENTS

Acknowledgments ix

1 The Point of Departure 1

What We Assume in Order to Do Political Science, 3
The Language of Political Science:
  Theories, Hypotheses, Concepts, and Variables, 6
The Cacophonous Sound of Political Science, 13
What Comes Next, 14

**2 Explaining Political Phenomena:
The Case of Turnout in National Elections** 17

The Classic "American Model":
  Wolfinger and Rosenstone's Analysis of Turnout, 18
Alternative Analyses of Turnout:
  Studies by Powell and Jackman, 28
Alternative Explanations of Turnout:
  Piven and Cloward's Analysis, 34
Sorting the Alternative Analyses of Turnout, 38
Examining the Alternative Analyses:
  Why Turnout in the United States Is Different, 39

3 Research Schools in Political Science 43

Rational Choice Theory, 45
Political Attitudes and Political Behavior, 52
Approaches from Anthropology, 57
Marx's Theory, 63
Weber's Social Science, 72
The Next Step, 80

**4 How Research Schools Structure Analysis
and Produce Conflicting Visions of Politics** 83

Marx and Weber on Revolution in Capitalist Societies, 85
The Analysis of Political Groups and Collective Action, 87
The Analysis of Vote Choice, 94

The Analysis of Demonstrations and Political Violence, 104
Conclusion, 112

5 How We Know When We Know: Testing Claims to Knowledge in Political Science — 115

Requisites for Empirical Propositions
 in Political Science, 117
Goals for Empirical Propositions About Politics:
 Strive to Make Strong Claims to Knowledge, 120
Methods to Accept or Reject Empirical Propositions, 122
Evaluating What We Know About the Relationship
 Between Party Identification and Vote Choice, 134
Evaluating the Utility of Detailed Case Studies, 138
The Limits of Empirical Tests of Propositions, 141
The Role of Theory in the Evaluation
 of Empirical Propositions, 143
Conclusions and Implications, 148

6 What We Mean When We Call Political Science a Science: Ambiguity and Certainty in the Pursuit of Knowledge — 151

All Sciences Seek Order in "the Multiplicity
 of Immediate Sense Experiences," 152
There Is No Knowledge Without Emotions:
 The Role of Passion in Science, 154
There Is No Knowledge Without Reason and Evidence, 157
In Science, Nonrational Factors Influence but
 Do Not Determine Claims to Knowledge, 162
Ambiguity and Certainty in Science, 167
Political Science as a Science, 177
Doing Political Science, 179

References — 183
About the Book and Author — 191
Index — 193

ACKNOWLEDGMENTS

Doing Political Science is the product of a dare. It is now more than a decade since my colleague Roger Cobb and I set out to prove that political science—not only politics but the abstractions and demands of the discipline—could be taught to undergraduate students. We chose to answer directly their sometimes stated and frequently implied question: Why do you teach us *political science* when we are interested in *politics*? In response, we constructed a course that directly addresses the intellectual puzzles of political science. That course, Brown University's "Foundations of Political Analysis" (Political Science 50), provided the basis for this book. Roger and I taught the course together in the spring and fall semesters of 1980. I am happy to acknowledge my debt for his partnership in creating the course and for teaching me how to keep the minds of students engaged in a lecture.

The course and the book stand as testimony to Brown University's policy of encouraging excellent teaching and research, which allows faculty to offer daring material. I am especially delighted to thank the many students, now more than one thousand, who have taken Political Science 50, struggling with the material and waiting for it to click. Several of these students provided assistance and comments on the book as I wrote it. Molly O'Rourke and Robert Greene were extraordinarily able research assistants; both pushed me hard, helping me to compose a more elegant and powerful exposition than I would have written without them. Their aid was the happy product of undergraduate teaching and research assistantships, and for that I would like to thank Deans Sheila Blumstein and Karen Romer. Janet Trafimow commented on an early draft of the manuscript and helped to convince me that I should write the book. And Nicholas Valentino directed me to important work on Albert Einstein's visions of science. The accomplishments of these students and their colleagues in Political Science 50 prove that Roger Cobb and I won the dare.

I take great pleasure in thanking several individuals for their contributions to *Doing Political Science*. The idea of the book first emerged in a conversation with Spencer Carr, senior editor at Westview Press. He has been indefatigable, generous, precise, demanding, and wise in seeing the volume to completion. Detailed criticisms of each line of the manuscript were provided by a number of people: Spencer Carr; Mary Ann Borrelli of Knox College, who served as one of the outside readers of the manuscript; Mark Irving Lichbach, my former student, who is now a friend and teacher and will soon be at the University of Colorado at Boulder; and two of my colleagues at Brown University, Roger Cobb and Darrell West. They provided help when I needed it, and I thank them while taking full responsibility for what I wrote.

I would not have started, kept to, or finished this book without the love and guidance of my wife, Roberta Zuckerman. Ricki, as I have been calling her since we were teenagers, knew from the outset that I should write this text. Whenever my interest faded, she helped to bring me back to the task. Here, as in every aspect of my life, her support is vital to me.

During the months of writing, my parents, Edith and Jack Zuckerman, passed away, dimming the lights of my world. They would have *kvelled* from this book, too. I am saddened to note that my friend Baruch Bokser also died during this period of time. My life is diminished by these losses.

I am dedicating *Doing Political Science* to our children, Gregory, Ezra, and Shara. Greg, a graduate of Brandeis University, now lives and works in Manhattan and helped to organize some of the material in the final chapter. Ezra, who is studying political science at Columbia University, took Political Science 50 during the summer of 1989. And Shara, who studies at the Maimonides School in Brookline, Massachusetts, will soon be attending New York University. Ricki and I thank God for our children.

Alan S. Zuckerman

CHAPTER 1

The Point of Departure

When we do political science, we set out to discover uniformities in the political world. We assume that the swirl of political events—wars, elections, coups, riots, incidences of corruption, and other political phenomena—can be understood in rather simple and precise ways. We develop concepts, hypotheses, and theories in order to describe and explain politics. Using the assumptions and methods of one or more of the research schools of political science, we are guided in our search by the rules of logic and the proper use of evidence. Political science, like any science, uses analytic techniques to posit and explore regularities in the world around us.

On first encounter, many students may find it strange that political science draws attention to both the general and the abstract. Some students come to the study of politics with a deep interest in current events. They expect to learn the particulars of politics: the relevant names, dates, and events; who said what to whom, and what did he or she mean by that? When they consider how we know what we know, they may believe analysis follows the principle that the closer one is to the phenomena, the more one knows. Other students seek to improve, perhaps even transform, the communities in which they live. Still others may pursue both of these goals. And all students may be puzzled by the effort to detect uniformities and offer hypotheses that apply to diverse cases of politics and by the methodological concerns that accompany this effort.

As a generalizing science, political science is not bound to the study of current events or to issues of political relevance. When we analyze something in the news, we do so with an eye to the more abstract theoretical issues at stake. We want to explain, for example, the collapse of the Communist regimes in Eastern Europe not only to know more about what we witnessed but also to address general questions, such as the formation of political movements and revolution in authoritarian regimes, revolution in industrial societies, and the conditions under which revolution occurs without violence. In political science, interest in the particular draws attention to general issues.

2 ■ THE POINT OF DEPARTURE

Neither citizenship training nor preparation for the revolution directs the study of politics. In the university, there is virtue in simply trying to know how the world works. At the same time, you have every right to care deeply about what you study. There is no rule that political scientists may have no preferences about the issues of war and peace or prosperity and poverty, just as there is no expectation that cancer researchers will be impartial about what they study. However, you must be objective, in the sense of being willing to test your ideas and accept the results of fair tests, even if they negate your preferences.

Political science offers theories that enable us to analyze political phenomena. Consider the goal of developing an explanation of revolution that can account for the transformation of power that occurred in Eastern Europe and Russia at the end of the 1980s, the Russian Revolution of 1917, and the revolutions in France, Cuba, and Germany, as well. To solve this puzzle, it is first necessary to decide what the concept "revolution" signifies. Are all of these events examples of the same concept? How would you define revolution so that we could decide which of these cases is a true revolution and which is not? You will ask the "what" questions: "What is a revolution?" or "What would indicate the presence of a revolution?" After all, no one actually sees a revolution as such, and we need to develop operations by which we can establish the defining characteristics of this phenomenon. Having defined revolution, you must then explain its presence by answering the "why" questions. These questions may come in simple or complicated form: "Why do revolutions occur?" or "What factors are present whenever a revolution occurs?" or "In what ways do the phenomena that designate the presence of the explanatory concepts vary so as to influence the phenomena that indicate the presence or absence of a revolution?" As you analyze, you decide what is important and what may be ignored. You move beyond the swirl of events and crises to search for underlying themes, and you offer concepts, hypotheses, and theories. As you do political science, you struggle to develop systematic and testable knowledge about politics.

There are several schools of research in political science, and alternative assumptions—about which questions to ask, concepts to use, hypotheses to test—and diverse views about the theories most likely to lead to powerful explanations characterize the discipline. Some political scientists focus attention on the behavior of individuals; others reason as if there were only groups. There is also disagreement over the relative importance of detailed descriptions of particular cases and over the power of abstract logic in analyses. No single approach to research represents all of orthodox political science.

WHAT WE ASSUME IN ORDER TO DO POLITICAL SCIENCE

All analyses entail assumptions about how the world should be studied. These suppositions lead us to ask particular kinds of questions, to use specific methods, and to propose certain kinds of answers. Clearly, you cannot seek to know the world without taking some principles as givens.

To do political science, you must accept the tenet that all knowledge is public. This apparently innocuous assumption implies several critical points.

1. There are no hidden truths, no hidden sources of truth, and no purveyors of truth who can never be wrong. "All must submit to the same base-line of evidence. Quite literally, this means that nothing is sacred" (Gellner 1985, 88–89). Because everyone can be mistaken, your effort to understand the world of politics should include an evaluation of the claims that are presented to you as knowledge. You have the right and, indeed, the obligation to assess whatever your teachers seek to teach you and whatever you read in articles and books. (Incidentally, you should judge the merits of this point, as well.) One of the most important goals of this book is to help make you a more critical reader and consumer of knowledge. When you do political science, you learn, evaluate, and, where appropriate, challenge claims to knowledge about politics.

2. Whoever analyzes politics must provide support that will convince other persons. Emotional attachments, personal hunches, and intuitive understandings do not adequately justify knowledge claims. The point is not that personal intuitions are wrong but that they are not necessarily relevant. To substantiate a claim that you have analyzed a political problem—interpreted the rate of voting in elections, accounted for the level of homelessness, or explained the outbreak of a war or revolution—you must present the credentials that warrant the analysis. Ultimately, you need to convince the reader or listener to accept your answer, but you should first persuade yourself of the merits of your analysis on rational grounds.

3. You should assess knowledge by standards that are beyond anyone's control. Logical coherence and adequate evidence are the most widely accepted criteria by which we judge claims to knowledge. Logical coherence entails precise definitions of key concepts, as well as careful and justified derivations of deductions (that is, the conclusions that are implied by initial principles), and inductions (the generalizations that are implied by empirical evidence). You also need to assess whether

the evidence assembled is adequate to the task at hand. As you read this book, you will encounter numerous examples that elaborate the principles of logical coherence and adequate evidence.

4. To do political science, you must assume that the political world is an orderly place. As Ernest Gellner instructs us, "Assume the regularity of nature, the systematic nature of the world, not because it is demonstrable, but because anything which eludes such a principle also eludes real knowledge: *if* cumulative and communicable knowledge is to be possible at all, then the principle of orderliness must apply to it" (1985, 89, emphasis in original). It is not possible to see, much less understand, something that is completely unlike anything else. And because you can only know something that displays recurrent patterns, you must begin with the assumption that there *are* regularities in our world.

5. Gellner describes another critical characteristic of the patterns that exist in the world: "The orderliness of the world is also assumed to be systematic: not only are there regularities to be discovered, but these form a system, such that if we are successful with our inquiries, the more specific regularities turn out in the end to be corollaries of more general ones" (1985, 89). This assumption urges you to extend your ideas, to push your ability to analyze the world to its limits. You need not assume that you will tie all the corollaries together, but you should be willing to expand your quest.

6. At the same time, you should not assume that order is self-evident. Do not suppose that all you must do to understand politics is read the newspaper or watch the news on television. Rather, you must analyze actively, proposing and testing ideas about the nature of the world's order. Only the active use of our intellects allows us to posit uniformities and bring logic and evidence to bear on our propositions and hypotheses.

7. Empirical sciences—like political science—recognize the centrality of our minds in the effort to know the world but insist that there is a reality outside our effort to know it. "In order to learn about the physical world through perception, we must be able to extract the relevant information from the items we perceive; and our available theories . . . permit us to do that" (Brown 1987, vi).

But even though theories enable us to observe the world, we are not caught in an infinite regress in which our thoughts determine what we observe. "Testing would be circular if what we observed were wholly determined by the theories under test, but observation always involves an interaction with an independent physical world that plays a crucial role in determining what we can observe in a given set of circumstances. Thus, even the most theory-laden observations can surprise us" (Brown 1987, vi).

Scientists assume a granular world, to borrow an image from Ernest Gellner (1985, 89)—that is, a world in which discrete phenomena exist in and of themselves, whether or not we posit their existence. They strive to bring our concepts and hypotheses in line with the discrete items, without necessarily ever seeing the granular matter.

8. The assumption of the granular nature of the world allows us to use the facts of the world (which really are no more than widely accepted descriptions) to test our explanations: "The very act of looking at data as *data*, as evidence for or against theories or interpretations which are inherently conjectural, *rather than as examples of theories as seen as inherently part of the very nature of things*, completely transforms the situation. It signals that everything is conjectural" (Gellner 1985, 22, emphasis in original). This assumption also precludes the view that the world out there is beyond our ken, a jungle of elements that we cannot explore.

9. You have the right, if not the obligation, to offer your own explanations of politics, as well. Remember that when we do political science, we offer concepts, hypotheses, and theories in order to discover the uniformities present in the world of politics. Hence, you should advance your own analyses, even as you learn, assess, and challenge those of others. And reason and evidence should guide your efforts.

Although you have enormous power over claims to knowledge, you are also tightly constrained by the rules of analysis. Gellner maintains that the effort to study the world as it exists—empirical analysis—requires that an individual be freed from the chains of intellectual orthodoxies. But this freedom is not unbridled license, which would entail that all claims to knowledge are equally personal and equally plausible. Rather, the rules of logic and evidence serve as checks to make sure that you adhere to standards that are beyond your control:

> Knowledge is and can only be about *my* experience, my *data*. . . . But it all depends on how you read this. Is knowledge about *my* data, or about my *data*? The reason why empiricism clings so to experience is not because it is mine . . . but because it is *outside my control*, because it is *given* to me and there is little or nothing that I can do about it.
>
> The point . . . is not that this or that self becomes the judge, but that there *is* a judge at all, some judge, for everything, that everything becomes subject to judgement, to conjecture. The self is introduced not in order to introduce private caprice, but for the opposite reason, to curb it: a *judge* is required to reduce all other participants to the status of mere witnesses, allowed to present evidence, which is then assessed (Gellner 1985, 20–21, emphasis in original; see also Newton-Smith 1981; Brown 1987).

By applying the rules of logic and evidence, not your unchecked hunches and personal experience, you can accept or reject the analyses offered by others and give others reasons to accept your interpretations. You thus use public standards to guide your decisions regarding claims to knowledge and to control your own explanations of politics.

There are several important implications in this discussion. First, because there is always a gap between the creations of our minds and the world itself, each of us is likely to analyze the world in a somewhat different way. Second, differences in how we interpret the world derive from and help to refine the various research schools of political science and the clashing theoretical systems and approaches that characterize all fields of knowledge. Third, we do not rejoice in these disagreements; instead, we strive to minimize their importance by following rules of analysis that enable us to demonstrate the meaning of our claims and the concepts and hypotheses of our analyses. Finally, although each of us analyzes the world somewhat differently, every perspective is not necessarily as good as all others. Indeed, the standard of public knowledge, the rules of analysis, and the specific requirements of logic and evidence help us to decide among the alternative visions. There can be no analysis without rules of analysis, and there can be no analysis without the evaluation of analysis.

THE LANGUAGE OF POLITICAL SCIENCE: THEORIES, HYPOTHESES, CONCEPTS, AND VARIABLES

Explanations—claims about how the world works—lie at the heart of political analysis. They answer the question, "Why did a phenomenon occur when it did or in the way it did?" with a response that is part of a general argument. W. H. Newton-Smith and Harold Brown tell us that "science begins when, having noted correlations, we seek an explanation of why they obtain" (Newton-Smith 1981, 211). We seek to discover "explanatory truths" in science, and "explanatory power comes from theories" (Newton-Smith 1981, 223). "A complete explanation is one that provides a set of premises that is acceptable in our current theoretical framework, and that is sufficient for deducing a description of the item to be explained" (Brown 1987, 140). We explain by demonstrating that the political phenomenon, event, or set of events that we are analyzing represents an instance of a general process.

Explanations answer "why" questions. "Why did the French Revolution occur?" seeks an explanation of a particular event. "Why do revolutions occur in industrial democracies?" focuses the analysis on a type of society or political system. "Why do revolutions occur?" points to the most general level, seeking to specify the conditions under which any and all revolutions occur. Although political scientists ask all these questions, the goal of providing abstract and general knowledge leads us to prefer questions about types of regimes and even about all regimes rather than questions about revolutions in particular countries. After all, when we explain why all revolutions or certain types of revolutions occur, we account for particular events as well, but the reverse is not true. When we explain, we claim that the world is organized in such a way that the phenomenon under question has to occur or is particularly likely to occur.

In political science and other empirical sciences, we explain by offering hypotheses. These statements specify the relationship among the phenomena being explained, the dependent variables, and the explanatory (or independent) variables. Each hypothesis requires a more general "covering hypothesis," which allows us to specify and justify the particular hypothesis as an instance of this more general claim. Hypotheses are situated within categories of related explanations or theories. They also require tests that assess the empirical adequacy of the hypothesis. And, as always, we use the standards of empirical knowledge—logic and evidence—to direct our efforts to know the world.

Hypotheses come in various forms, specifying that the explanatory variable influences, affects, predicts, rises with, is inversely related to, is a necessary condition for, is a sufficient condition for, is both a necessary and sufficient condition for, accounts for the variation in, or is tied in some other way to the dependent variable. In the next chapter, you will examine a hypothesis that attempts to account for variations in the level of voting in national elections—the dependent variable—by relating it to variations in the level of education—the explanatory variable. This hypothesis suggests that the higher the level of education is, the higher the level of turnout will be. You will also consider a hypothesis that accounts for turnout by relating it to specific characteristics of the political system, contending that the more the electoral rules facilitate voting and the greater the level of electoral competition among the political parties is, the higher the level of turnout will be. Hypotheses detail the precise relationship among the explanatory variables and that which is to be explained.

You must be able to test your hypotheses with empirical evidence. Barrington Moore, Jr., emphasizes the centrality of this simple but absolutely critical statement: "The effort requires constructing the argument in such a way that disproof is possible through resort to evidence" (1978, 381). Harold Brown tells us that "the ability to recognize that a particular set of items has the requisite properties

. . . constitutes the critical step in theory construction" (1987, 28). Similarly, W. H. Newton-Smith notes, "In the long run . . . the ultimate test of the superiority of one theory over another is observational success" (1981, 224). Referring back to the previous example, you must be able to observe whether turnout rises as a direct function of education. Hence, hypotheses must include precisely defined and measured variables. It follows, as well, that you must be able to specify the meaning of the linking verbs, such as influences, predicts, varies with, or any of the other words you might use to relate a set of explanatory and dependent variables. If you cannot test the hypothesis directly or derive testable implications, you do not have a hypothesis. And if you do not have a hypothesis, you do not have an explanation.

Political scientists work with *nominal* definitions, which indicate how the concept is to be used. In other words, we specify that *for our purposes* something is this and not that. Such definitions do not provide the true or essential characteristics of the political phenomena in question—this could only be done if the concept were a perfect representation of the component of the world that we claim it represents. Because we cannot be sure of this claim and because we have reason to think that we can never provide a concept with this kind of power, we strive to offer concepts that come closer and closer to that reality, to the "grains" of our granular world. But we do not claim that they are abstract equivalents, or a representation in words, of the world as it exists. We work by the rule that precisely defined concepts allow us to think clearly.

It is useful to distinguish between *abstract* and *operational* definitions. Abstract definitions correlate terms and sets of characteristics without connecting either to observable phenomena. If we define turnout in an election as participation in the voting process, we have a reasonable abstract definition. But if we want to make the concept of turnout empirically useful, we need to provide an operational definition. We need to provide a technique, method, or measure—an operation—that will connect the abstract concept with what is observable and verifiable. We must devise an operation, such as determining the percentage of adults with the right to vote who go to the polls. This figure can be calculated, verified, and compared over time.

Notice that we do not see turnout as such, just as we never directly see an election, a revolution, a government, a war, or any other of the abstractions we deal with in political science. (We only see people voting, fighting, holding meetings, and so forth.) But because we want to make the study of political science objectively verifiable, we use operational definitions to connect unobservable abstractions to publicly observable phenomena. In this way, we specify the variables in our hypotheses.

To assess the utility of an operational definition, you should examine the validity and reliability of the measures or indicators you use. When you can show that the indicators adequately detail the presence of the concept's defining characteristics, you have reason to use the hypotheses that contain these variables.

Validity examines whether the indicators come sufficiently close to the concept's abstract definition. For example, let us assume that the abstract definition of education is the process of learning about the world and the operational definition is the number of years of formal schooling. (Notice that it is relatively easy to observe the characteristics of the operational definition but not those of the abstract definition.) You weigh the validity of this operationalization when you ask whether there are other ways of learning about the world and whether the omission of learning that takes place at home or on the streets—to name two such alternatives—invalidates the operational definition. Questions of validity might also be used to ascertain whether the concept of party identification, defined abstractly as a psychological attachment to a political party, is properly measured by the answer to the question, "Generally speaking, do you think of yourself as a Republican or Democrat or—?" Similarly, those who deny that scores on the Scholastic Aptitude Tests really measure intelligence are raising questions about the adequacy of this particular operational definition. Note that in order to assess a concept's validity, you must know its abstract definition. Questions of validity examine the gap between the abstract and operational definitions of a concept.

To assess the reliability of a set of measures, you must first determine if the information in the operationalization is dependable. You must ask whether the techniques used to measure the components of the concept produce consistent and accurate results. As an example, imagine the problems that could result from defining political corruption as an affirmative response to the question, "Have you ever taken a bribe?" After all, it is unlikely that a corrupt person would answer in the affirmative. We also assess reliability when we decide if we should accept the answers people give in surveys asking whether or not they voted in the most recent election. We must consider the possibility that a significant number will say they have voted even when they have not, in hopes of appearing to be good citizens. But just because you can raise questions about a measure's dependability does not mean that the operationalization is useless. You need to draw reasonable conclusions, knowing that there are no perfect operationalizations.

As long as you keep in mind that our measures are efforts to make our concepts and hypotheses useful—not exact equivalents of the abstract definitions—you will make the most of your ability to analyze politics without violating the distinction between what is in our minds and what is real. Remember this rule: *Measurements must be made, and all measures have problems.*

Hypotheses in political science specify the relationship among the explanatory variables and that which is being explained; variables that specify the motives of the actors or that establish causal relationships are not necessarily included. Some students are puzzled by this point because it violates their implicit understanding of the meaning of explanation. Consider the justifications for hypotheses that do not refer to motives or causes. First, it is not always possible to attribute motives to actors, to test for the presence of those motives, or to make the link between the presence of the motive and the action. Furthermore, the stated motives—which are all we ever get from surveys, interviews, or discussions—are sometimes really justifications that follow and rationalize actions. In addition, a causal explanation is not the only form of explanation. Cause implies constant conjunction, temporal precedence, and nonspuriousness. This means that the explanatory variable precedes in time and is always associated with the presence of the dependent variable and that the dependent variable is brought about by *that* explanatory variable and no other. However, a successful explanation in political analysis does not have to meet such stringent conditions.

Given the need to test our hypotheses and the assumption that the world is an orderly place, we should keep our hypotheses as simple as possible. There is no reason to search for what are sometimes called "full" explanations if that implies including all possible explanatory factors. Politics is not so complicated that it excludes parsimonious analyses. Indeed, the guiding rule leads us in the opposite direction: Search for the simplest explanation, the one with the fewest number of explanatory variables. We use this preference for simple hypotheses to choose among competing explanations when all are equally able to solve the problem at hand. Here, as in many aspects of your life, strive to keep it simple.

Hypotheses are strengthened when they are tied to strong theories. A theory is a set of propositions that are deductively connected to each other in ways that explain the phenomena in question. Newton-Smith defines a "successful" theory as "one whose success includes not only observational success but theoretical success. Theoretical success is a matter both of the generation of novel predictions which themselves are theoretical and of the explanation of accepted theories" (1981, 224).

The more a particular hypothesis is logically implied by and leads to other hypotheses, the more reason we have to use it and accept its explanation of the phenomena being studied. And the greater the theoretical scope of a hypothesis, the more reason we have to think that it is part of an interrelated set of ideas that helps us understand a larger portion of the political world. This does not contradict the standard of parsimony, which should be applied to each hypothesis but not the set of related hypotheses. Indeed, we strive to place our simple hypotheses in a complex and wide-ranging web of ideas.

Philosophers of science often use the metaphor of a net to describe the relationship among the hypotheses of a theory. Karl Popper, for example, compares theories to "nets in which to capture the world," suggesting an image of tightly woven intellectual systems. "The finer is the mesh," he says, the more of the world that we capture with our ideas and the more we can claim to know about the world (Popper, cited in McGaw and Watson 1976, frontispiece). In other words, by linking more and more hypotheses and propositions together, we improve our understanding and explanation of the world around us. David Hull (1988, 493) prefers the image of "patchwork nets" as a more realistic description of the weave of intellectual systems. Theories vary in the extent to which their sets of propositions and hypotheses are tightly and precisely linked to each other.

Let's look at some illustrations of hypotheses and theories. (a) The statement, "The stronger a voter's identification is with a political party, the more likely he or she is to vote for that party" is a hypothesis in which party identification—a psychological state—is used to explain vote choice—a political act. (b) The statement, "When parents share the same party identification, their children have a very strong identification with that party" is a hypothesis in which the party identifications of the parents explain the strength of the voter's party identification. (c) The statement, "The stronger a person's attachment to a social group is, the more likely the person is to act in accordance with the expectations of that group" is yet another hypothesis, which may be used to explain the first and second hypotheses. It covers them with a more general claim, and in so doing, it explains and provides the justification for each.

Together, the three hypotheses compose a theory of the relationship between psychological attachments to social groups and vote choice. Given statement c and the proposition that identification with one's parents' loyalties is an example of such a psychological attachment, it follows that where parents have the same party loyalties, their children will also have those political identifications. Given statement c and the proposition that identification with a political party is an example of a psychological attachment, it follows that persons who identify with a political party will vote for that party.

Another theory explains the pattern of working-class politics under capitalism. Hypothesis (*a*) holds that the greater the level of economic organization is among the working class, the greater the level of electoral support for socialist parties is among that class. Hypothesis (*b*) holds that the greater the proportion of the working class who labor in large factories is, the greater the economic organization of that class is. Hypothesis (*c*) holds that the greater the level of capitalism is, the greater the level of revolutionary activity among the working class is. Here, too, we have a general hypothesis that specifies the relationships among a set of variables, while covering other hypotheses.

To explain or analyze, we must propose specific hypotheses, place them into theories by linking them to more general hypotheses, and test the hypotheses. By examining the logical power of the derivations, testing the hypotheses with relevant empirical evidence, and examining rival explanations, we determine if our hypotheses can explain the political phenomena in question. As more tests are passed—tests of logical coherence, of validity and reliability of measures, or of observations about the strength and nature of the relationships proposed—our reasons to accept the explanations are strengthened.

These standards for the acceptance of claims to knowledge are the criteria used by the community of scholars that studies politics. Hence, when we demonstrate that an explanation of the rate of turnout conforms to data from national or state elections, we are testing and supporting the knowledge claim. When we demonstrate that the explanatory hypothesis is properly deduced from a more general law, we are showing that our analysis accords with the rules of logic. Other members of the community of scholars who share these criteria for the acceptance of knowledge claims can then assess and decide whether to agree with our analysis.

Two related conclusions follow: First, those outside the circle of scholars need accept neither the explanation nor the criteria by which it is assessed. Second, all knowledge is relative to the methods that produce and evaluate it.

There is no claim that political scientists produce absolute truth about politics. All that is claimed is that successful analyses meet the criteria of knowledge established by those who study politics. Lest you be dismayed by the limited nature of this claim, I should point out that it applies, as well, to other sciences. All knowledge that fits under the heading of science is relative to the theories and fields of study from which it comes. Consider Harold Brown's admonition: "We have excellent grounds for taking the well-tested claims of current science to be true, while remembering that these results remain tentative and subject to reconsideration, and that the best established scientific knowledge of our day may yet have to be revised" (1987, 220). The standards of a discipline can come under attack and can change, but they do so only when they are challenged by those who have mastered these very standards. The goal of this book is to help *you* master them, as well.

Some scholars offer a stronger defense of these standards. Gellner insists that they, more than any other form of reasoning, provide the means to increase our knowledge of the world. He argues that they are the standards of "science—of that transcultural, cumulative and qualitatively superiour form of knowledge which has so totally transformed the modern world" (Gellner 1985, 53; Newton-Smith 1981, and Brown 1987, make similar claims). He and others contend that we must accept the principle of public knowledge and use the rules of logic and evidence to test claims about the world; if we ignore these standards, our ability to understand and explain political phenomena is diminished.

THE CACOPHONOUS SOUND OF POLITICAL SCIENCE

Political science appears to contain a fundamental paradox. Political scientists share a language of analysis—which emphasizes concepts, variables, indicators, hypotheses, and theories—and a vision of the discipline that focuses on the explanation of political phenomena. However, they display deep conflicts over appropriate assumptions, foci, and methods of analysis, and they offer hypotheses and theories that directly contradict one another. They frequently describe the same phenomenon but offer very different analyses of it. They may even observe the world in different ways. And the research schools of political science voice much agreement on the methods and goals of analysis but much disagreement on the results of analysis.

In a field like political science where there are multiple and competing theories, there are also multiple and competing analyses. This is true because each theory contains concepts, variables, and hypotheses that necessarily depict politics in a particular way. Consider the two examples of theories that I presented earlier. In the first theory, the decision to vote for a particular party is explained as the result of a psychological attachment to that party. In the second theory, vote choice is explained as the result of the voter's position in a particular social class. Such multiple theories characterize the analysis of electoral choice and almost all other political phenomena. The diversity of political science derives, as well, from the multiple and competing schools of research that encompass the various theories.

In the next chapter, we will explore four alternative analyses of turnout in national elections. As you will see, some of the studies focus on the calculations and behavior of individual voters; others direct us to look for answers in the characteristics of political and social institutions. The following chapter ties these alternative analyses of turnout to more general differences in the modern approaches to political science. These intellectual structures are broader and more basic than theories, and they address a wide range of issues, including: the relative importance of logical proofs and empirical evidence in analysis; the role of data organized in the form of statistics; the value of explanations that include motives; the importance of locating a hypothesis in a well-developed theory; and the appropriate level upon which research should be focused. Throughout our explorations in the pages ahead, you will see clearly that political scientists disagree on how best to do political science.

Within the research schools of political science (and all sciences), there is intellectual order. For those who speak the same language of theory and method, the conversations are complex and fascinating, yielding powerful analyses. But you must resist the temptation to merge the approaches. They are offered as alternatives to one another, and you need to understand them as different and sometimes contradictory ways to analyze politics. As you do political science, you will gradually decide which you prefer.

Some of the challenges of political science stem from the diversity of the discipline itself. Political science has no theoretical orthodoxy. There is no approach that you must select and no theory that you need accept as true. You may even choose to use some methods of analysis while ignoring others. Some see this as a virtue because there is little that must be accepted uncritically as truth and because there are no defenders of a holy writ. Others see this as a problem because there is little evidence of an accumulation of accepted knowledge claims about politics. As a result, it may seem as if each analysis treats its problem as if it were the only analysis. Whatever your preferences in this regard, you must understand and evaluate each of the competing theories and assess the relative merits of the competitors. And when you submit your own hypotheses, you must be ready to justify your analyses in the face of powerful criticisms within the discipline.

WHAT COMES NEXT

This book directly confronts the challenge of doing political science by examining research that exemplifies this field. I will not discuss any work that focuses only on current events to the exclusion of more general analytic issues. Nor will I focus on studies that are not bound by the desire to apply empirical evidence. I will not discuss the work of political philosophers. I will, however, help you to examine some of the puzzles that captivate political scientists who seek to apply analytic techniques to the explanation of political phenomena. As you grapple with these puzzles, you will learn how political scientists think.

I have organized the book around three challenges to political science. The first involves the diversity of the discipline. The second examines the issue of mandates to knowledge, exploring the ways in which political scientists claim to know what they know. The final theme locates political science in the context of all the sciences. The book portrays a discipline that is, at the same time, relatively divided, relatively orderly, and relatively successful in pursuing the systematic and verifiable claims to knowledge about politics.

The next three chapters explore the diversity of political science. In Chapter 2, we discuss the seemingly paradoxical fact that political scientists share a language of analysis but produce alternative, even conflicting, theories of politics. We study analyses of turnout in national elections, in order to understand what else political scientists share and what they do not share. The following two chapters move more deeply into this intellectual thicket.

Chapter 3 summarizes five approaches to doing political science: (1) rational choice theory, which emphasizes the utility of analyzing politics as if all persons rationally pursue their self-interests, has intellectual roots in economics; (2) the study of political attitudes and behavior, which explores how variations in these beliefs and perceptions affect the ways individuals take part in politics, borrows methods, questions, and hypotheses from psychology; (3) studies drawing on anthropology emphasize the utility of looking at communities and realizing that cultures vary across time and space; (4,5) structural theories—the work of Karl Marx, whose theories have had the greatest impact on the world outside the university and have influenced the research of many social scientists, and the research and methodology of Max Weber, who composed a direct response to Marx and whose philosophy of social science has influenced generations of sociologists and political scientists.

Chapter 4 reapplies these perspectives to a set of topics. We will see that Marx and Weber offer diametrically opposed analyses of revolution in capitalist societies; Marxist and rational choice theorists disagree fundamentally on the conditions for the formation of political groups and collective action; and students of political attitudes and behavior adamantly oppose the structural analyses of vote choice. The chapter concludes by contrasting rational action, political attitude, and structural analyses of demonstrations and political violence in democracies. The cacophony of political science echoes through these pages.

Given the presence of alternative claims to knowledge about politics, Chapter 5 establishes criteria by which the different descriptions, hypotheses, theories, and research schools may be assessed. Each political scientist—professor as well as student—must decide when to accept and when to reject a claim. Here, we solve the paradox of alternative approaches to political science not by deciding which one is best but by evaluating ways to select strong hypotheses and draw compelling conclusions from empirical information, even where experiments are not possible. We also discuss the limits inherent in all efforts to assess claims to knowledge.

The final chapter directly confronts the issue of political science as a science by exploring other disciplines. All sciences assume the reality of the world and seek to devise ways to understand it. And all scientists are motivated by rational, nonrational, and sometimes irrational drives as they pursue their goals. Sciences vary in the extent to which they display diversity, consensus, and conflict, but all knowledge derives from and is limited by the questions asked and the methods used to answer them. In political science, as in other disciplines, the point is not to *be* a science, but to *do* science, by offering systematic and verifiable analyses of the world.

CHAPTER 2

Explaining Political Phenomena: The Case of Turnout in National Elections

Free and contested elections are critical to all definitions that distinguish democratic systems from other forms of government. Picture the placards and remember the demands voiced in the mass rallies that rocked China and Eastern Europe in the last half of 1989. And recall that the first actions taken by the new authorities in Eastern Europe established elections among competing political parties as the mechanism to select governments. In the popular imagination, as well as in the work of political scientists, free elections define democracy.

Voting typifies the way in which most people take part in democratic politics. Indeed, in the democracies of Western Europe and North America, going to the polls is the most frequent form of political participation. Only 10 to 15 percent of people contribute money to electoral campaigns, and no more than one-fourth to one-third of the citizens of these countries contact government officials for assistance or attend political meetings. But roughly three-fourths cast ballots on election day (Verba, Nie, and Kim 1978; Dalton 1988).

In democracies, those who would rule can only reach their goals by convincing enough citizens to cast ballots for them and not for other would-be rulers. Consequently, candidates expend extraordinary resources—devoting enormous amounts of time, money, and energy—to attract voters. No wonder, then, that questions of who votes and how many vote are central to democratic politics.

Why do people vote? Why are there variations in the levels of election turnout in the same country over time and for different offices within one country? And what explains the variations in the rate of voting across democracies? These questions structure the study of turnout, the technical term for the rate of voting in elections.

The issue of turnout is important in its own right. For our purposes here, however, the study of turnout also has the advantage of illustrating different ways in which political scientists do political science. They use the language of concepts, variables, indicators, hypotheses, and theories when they describe what they claim to know about turnout. They present explanatory hypotheses that are tied to broad theories of political participation. They also codify the results of surveys of national population samples and other information into precise categories in order to operationalize the explanatory variables, as well as turnout itself. At the same time, their studies of turnout display the diversity within political science. Many theorists focus their analysis on one country, usually the United States. Others analyze variations in the levels of turnout in all democracies, striving for more general conclusions. Some extend their analyses to examine how variations in the levels of turnout influence other elements of democratic politics. Some offer explanations that rely on attitudinal variables to explain turnout, and others organize their analyses around structural factors. Political scientists differ, as well, on the relative importance of theoretical scope, precisely determined statistical measures of association, and the ability to present a coherent historical narrative as definitions of explanation. No matter how similar the concepts and measures are and no matter how much agreement exists on the importance of answering the "why" questions, the field of political science is characterized by rich diversity, as the analysis of turnout demonstrates.

My goal in this chapter is not to analyze turnout per se but to explore how some political scientists—chosen because their analyses speak directly to each other—analyze a typical problem in their field. By addressing this question about a question, we can examine the standards of the discipline. And in the process, you will become a more conscious thinker. You will learn how to assess the strengths and weaknesses of any claim about how the world works—even (and perhaps especially) your own claims to knowledge.

THE CLASSIC "AMERICAN MODEL": WOLFINGER AND ROSENSTONE'S ANALYSIS OF TURNOUT

In *Who Votes?* (1980), Raymond Wolfinger and Steven Rosenstone illustrate how the standard research school of U.S. politics analyzes turnout. They study a large national sample (in this case, drawn from census data); they correlate various social and psychological characteristics of the citizens with the level of turnout; and they relate their results to more general claims about politics in the United States. They do not, however, attempt to tie their findings to the issue of turnout in other countries.

On the first page of *Who Votes?*, the authors specify a set of analytic questions to guide their work: (1) Why is turnout low? (2) Why has it declined in recent years? (3) Why do people vote? and (4) Why are there such pronounced differences in turnout among different sorts of people?

These "why" questions presuppose "what" questions, which call for descriptions: What is the level of turnout now? What was it in the recent past? Wolfinger and Rosenstone define turnout as the percentage of the voting age population that takes part in an election and find that "while 62.8 percent of the voting age population participated in the 1960 election, only 55.5 percent in 1972 and 54.4 percent in 1976 went to the polls" (1980, 1). We can further detail the turnout levels in recent presidential elections in the United States, demonstrating that this decline has persisted: Data from CBS polls and the Federal Election Commission display levels of 62.77 percent in 1960, 61.92 percent in 1964, 60.84 percent in 1968, 55.21 percent in 1972, 53.55 percent in 1976, 52.56 percent in 1980, 53.1 percent in 1984, and just over 50 percent in 1988 (Kimberling 1988, 23). These data clearly reinforce Wolfinger and Rosenstone's point that the proportion of adults who have voted in recent presidential elections has dropped. Furthermore, elections for Congress that occur in years without presidential contests— off-year elections—display a similar pattern. In 1962, 47.1 percent voted, as did 48.2 percent in 1966, 46.6 percent in 1970, 38.2 percent in 1974, 37.2 percent in 1978, 39.8 percent in 1982, and 36.4 percent in 1986 (Kimberling 1988, 23). These data answer the "what" questions regarding voter participation in recent U.S. elections.

Who Votes? focuses, however, on the "why" questions. Empirical analysis attempts to explain why the world is as it is, and Wolfinger and Rosenstone's study falls squarely into this mode. Let us look more closely at these "why" questions:

The first and second questions (Why is turnout low? Why has it declined in recent years?) concern the electorate as a whole. They ask about the aggregate level of voting in the United States. Direct answers to these questions specify the characteristics of the entire electorate that account for variations in the levels of turnout. The explanatory hypotheses come in the form of "the higher the level of x is in a society, the higher the rate of voting will be," where x specifies some characteristic of the members of the society. As you will see, Wolfinger and Rosenstone emphasize the explanatory importance of variation in levels of education, which is claimed to influence, to be associated with, or to predict the level of turnout.

By asking the third question (Why do people vote?), these political scientists draw attention to the individuals' motives for going to the polls. They are seeking a reason, or a disposition, that will motivate a citizen to cast a ballot. The answers provide a way of explaining turnout that is very different from that obtained by looking at aggregate voting totals. Rather, they indicate a psychological characteristic or a personal attitude that brings about the decision to vote.

There are other ways to distinguish the first and second questions from the third. First, they are posed at different levels of analysis. When we discuss the behavior of individuals, as we do in answering questions about why people vote, we address the micro level of analysis. Here, turnout is a nominal variable: Either you voted or you did not vote. Questions about aggregates, which examine rates and levels of turnout, direct attention to the macro level. And how we ask the question strongly affects our analyses.

The fourth question (Why are there such pronounced differences in turnout among different sorts of people?) indicates how Wolfinger and Rosenstone propose to explain turnout. By asking how to categorize voters, so that they can distinguish sets of persons with high rates of voting from those with relatively low rates, they imply the hypothesis that persons vary with regard to particular characteristics that affect the likelihood they will vote. As a result, the analysis seeks to group persons into categories that exhibit different rates of voting, and it determines the relative importance of these categories in the explanation of turnout. Explanation implies the need for an unambiguous correlation between the explanatory and dependent variables.

The standard demographic characteristics that abound in surveys of U.S. society and politics define the sets of persons based, for example, on education, income, occupation, employment status, type of employer, age, sex, marital status, race, city of residence, state of residence, whether registered to vote, whether voted, reason given for not voting or registering, Hispanic ethnicity, length of residence at present address, length of unemployment, or residence in a trailer (Wolfinger and Rosenstone 1980, 3). Wolfinger and Rosenstone obtain most of their data from a survey of nearly 90,000 U.S. citizens taken by the Bureau of the Census in 1972. They also add information on the political environment that surrounded each respondent—"concurrent gubernatorial and senatorial elections, political culture, and state registration provisions in effect in his state in 1972" (Wolfinger and Rosenstone 1980, 4–5). In their analysis, they seek to relate variations in these demographic characteristics to differences in the rate of voting.

These political scientists also include information on the motives and psychological attributes of voters. Even though the fourth question would seem to focus on groups or categories of persons, which are properly placed at the macro or structural level of analysis, Wolfinger and Rosenstone believe that the explanation of political phenomena requires micro or individual-level variables. As a result, they complement the data taken from the census surveys with information from a study conducted by the Survey Research Center at the University of Michigan, which includes data on "political interest, information, sense of citizen duty, attitudes about issues, political disaffection, party identification, [and] other individual perspective[s] on politics" (Wolfinger and Rosenstone 1980, 4). Their guiding question leads them to the analysis of categories of voters, but their theoretical perspective insists that they include motives for political participation.

A first step in analysis is the evaluation of the accepted explanations for the problem being examined. Wolfinger and Rosenstone do this by testing the standing wisdom as encapsulated in a hypothesis by Sidney Verba and Norman Nie: "Probably the best known finding about turnout is that 'citizens of higher social and economic status participate more in politics.' This generalization . . . holds true whether one uses level of education, income, or occupation as the measure of social status" (Wolfinger and Rosenstone 1980, 13, citing Verba and Nie 1972, 125). This hypothesis relates political participation to the social class structure of a democracy. By implication, it draws theoretical support from the hypotheses and theories offered by two founders of social science, Karl Marx and Max Weber. (We will examine their work in the next chapter.) Both theorists maintain that variations in social status affect participation in politics, but, as we will see, Marx's and Weber's concepts imply different operationalizations. Verba and Nie offer their own definition of the concept of social and economic status: a set of indicators, joining level of education, level of income, and the status of the person's occupation. Wolfinger and Rosenstone begin their analysis of turnout by examining the most widely accepted hypothesis available.

But no matter how central this hypothesis is to literature on political participation, they reject it. The standard measures of the concept of social and economic status, they maintain, are not valid, and so any hypothesis in which it is found has no meaning. "We will see that the assumptions implicit in the procedure used by Verba and Nie are wrong: (1) the three components [education, income, and occupation] are not equally related to turnout, (2) their effect is not additive, and (3) the relationships are often not linear" (Wolfinger and Rosenstone 1980, 16). In short, they demonstrate that Verba and Nie's concept fails a particular test of validity, known as predictive validity, that seeks to determine whether the score on each item of a multiple measure of the same concept predicts the other scores. As a result, Wolfinger and Rosenstone examine the effect of each of the components—education, income, and status of occupation—on variations in the level of turnout. By dropping the concept of social and economic status from the analysis, they forego the theoretical power that Verba and Nie's concept obtained from its association with the theories of Marx and Weber. Instead, they seek greater explanatory precision by specifying the relationship between each component and turnout and the relative effects of the explanatory variables on the dependent variable.

Let us observe Wolfinger and Rosenstone's tests of these hypotheses. Citing several scholars, they hypothesize, "Education has usually been found to be the demographic variable most strongly related to turnout" (Wolfinger and Rosenstone 1980, 17). Examining the survey data, they present evidence that supports this proposition. With slight exception, they find a direct line between rising levels of education and turnout. Some 38 percent of those with zero to four years of schooling reported voting in the 1972 presidential election, compared to 91 percent of those who had more than five years of a university education. Next, Wolfinger and Rosenstone present a graph showing a direct association between turnout and variation in the level of income. Finally, they scale occupation, placing those who work in agriculture into the lowest category, followed by members of the working class, clerks and salespeople, and, finally, professionals and managers. Here, too, the analysis in *Who Votes?* shows that as occupational status rises so does the rate of turnout. The bivariate relationships, the association between each explanatory variable and turnout, are strongly positive.

In the previous chapter, I noted that each hypothesis is embedded in a theoretical structure that supports its explanatory power and makes it worthy of empirical testing. The more general hypotheses explain why we would expect to find a positive association between education and turnout, income and turnout, and occupational status and turnout in the absence of a hypothesis that associates a more general concept (like social and economic status) and turnout. I will present each set in turn to illustrate how hypotheses are tied together in a theory.

Hypothesis: The rate of turnout is directly related to level of education. Wolfinger and Rosenstone provide several broad points to substantiate the theoretical power of this hypothesis: (1) Much time is spent in U.S. schools to exhort students to be good citizens, and voting corresponds with the obligations of citizenship—going to the polls derives from the moral suasion that one has received from many years of schooling; (2) "Perhaps more important, education imparts information about politics and cognate fields and about a variety of skills, some of which facilitate political learning. . . . Schooling increases one's capacity for understanding and working with complex, abstract, and intangible subjects, that is, subjects like politics" (1980, 18). In other words, the relationship between turnout and education is subsumed under the more general association between the ability to handle abstract subjects and the tendency to take part in politics.

Hypothesis: The rate of turnout is directly related to the level of income. General hypotheses: (1) The very poor do not have the time or emotional energy to engage in activities like politics, which are not directly related to their survival; (2) The wealthy learn skills at their jobs that aid their participation in politics; (3) People who live in wealthy neighborhoods tend to have friends and associates who frequently participate in politics; (4) Those who have become wealthy without much education tend to have the personal drive to keep them involved in politics; and (5) The wealthy have a relatively greater stake in the system and are motivated to take part in politics to defend their place (Wolfinger and Rosenstone 1980, 20–22).

Hypothesis: The rate of turnout is directly related to occupational status. General hypotheses: (1) Jobs at the top of the occupational status scale involve persons in superordinate work relationships that give them a general sense of mastery and high levels of political efficacy, and high levels of political efficacy are, in turn, directly related to turnout. (2) High-status occupations are associated with frequent conversations with officials and discussions of politics, both of which are related to turnout; and (3) Persons in high-status occupations have the time to read about politics and to participate in politics, two factors that are related to turnout (Wolfinger and Rosenstone 1980, 22, 28–29).

Where three related variables have similar effects on a dependent variable, you should try to establish the relative explanatory power of each. Wolfinger and Rosenstone use multivariate techniques (that is, statistical tests that sort the relative effects of many explanatory variables) to test each hypothesis. They look for the relationship between education and turnout, income and turnout, and occupational status and turnout, after removing the association between each of the other two variables and turnout.

Wolfinger and Rosenstone's findings are clear and stable. They found that rising levels of education are consistently and strongly associated with increasing levels of turnout, even after they control for the effects of income and occupation. Once education is taken into account, however, rising levels of income are weakly associated with higher levels of voting. In addition, after removing the effects of education, persons in high-status occupations are not especially likely to vote.

Farm owners and persons who work in clerical and sales occupations have the highest rates of turnout, net of the effects of education.

The analysis draws general conclusions from these tests: First, it denies the utility of hypotheses that employ a general concept of social and economic status. Second, by supporting the effect of education on turnout, Wolfinger and Rosenstone maintain that they are corroborating the more general association between those who possess skills in dealing with abstract issues and those who participate in politics. Conversely, the finding that income has no relationship with turnout (net of education) *negates* the claims that having a stake in the system or having much free time are associated with high levels of participation. The authors also maintain that all nonmanual occupations impart the ability to deal with abstractions and that this skill accounts for both the general association between some occupations and turnout and the absence of a direct relationship between occupational status and participation in politics. Thus, Wolfinger and Rosenstone move between the hypotheses and the general theories in which they are located as they discuss the results of their empirical tests.

The analysis in *Who Votes?* uses the same techniques to examine the relationship between age and turnout. The simple bivariate relationship may be summarized as a slightly curvilinear relationship between these two factors. In other words, as people age, their rate of voting increases, until a point where it tails off slightly. Lester Milbrath and M. L. Goel suggest a more general hypothesis that subsumes this finding: "In the twilight years, physical infirmities probably account for a modest decline in participation" (Wolfinger and Rosenstone 1980, 37, citing Milbrath and Goel 1977, 116). Wolfinger and Rosenstone deny this hypothesis by showing that it confuses the relationships among age, sex, marital status, education, and income, all of which are related to turnout. Using the techniques of multivariate analysis, which allow the researcher to assess the relative importance of many explanatory variables, they show that when these variables are sorted there is a positive relationship between age and turnout.

Having located this direct positive relationship, Wolfinger and Rosenstone place this finding into a more general theoretical context. They must eliminate the possibility that the relationship is nothing more than a coincidence and that age somehow offers an alternative explanation of turnout. The goal of maximizing theoretical scope drives them to place the relationship between age and turnout under the same general hypothesis that accounts for the relationship between education and turnout and various occupations and turnout. As a result, they offer a general hypothesis to account for the positive age/turnout relationship.

> We have argued that people who have skill and experience in dealing with complex and intangible subjects are more likely to vote. . . . Our findings about the greater effect of aging on the uneducated point to another source of these skills—exposure to life in general and politics in particular. . . . Life experience is a substitute for school. . . . Consistent with this assertion is the previously noted increase in political interest, information, and use of the mass media among older people without the benefit of a college education and the lack of any change in those who have gone to college (Wolfinger and Rosenstone 1980, 59–60).

Both aging and attending school, reason Wolfinger and Rosenstone, impart skills and interests which increase the likelihood of political participation.

Throughout *Who Votes?*, they emphasize the importance of the attitudinal dispositions of voters in explanations of turnout. As you have seen, they consistently strive to relate the demographic characteristics of voters to psychological and motivational concepts. Even as they accept the apparent importance of election laws and specify the effects that these laws have on turnout, they link the significance of these factors to variations in the voter's disposition to vote. Wolfinger and Rosenstone determine that if all voters lived in the state with the least restrictive laws—where there was no closing date for registration, where registration offices were open during the workweek as well as evenings and Saturdays, and where absentee registration for the sick, disabled, and absent was permitted—then *"turnout would increase by approximately 9.1 percentage points"* (1980, 73, emphasis in original; see also Table 4.2, 74–75). Nonetheless, they insist that this finding has no explanatory power. By itself, it does not solve the problem of the low level of turnout in the United States. And even if registration was made as easy as possible, the level of turnout would still be low. In addition, they maintain that this finding is really nothing more than a substantiation of the general hypothesis. The effects of variations in the electoral laws on the level of turnout are filtered through the broader importance of skills that enhance or impede voting: "To put it another way, the difference in turnout produced by variations in registration laws is an indication of the varying commitment and capacity to vote of different kinds of people" (Wolfinger and Rosenstone 1980, 80). It follows, they maintain, that registration laws have a relatively small impact on the rate of turnout, and even this effect relates to the personal characteristics of the voters.

We can now summarize the answers to the questions that formed their analysis. Why do people vote? Persons with the attitudes and skills that facilitate learning about politics have the motivation to go to the polls. Why are there such pronounced differences in turnout among different sorts of people? When we categorize people with regard to their ability to learn about politics, we can sort them into groups with different motives for voting and, therefore, different rates of turnout. This enables us to account for variations in the rate of turnout within an electorate.

Notice the general hypothesis that underpins their reasoning: "The personal qualities that raise the probability of voting are the skills that make learning about politics easier and more gratifying and reduce the difficulties of voting" (Wolfinger and Rosenstone 1980, 102). Through many years of schooling, owning a farm, working in nonmanual jobs, and exposure to politics, citizens obtain the skills that increase their political participation. And just as education, age, and particular occupations specify the general concept of the personal qualities that enable a person to deal with complex laws and bureaucrats, turnout specifies the general concept of political participation.

Wolfinger and Rosenstone strengthen their theory by denying the explanatory power of hypotheses drawn from alternative approaches, such as those that rely on the power of variations in physical infirmities, free time, or stake in the system; specifically, they do this by demonstrating that the slight influence that variations in electoral laws have on turnout is really another specification of the general hypothesis. In relating specific hypotheses to general theories, showing how these hypotheses conform to the available data, and negating hypotheses that present alternative explanations of turnout, Wolfinger and Rosenstone provide credentials that warrant acceptance of their analysis.

They also ask, "Why does it matter that so many Americans fail to vote?" (Wolfinger and Rosenstone 1980, 104). This question expands the study's focus beyond turnout. The rate of voting becomes an explanatory variable when Wolfinger and Rosenstone ask how the low level of turnout influences other aspects of U.S. politics. This question lends itself to many answers. As the authors suggest, they could have used the results of their analysis to discuss the quality of U.S. democracy. They could have explored other forms of political participation, determining whether their theory of turnout applies to participation in demonstrations, petitioning, and working in electoral campaigns. They could have studied whether their analysis of turnout applies to state as well as presidential elections and to participation in the electoral contests of other democracies. Wolfinger and Rosenstone address a different issue: What effect does the low level of turnout have on the expression of political preferences in U.S. elections? Is the electorate a skewed distribution of U.S. citizens? Does the half of the population that votes hold different political views from the half that does not go to the polls?

To answer these questions, they compare a sample of voters with a sample of the population at large, finding that those who cast ballots are not a proper representation of the demographic characteristics of the general population: "In short, voters are not a microcosm of the entire body of citizens but a distorted sample that exaggerates the size of some groups and minimizes that of others. . . . The most underrepresented Americans include those who are disadvantaged in other ways as well: the poor, the uneducated, and racial minorities. (Also underrepresented are people whom it is difficult to consider disadvantaged, such as youth and people who are not married or have moved shortly before the election.)" (Wolfinger and Rosenstone 1980, 108). As a result, there are marked differences between those who vote and those who do not.

At the same time, Wolfinger and Rosenstone maintain, there are no significant differences in the political attitudes held by those who vote and those who are not part of the electorate. First, they compare the party attachments among the population at large and among voters, discovering that the rate of turnout produces nearly a 4 percent bias toward Republicans. In 1972, "51.4 percent of all citizens and 51.3 percent of voters identify with the Democratic party," and "Republicans comprise 36.0 percent of the total population and 39.7 percent of voters" (Wolfinger and Rosenstone 1980, 109). What about other measures of political preferences? They find that all differences between those who vote and the rest of the population are very small, falling below this gap of 3.7 percent, and do not consistently favor liberal or conservative positions (Wolfinger and Rosenstone 1980, 109–113). They see no political consequences that derive from variations in the rate of turnout among citizens with different demographic characteristics.

This conclusion snaps the thread connecting turnout and measures of political preferences in the United States. "If future political cleavages more closely parallel education, income, age, and race differences, then the consequences of turnout will be felt in the policy proposals" (Wolfinger and Rosenstone 1980, 114). Put differently, although variations in these phenomena explain turnout, they do not account for the political views held by U.S. citizens. The study implies that political preferences do not explain the rate of turnout and that these two concepts must be treated as independent of each other, not as dimensions of political behavior. Like all well-crafted studies, *Who Votes?* points to new hypotheses that need testing, new threads that may be woven into the analytic tapestry.

How should you decide whether to accept Wolfinger and Rosenstone's analysis of turnout? One way to assess their interpretation is to apply their own standards to it. Have they succeeded in showing a strong relationship between education, age, certain occupations, and turnout? What criteria do they use to judge the strength of the relationship? Do their data demonstrate that there is a strong relationship between these explanatory variables and turnout? Wolfinger and Rosenstone contend that the theoretical source of these explanatory variables is the more general phenomena captured in the concept of abstract skills and the ability to deal with bureaucracies. Is the general concept precise enough to be specified by high levels of education, age, owning farms, and working in white-collar occupations? Are you convinced of the reliability and validity of each of the indicators of the explanatory variables and of turnout?

A second way to assess the power of their analysis is to compare it with other efforts to explain turnout, which will raise a host of new questions. How can two analyses of turnout provide support for different explanations while denying the claims of the other interpretations? How do we resolve contradictory analyses of the same subject? How do different theories produce different explanations of turnout? How do analyses of turnout relate to explanations of other forms of political participation? To answer these questions, we must move from a single study of turnout to other analyses of the same subject. Moving in this direction will also draw us deeply into questions about the bases of knowledge in political science.

ALTERNATIVE ANALYSES OF TURNOUT: STUDIES BY POWELL AND JACKMAN

In articles in the *American Political Science Review*, G. Bingham Powell, Jr. (1986) and Robert Jackman (1987) offer explanations of turnout that differ from and compete with those in *Who Votes?* Although they also rely on various forms of statistical analyses to demonstrate the strength of relationships among their explanatory variables and turnout, both Powell and Jackman move beyond the examination of one case, introducing evidence from some fifteen other democracies. Their results cast doubt on the explanatory power of individual-level variables, such as abstract skills, that are defined by indicators like education or age. Instead, they argue that political institutions are determinants of the rate of turnout. Simply put, they maintain that the more institutions there are that encourage voting, the higher the level of turnout will be. Thus, Powell and Jackman represent an approach to doing political science that emphasizes both the testing of hypotheses with evidence drawn from many nations and the relative importance of structural over attitudinal variables in the analysis of politics.

Powell structures his analysis around the resolution of a paradox: "Americans seem to be more politically aware and involved than citizens in any other democracy, yet the levels of voter turnout in the United States are consistently far below the average" (1986, 17). Relating this observation directly to Wolfinger and Rosenstone's study, he doubts that turnout is a function of the skills that facilitate learning about politics and increase a person's awareness of that field. If being involved in politics is closely related to these skills and if U.S. citizens have especially high levels of these skills, Powell asks, why is the rate of turnout in the United States well below that of other democracies? Following Verba, Nie, and Kim's argument (1978), he suggests that voting has different determinants than other forms of political participation, and he argues that the institutional context of politics is better able to explain this form of political behavior. In the United States, Powell shows, the institutions of politics depress the level of voting to a far greater degree than the attitudes of Americans increase turnout.

Powell distinguishes two sets of explanatory variables—"attitudes and characteristics that individuals bring to the participatory arena" and the "institutional context" of politics. His measures of the individual-level variables overlap somewhat with the indicators used in *Who Votes?* He, too, includes education, age, and occupation, but he adds partisanship (measured as the percent who "mention a party they usually feel close to"), political efficacy (the percent who "reject: people like me have no say in what the government does"), political trust (the percent who report that they "trust the national government to do what is right most or all of the time"), and interest (those who claim to "possess at least some interest in politics") (Powell 1986, 19). To define the institutional context of politics, he introduces a new set of variables: (1) the extent to which the registration laws impede voting; (2) the competitive context, as defined by two indicators—"the frequency with which the control of the national chief executive, by a party or a coalition of parties, changed after an election in the twenty-year period from 1961 to 1980" and the kind of electoral constituencies present (1986, 21); (3) "the linkage between political parties and social groups," measured by the extent of overlap between occupation and religion and vote choice (1986, 22). Like Wolfinger and Rosenstone, Powell organizes the analysis of turnout around carefully defined and measured variables.

The differences between the United States and other democracies with regard to these attitudes and institutions structure his analysis:

"With few exceptions . . . the evidence on American political culture suggests that it should facilitate all kinds of individual political activity. With one exception, the institutional factors would seem to make the act of voting more difficult, and to impede the ability of parties and activists to mobilize supporters through appeals or through election day efforts to get them to the voting booth" (Powell 1986, 23). He finds that U.S. citizens have attitudes that facilitate going to the polls, but they live in a political system whose laws and structures inhibit voting. Because the level of turnout in the United States is considerably below that of the other democracies, it would seem, then, that variables associated with political structures have a greater impact on the rate of turnout than variables that tap the motives of individual voters. Powell tests the general hypothesis embedded in this summary: Variations in the institutional context are more important than individual-level variables in explaining the differences in the rate of turnout between the United States and other democracies.

The analysis uses various statistical techniques to explain variation in the cross-national level of voting. First, Powell combines survey and other data from twenty democracies (Canada, Israel, Japan, the United States, as well as the countries of Western Europe, excluding Portugal) into two time periods—the 1970s and the 1960s. The dependent variable is the average rate of voting among the adult population. He suggests that a set of variables posed at the aggregate level explains turnout: the institutional characteristics cited above, the percentage of the population above the age of thirty-four, and the percentage employed in white-collar occupations. Powell uses the technique known as multiple regression analysis to establish the relative effect of each of the explanatory variables on turnout. Finally, he uses the statistic known as the R^2 to assess the ability of all the explanatory variables to account for variation in the level of turnout across all the democracies.

The result establishes the primacy of specific structural factors in accounting for variation in turnout level. Two variables—the extent to which there are nationally competitive election districts and party-group linkage—are best able to explain the variation in turnout across all cases. Another result indicates a fundamental disjuncture between the political institutions of the United States and those of Switzerland and the other democracies. He then expands his study to negate hypotheses that associate the proportion of the population that is employed in white-collar occupations and turnout. In each explanatory model, the variables associated with the political institutions, along with age, account for 90 percent or more of the variance in turnout. By the definition of explanation used here—the ability to account for variation in that which is being analyzed—these variables explain who votes.

Returning to examine the U.S. paradox, Powell then analyzes the effects of the individual-level variables on turnout in the United States and other democracies. He poses two questions: "First, are the processes of voter involvement in the United States similar to those in other countries despite the differences in context? Second, if not, are there reasonably similar processes operating in other democracies, so that we could estimate the relative importance of various individual-level variables if the United States did have electoral and party contexts more comparable to those in other countries?" (Powell 1986, 26–27). He draws on surveys of electorates in eight European democracies and the United States to provide a negative answer to the first question. Only in the United States do all the variables that apply to a particular voter—education level, sex, age, party identification, political interest, and political efficacy—have a consistently positive and strong influence on the rate of turnout. In Italy and Austria, these variables do not vary with the level of turnout at all. In six other democracies—Britain, West Germany, the Netherlands, Switzerland, Finland, and Austria—neither education nor sex has an impact on turnout. "But in each country we see sharp, slightly curvilinear effects of political interest and, less consistently, efficacy. Party identification . . . is a significant direct predictor of turnout in each country. Age has a positive and generally curvilinear effect" (Powell 1986, 30–31). In sum, he finds that the consistent and strong effects of individual-level variables on turnout distinguish the United States from other democracies.

The final step examines the relative effects of individual and institutional variables on voting: "If the average democracy had a political culture as facilitating to voter turnout as American education and attitudes, we would expect turnout to increase by 5%. If the other democracies had the American levels of competition-encouraging constituencies and party-group linkages, their turnout would decrease by about 13%" (Powell 1986, 33–34). On average, then, the contextual effects of political institutions have three times more impact than the individual-level variables on the rate of turnout. Like Wolfinger and Rosenstone, he maintains that easing the registration laws in the United States would increase voting by about 10 percent (Powell 1986, 35). But unlike the authors of *Who Votes?*, Powell does not interpret this evidence as support for explanations that emphasize attitudinal variables. Rather, he uses this finding to underline the importance of structural, rather than attitudinal, variables in the analysis of turnout.

Thus, Powell offers an alternative to Wolfinger and Rosenstone's explanation of the low level of turnout in the United States. By examining other democracies and by testing variables associated with the characteristics of political structures as well as the attitudes of voters, this political scientist demonstrates that Wolfinger and Rosenstone's hypothesis, explaining turnout by education, age, and specific occupations, applies only to the United States. He shows that structural variables have an average of three times the influence of attitudinal variables on the rate of turnout. Consequently, he argues that political institutions—not attitudes and skills—are the primary determinants of the relatively depressed level of voting in the United States and of variations in the level of turnout among democracies.

Robert Jackman draws directly on Powell's research but modifies the analytic question and the explanation. First, he strives to account for the cross-national variation in the level of voting (Jackman 1987, 405), rather than the similarities and differences between the rate of voting in the United States and other democracies. Second, Jackman maintains that structural factors, by themselves and without regard to attitudinal variables, account for this variation. Rejecting the theory that relates turnout to the presence of a "participatory political culture," which *Who Votes?* illustrates so well, Jackman notes: "My purpose is to demonstrate that different institutional arrangements have a major and predictable impact on national rates of voter turnout" (1987, 406). He presents the set of variables best able to account for variation in the dependent variable, and he shows that a theory that limits itself to variables associated with the institutions of electoral politics explains variation in the rate of turnout in democracies.

Drawing on much of the data already analyzed by Powell, Jackman alters the indicators of the set of explanatory variables that define electoral institutions. Initially, he adds "multipartyism," which is measured "by the number of effective political parties in the legislature" (Jackman 1987, 410, citing Laakso and Taagapera 1979). Then, unicameralism (the existence of only one house in the legislature) joins the list. His general hypothesis—that the more direct the voter's impact is on the selection of governments, the more likely he or she is to vote—justifies these additions. Hence, where there are many parties and a coalition must be formed in order to govern, reasons Jackman, voters do not have a direct impact on the selection of the government and are less likely to vote. Similarly, where there is but one house in the legislature, voting will be high (Jackman 1987, 408). Finally, Jackman adds the presence or absence of mandatory voting laws. He also removes Powell's party-group linkage, arguing that this variable is poorly defined and measured, and denies that age has any explanatory value even in Powell's own model (Jackman 1987, 414). He uses his own group of variables to assess the effects of institutional structures on the levels of turnout in the 1960s and 1970s.

Jackman's results reaffirm the general importance of structural variables, which we first observed in Powell's analysis. As a set, he finds that the explanatory variables account for three-fourths of the variation in turnout across all democracies in the 1970s. When a distinction between the United States and Switzerland and the other nations is added, the model accounts for 96 percent of the variance in turnout in the 1970s and 97 percent in the 1960s. In other words, political institutions are seen to explain turnout.

Given these results, Jackman rejects the need to test hypotheses drawn from a theory of political culture (1987, 416–417). "The results of my paper suggest that the . . . odds that citizens will vote vary with the structural incentives that they confront." This implies that "high rates of turnout cannot be taken in themselves as evidence of participatory norms" (Jackman 1987, 419). In direct contradiction to Wolfinger and Rosenstone, Jackman claims that the rate of turnout assesses not the norms of the citizens but the opportunities offered to them by their nation's political institutions.

Powell's and Jackman's analyses not only offer alternative explanations of turnout, they alter the mode of turnout analysis itself. They shift the level of analysis from the individual to the characteristics of the nation's political institutions. Jackman maintains that explanations of political phenomena need not include motives at all. He suggests that analyses of aggregates of persons do not require and, in fact, usually eschew claims about dispositions, attitudes, and motives; they include the ability to account for variation in the dependent variable as the definition of explanation. Furthermore, both of these analyses challenge Wolfinger and Rosenstone's decision to limit the study of turnout to data drawn from only one country, particularly a country that stands apart from other democracies with regard to turnout. Indeed, they imply that Wolfinger and Rosenstone's book might more accurately have been entitled *Who Votes in the United States?*—perhaps even *Who Voted in the United States in the Presidential Election of 1972?* By extension, they maintain that Wolfinger and Rosenstone's analysis understates the institutional factors and overstates the importance of attitudinal variables in determining the turnout level in the United States.

This challenge to our first study of turnout brings our discussion to more basic questions. Because the authors offer not only alternative but competing modes of analysis and explanations, do students of turnout therefore need to choose among them? And if we must choose, how do we choose? But before we turn to these questions, we must examine another analysis of turnout that will introduce still other fundamental questions.

ALTERNATIVE EXPLANATIONS OF TURNOUT: PIVEN AND CLOWARD'S ANALYSIS

Frances Fox Piven and Richard A. Cloward present a quite different analysis of turnout in *Why Americans Don't Vote* (1988). Although their study accepts many of the findings that we have examined, these authors deny Wolfinger and Rosenstone's standard interpretation: "The point is not that the political context sometimes *offsets* the effects of demographic or social-psychological factors on turnout, but the political context *determines* whether these factors will have a significant effect on participation, and just what those effects will be. The evidence strongly suggests that who votes and who does not vote has no inherent relationship to either variations in attitudes or socioeconomic status" (Piven and Cloward 1988, 117, emphases in original). Instead, they explain the correlation between education and turnout in the United States by linking it to the more general pattern of party politics and relations among the social classes. The poorly educated display low levels of voting, they maintain, because lack of education is tied to poverty and membership in the lower and working classes; it is not an attitudinal variable. In the United States, electoral competition gives the parties much incentive to campaign for the votes of the middle and upper classes, not the poor, and the electoral rules make it very difficult for the poorly educated to get to the polls. As you examine the work of Piven and Cloward, you should keep in mind the issue of how analysts can "see" the same phenomena but explain it in different ways.

Piven and Cloward offer more than just another explanation of turnout. Accepting the claim that electoral rules determine the level of voting (an explanatory variable that you have already encountered in both Powell's and Jackman's analyses), they seek to explain *why* the political institutions are as they are. They address this problem with the concepts, variables, and hypotheses of Marxist theory. They also offer an alternative standard for the evaluation of explanations in political science by presenting a coherent historical narrative rather than graphs, tables, and measures of statistical association. *Why Americans Don't Vote* displays a wide theoretical scope and describes the changing flow of events.

In addition, Piven and Cloward introduce the policy and evaluative— or normative—aspects of political science. In *Why Americans Don't Vote,* they argue that low levels of turnout have negative consequences for the United States, deeply hurting the poor and increasing the tilt in the distribution of jobs, housing, and other opportunities that already favors the wealthy. And they contend that, because the poor usually do not vote, the political parties have no incentive to appeal to them. (None of the authors we discussed earlier takes an explicit stand like this on the normative aspects of low levels of turnout in the United States.) Furthermore, Piven and Cloward guide policymakers to ways of increasing turnout. Not only do they introduce the problem of why the political institutions are as they are but they also suggest how to streamline the process of voter registration and thereby raise the level of turnout. In particular, they deny Wolfinger and Rosenstone's implicit policy recommendation that the best way to increase turnout in the United States is to get people to stay in school longer. Rather, Piven and Cloward contend that this suggestion will not work and will actually delay implementation of the simple changes in election rules that will increase turnout. In sum, *Why Americans Don't Vote* introduces us to the relationship between political analysis and policy recommendations, while presenting an explanation and critique of U.S. politics linked to Marxist theory.

At the beginning of their second chapter, Piven and Cloward describe the theoretical net that surrounds their analysis:

> Toward the end of the [nineteenth] century, however, wrenching economic change provoked a series of popular mobilizations that overtaxed the earlier methods of political incorporation that had sustained high electoral participation but limited its influence. Popular demands, especially popular economic demands, began to emerge into electoral politics, and even to dominate some contests. As the possibilities of popular electoral mobilization began to threaten the interests of ruling groups in the United States, they responded by sponsoring something like a democratic counterrevolution. A series of "reforms" were introduced which weakened the ability of local parties to maintain high participation among lower-strata voters, and which impeded voting by lower-strata peoples. The effect of these changes was to marginalize potentially contentious groups from the electoral system (1988, 27).

Notice the importance they give to concepts derived from Marxist political theories that emphasize class conflict in capitalist democracies. They speak of "wrenching economic changes," "the ruling class," and "lower-strata peoples." They maintain that the beginnings of capitalist industrialization destroyed the existing bases of political participation, while fostering the rise of conflict over economic demands—that is, "popular mobilization." The early successes of political alliances among farmers and an outburst of strikes by railroad workers, miners, and steelworkers, along with the appearance of the Populist movement, "threatened" the industrialists and bankers, the nation's capitalists.

Responding to this attack, the ruling elites poured resources into the Republican party and manipulated the rules of elections in order to keep the poor, the illiterate, and the industrial workers of the lower strata from voting. And a "counterrevolution" inhibited the formation of class politics. The guiding hypotheses of Marx's theory structure the analysis of turnout in *Why Americans Don't Vote*.

Piven and Cloward define their concepts by illustration; they do not provide rigorous abstract and operational definitions. Industrialists, bankers, and leaders of the Republican party exemplify the "ruling groups" or "ruling elites." The "lower strata" are exemplified by the blacks and poor whites in the South and by steelworkers, miners, and immigrants in the big cities of the North. In this analysis, issue politics is the conflict over economic demands, but Piven and Cloward do not directly assess the reliability and validity of these definitions.

These political scientists imply that the theoretical richness of their analysis enhances the validity of their measures. Put another way, they use their ability to provide so many explanations of so many events during the last century of U.S. electoral politics to strengthen the validity of any and all measures of their variables. The logic of this justification runs as follows: Where a theoretical system has been shown to be useful in the analysis of one set of democracies, as Marxist theory has in the analysis of the politics of European democracies, there is good reason to use it in the study of another democracy, such as the case of turnout in the United States. Wide theoretical scope, they imply, overcomes the validity and reliability problems that might be attached to any single element of their study. Consequently, *Why Americans Don't Vote* relies on a powerful theory and the ability to provide a coherent narrative of disparate historical events to justify any one claim to knowledge.

Consider how Piven and Cloward substantiate the critical claim that the level of turnout among the lower classes declined after 1896. Drawing on the literature on this period in U.S. politics, *Why Americans Don't Vote* presents information about various kinds of poor people, blacks, immigrants, and industrial workers to illustrate their concept of the working or lower classes. Citing available research, they point to rapid and marked declines in turnout in Arkansas, Mississippi, and South Carolina between the 1880s and 1900. They present a table that locates many of these changes among blacks in the South and among whites living in the black belt, the poorest counties of the region (Piven and Cloward 1988, 84). Workers in the cities of the North also fall within the boundaries of their concept of working and lower classes. Indeed, given Piven and Cloward's reliance on the systematic import of Marxist theory, these categories of persons are actually closer to

Marx's concept of the proletariat than are blacks and poor whites in the South.

How do they show that turnout declined among the working class of the industrial United States? They provide no direct information on voting levels in northern districts that were heavily populated by industrial workers. Instead, they reason that members of the ruling class all across the United States were engaged in the same process of reducing the electorate. Therefore, they contend, data displaying overall declines in the level of turnout may be combined with information on blacks and poor whites in the South and the presence of tougher registration laws in many parts of the North and South to provide enough evidence to justify their basic claim—that there were declines in turnout among the U.S. proletariat following the presidential election of 1896. "Inevitably, over the long run, these . . . barriers tended to exclude those who were less educated and less self-confident, and in any case were often administered so as to secure that effect" (Piven and Cloward 1988, 94). They rely on a form of validity known as construct validity, in which the results of the analysis are in line with predictions derived from a theory. As you evaluate such an analysis, you must consider the relative importance of direct and indirect measures of concepts and variables.

Although Piven and Cloward frequently echo Wolfinger and Rosenstone's descriptions of the U.S. electorate, they offer contradictory interpretations of what they see. The authors of both *Who Votes?* and *Why Americans Don't Vote* recognize that the poor and uneducated are the least likely to vote, producing an electorate that is a skewed sample of the general population. But Piven and Cloward deny Wolfinger and Rosenstone's claim that these differences in turnout have no influence on the outcome of elections and the distribution of political preferences. Citing surveys of the 1980 presidential election, they maintain that 52 percent of voters preferred Ronald Reagan and 38 percent backed Jimmy Carter, while nonvoters had approximately the opposite preferences; they also use these data to conclude that "the Reagan victory of 1980 was literally made possible by large-scale nonvoting" (Piven and Cloward 1988, 12). The two sets of authors examine different elections, develop contradictory generalizations, and describe clashing patterns in U.S. elections.

Piven and Cloward also deny the theory from which Wolfinger and Rosenstone derive their explanatory hypotheses: "Of course, it is obvious that less educated or poorer or younger Americans in fact vote less. But the social or psychological differences between voters and nonvoters do not constitute explanations of nonvoting" (1988, 115). The standard account of turnout in the United States fails, they argue, because it highlights a spurious relationship. Its covering hypothesis cannot explain high levels of turnout in other democracies or in U.S. elections during the 1800s and early decades of the current century. And in none of these cases is there evidence that turnout rises and falls with variation in the level of education or the skills that facilitate dealing with complex rules and bureaucracies.

Piven and Cloward are deeply committed to erasing the bias in the electorate that favors the middle and upper classes. In their view, drawing large portions of the nonvoters to the polls will significantly increase the number of poor and workers in the electorate. The parties will then have to appeal to the interests of these voters, and, over time, government policies will tilt toward the poor and working class and away from the wealthy and well educated. In reality, *Why Americans Don't Vote* is as much a clarion call for bringing the poor and less educated to the polls as it is an alternative explanation of turnout.

What policy change would have the greatest and most direct impact on turnout according to Piven and Cloward? Raising the level of commitment to democracy or the sense of political efficacy will not succeed, they say, because attitudes only follow and justify behavior; voting behavior will change only after the surrounding institutions change. To get more of the poor and the workers to the polls in the next election, they recommend easing registration rules. To support this recommendation, Piven and Cloward cite surveys that demonstrate that nearly 90 percent of those registered to vote actually vote, and they claim that "nonvoting is almost entirely concentrated among those who are not registered" (1988, 260). They maintain that data on registrants supplied by secretaries of state overcount those who are registered by failing to remove from the lists the names of those who have moved. As a result, these data deflate the rate of voting among those who are registered (1988, 267). They also claim that the gap between the poor and the wealthy first appears on the registration lists; closing this gap will begin to ease the class bias of U.S. politics.

SORTING THE ALTERNATIVE ANALYSES OF TURNOUT

The four analyses of turnout that we have reviewed display both strong similarities and marked differences. They draw the same portrait of the levels of turnout in the United States and other democracies, but their explanations frequently contradict each other. Given these discrepancies and disagreements, you must evaluate each by itself and in relation to the others prior to accepting any one. Before discussing how that might be done, let's review where the four analyses join and part company.

1. All share the technical language of hypothesis, concept, variable, and theory.
2. All describe the same level of turnout in the cases examined, frequently citing the same sources.
3. Powell, Jackman, and Piven and Cloward specify the need to account for cross-national evidence on turnout.
4. Piven and Cloward stress the importance of being able to plausibly account for events over a broad sweep of time.
5. Wolfinger and Rosenstone, Powell, and Piven and Cloward agree that individual and aggregate variables are associated with variations in the level of turnout.
6. Wolfinger and Rosenstone emphasize the importance of individual-level variables in the explanation of turnout.
7. Powell, Jackman, and Piven and Cloward emphasize the importance of political institutions in the explanation.
8. All use information drawn from national surveys to obtain data on turnout and explanatory variables, and Piven and Cloward add the reports of historians.
9. All assess the power of the explanations offered by searching for correlations between turnout and the explanatory variables.
10. Wolfinger and Rosenstone, Powell, and Jackman move beyond correlations to examine the net and total effects of a set of explanatory variables by using forms of regression analysis, while controlling for random results. These techniques enable them to assess the influence of each and all the variables on turnout.
11. Piven and Cloward imply that explanations should explain the ebb and flow of historical events in terms of a full-fledged theory.
12. The approaches differ in the extent to which their particular hypotheses on turnout are deduced from general theories of politics.

EXAMINING THE ALTERNATIVE ANALYSES: WHY TURNOUT IN THE UNITED STATES IS DIFFERENT

Let us move beyond the list of similarities and differences to examine how each of the authors treats a theme common to all the studies—the exceptional qualities of turnout in the United States. First of all, no one disputes that U.S. citizens are much less likely to vote than citizens in other democracies. Indeed, everyone accepts the reliability of the available data, which places the U.S. level of turnout approximately twenty percentage points below the average of all other democracies. Furthermore, they all agree that variations in level of education and age correlate with turnout in the United States. The disputes involve more fundamental dimensions of analysis: What hypothesis best explains turnout in the United States and what is the relationship between that hypothesis and the explanation of turnout in all democracies?

Wolfinger and Rosenstone place the association between education, age, and turnout under the more general hypothesis that relates political participation and the possession of abstract skills that facilitate an understanding of political issues and dealing with bureaucracies. Although they analyze only U.S. data, the more general theory would extend the hypothesis to other democracies as well. Indeed, Powell, Jackman, and Piven and Cloward all maintain that Wolfinger and Rosenstone exemplify the political culture approach, a mode of thought that emphasizes the explanatory importance of motives, dispositions, and attitudes. Wolfinger and Rosenstone imply, therefore, that the theory that explains turnout in the United States will work as well in other democracies.

By extending their analyses to include other democracies at several points in time, Powell and Jackman address the similarities and differences between the determinants of turnout in the United States and other democracies. Powell accepts the view that hypotheses employing elements of political culture account for turnout in the United States, but he denies that they satisfactorily explain who goes to the polls in other democracies. According to his presentation, individual-level variables are particularly important in the United States only because of the nature of U.S. political institutions. Jackman believes that there is something peculiar about the determinants of turnout in the United States, but he denies that political culture explains anything about cross-national variation in the level of voting. Both theorists insist on the fundamental importance of political institutions in explaining turnout.

Piven and Cloward move beyond Powell's and Jackman's claims by placing the peculiarities of U.S. politics into the theoretical context of "American exceptionalism," drawing once again on Marxist theory:

> In Western Europe . . . the working classes were enfranchised at the beginning of the twentieth century, and their enfranchisement led to the emergence of labor and social democratic parties that ultimately exerted considerable influence on the policies and political culture of

their nations. In the United States, by contrast, the partial disenfranchisement of working people during the same period helps explain why no comparable labor-based political party developed, and why public policy and political culture remained more narrowly individualistic and property-oriented. . . .

These assertions bear on the large debate in the literature regarding "American exceptionalism," which tends to blame the culture of the working class, especially its lack of class consciousness, for the distinctive pattern of political development in this country. But political attitudes are formed in the context of political institutions. We are proposing that the electoral arrangements that evolved at the turn of the century at least partly explain the path of American political development (1988, 8).

They argue that the political institutions that produced the peculiarities of U.S. political culture are the result of the victories of the U.S. capitalists over the poor and workers since the late nineteenth century. Comparing the United States and the European democracies, they say, reveals an especially powerful ruling class in this country that moved workers out of the electoral system and blocked the formation of a powerful Socialist movement. The peculiarities of U.S. politics, therefore, derive from the exceptional strength of U.S. capitalists and the weakness of U.S. workers.

The diverse analyses we have studied here derive from alternative research schools and theories, which provide very different variables, concepts, and hypotheses. I will now turn to the analysis of whole systems of thought used in political science. These general approaches propose explanatory "nets" from which particular hypotheses may be developed. Our focus will therefore shift from an analysis of the single problem of turnout to the modes of thought used to examine politics. We will move from the study of single knots to examine whole nets of explanatory ideas; the assessment of any analysis requires a review of the theory and research school from which it comes.

CHAPTER 3

Research Schools in Political Science

Research schools teach us how to observe the world. Their concepts and variables depict what is "out there"; their hypotheses detail how the components of the world relate to each other; and where the hypotheses are tightly knit, they produce theories with wide scope. Their methods instruct us how to confirm or negate descriptions and explanations. After establishing what exists, the research school determines what else we need to know.

All analyses require theoretical contexts, for no analysis stands by itself. When Wolfinger and Rosenstone describe low turnout in the United States, against what standard do they measure this turnout to determine that it is low? There are three possible answers, each of which implies that there can be no knowledge about a single case without knowledge drawn from other cases or from an abstract standard of some sort. First, turnout in the United States may be low relative to the scale on which it is measured. On this scale, 100 percent is the maximum, 0 percent is the absolute minimum, and 30–40 percent is a more likely real minimum. In this context, it is reasonable to describe a case with a turnout rate of 50–60 percent as low. Second, turnout in the United States may be low relative to that of other democracies, and, although *Who Votes?* does not display the relevant sources, you have seen Powell's and Jackman's data on other democracies that substantiate this claim. Third, turnout may be low relative to an ideal of democratic participation in which all or nearly all citizens take part in politics. This illustration makes a general point: Any effort to describe and measure requires a standard that lies outside the particular study. Without general hypotheses, we cannot move from the particular to the general; indeed, we cannot even discuss the particular.

Explanations necessarily take on the assumptions, concepts, language, and mode of analysis of the covering hypotheses, the theories to which they are tied, and the research schools from which they come. For example, Jackman posits that the number of parties is likely to be inversely related to the rate of voting. He derives this hypothesis from a general principle of behavior: Persons seek to maximize their benefits while minimizing their costs. Therefore, he reasons, if more people believe that their ballots will have an effect on the outcome of an election, the rate of voting will increase. He also finds it reasonable to suppose that the greater the number of political parties there are, the less voters will believe that their votes will affect which party wins the election and forms the government; consequently, Jackman contends that turnout will be higher in two-party systems than in democracies with many political parties. He applies the principles and modes of reasoning contained in an approach to political analysis known as rational choice theory. Piven and Cloward, on the other hand, use the conceptual language of Marxist political theory. They derive their claim that class conflict is at the heart of electoral politics in the United States from Marx's general hypothesis that class politics is central to all politics in capitalist democracies. Thus, we can see that the concepts and explanations of general theories of politics drive particular analyses.

In essence, research schools teach us how to do political science. They answer questions about: (1) the appropriate level to focus upon— be it the individual, the group, the structure, the aggregate, or a combination of the individual and the group; (2) the mode by which evidence should be obtained, which usually entails choosing between the quantitative data of surveys and statistical sources or the discursive reports of historians, anthropologists, and other careful observers; (3) the relative importance of detailed analyses of single countries or cases and cross-national analyses, whether by quantitative or qualitative data or both; (4) the relative importance of hypotheses arranged into the tight web of full-fledged theories and single hypotheses loosely associated with each other; and (5) the relative importance of theoretical power and empirical evidence in the defense of claims to knowledge.

The research schools of political science vary in the extent to which they offer closed theoretical systems. Some approaches take a hard and fast position on one or more of the dimensions of analysis. Others offer stances that more closely resemble suggestions for research rather than strict requirements for analysis. Rational choice theory, for example, insists on the importance of analysis at the individual level and the requirement of theoretical power—the ability to account for many and diverse phenomena, especially through the use of deductive logic. Empirical evidence is employed to illustrate but not test the propositions of rational choice theorists. Marxist theory organizes analyses around the concept of social class and the goal of theoretical power, though usually without the mathematization that accompanies rational choice theory. This research school also presents detailed empirical analyses of political change. Studies that focus on political attitudes and behavior, as well as those that draw on Max Weber's approach to social science, are much less restrictive. Thus, Wolfinger and Rosenstone rely on quantitatively organized empirical studies of one case but do not strive to establish hypotheses with wide theoretical scope. They sometimes borrow propositions from rational choice theory and also apply hypotheses drawn from the study of political attitudes and behavior. Those who, like Powell, follow Weber's insights strive to combine empirical studies, the analysis of motives, and hypotheses that apply to a host of cases. They do not make consistent use of deductive logic. Finally, those who apply the strictures of anthropology to the analysis of politics use a distinctive methodology but do not offer a set of deductively related hypotheses. Indeed, many who work in this research school deny the possibility of general theories of politics. Among the research schools of political science, rational choice theory and Marxist theory offer the most defined visions of politics.

RATIONAL CHOICE THEORY

The approach known as rational choice or rational action theory offers a distinctive strategy for political analysis. Members of this school make radical simplifications and use formal mathematical models to explain and interpret political phenomena. Rational action models are word pictures of how politics would look if the model's assumptions were true. Empirical evidence usually illustrates the extent to which politics fits the hypotheses that are deduced from these assumptions. This approach has been applied to a wide range of political phenomena—for example, the formation of cabinets in parliamentary democracies where no party controls a majority in the legislature; the outbreak and conclusion of wars; vote choice; the formation of political parties and interest groups; policy outcomes of governments; and turnout at elections. Rational choice theorists maintain that good political analysis need not include information on the particular political culture or the details of politics—the names, dates, and places or the stories that interest so many students in the field. These political scientists promise that you will enhance your knowledge of politics by thinking about the subject in ways that may appear counterintuitive but are really very powerful.

Individuals and Their Personal Goals

Rational action theory assumes that all persons are rational maximizers of self-interest, calculating the value of alternative goals and acting efficiently to obtain what they want. In *The Politics of Private Desires*

(1981), Michael Laver outlines the basic principles of this approach (see also Frolich and Oppenheimer 1978 and Elster 1986):

1. Reason as if the political world were composed only of individuals and their goals;
2. Assume that individuals choose rationally among their goals. Rational decisions involve selecting the most appropriate means to reach the desired goals. In the words of another exponent of this research school, Mancur Olson, Jr., "rational" implies that individuals pursue their goals "by means that are efficient and effective for achieving these objectives" (Olson 1968, 65).
3. Goals are intrinsic—valued in and of themselves—or instrumental—useful for reaching intrinsic goals.
4. Intrinsic goals are personal and asocial; instrumental goals are social. Personal goals are those that we can obtain for ourselves, for example, more money, a bigger house, a new job; social goals pertain to others—housing for the homeless, defense for the nation—and encompass phenomena such as respect and popularity, both of which depend on the views of other people. This assumption enables rational choice theorists to avoid the bloated and useless claim that any and all behavior is rational, because it might derive from any supposed goal (Laver 1981, 29).
5. Because individuals always value personal goals and almost everyone wants to improve his or her economic condition, self-interest is usually defined as "the enhancement of the economic well-being of the individual concerned" (Laver 1981, 110).

Mark Irving Lichbach reiterates these points. Rational action theory "assumes that preferences over outcomes are not other-regarding, but rather are self-regarding. . . . Rational actors, in other words, care about their own income and wages relative to what they can do, not relative to what others receive" (Lichbach 1989, 460).

These political scientists insist that politics begins with the behavior of individuals. Groups and nations do not act; policies are not made by governments as such but by persons in particular positions. Explanations of politics must, therefore, focus on the behavior of individuals, and posit the individual's goals. "The implicit assumption . . . is that explanations of phenomena in one realm (the political), on the basis of motivational assumptions defined entirely in another realm (the individual), are somehow 'deeper' than explanations of the political in terms only of the political" (Laver 1981, 14). Consequently, the rational choice approach constructs models of politics at the individual level of analysis.

At the same time, rational choice theory maintains that it is reasonable to assume that individuals know what they most desire, sift through alternatives, and act efficiently and effectively to reach those goals. It denies the need to directly examine the goals of each person. Positing that all people seek to maximize their self-interest resolves the need to tap each person's goals and values.

But what justifies the claim that we should analyze everyone as if they were always seeking to enhance their self-interest? Why should we not assume that most humans are altruists, willing to help others at their own expense, or, perhaps more plausibly, that they are social animals for whom personal and group goals are one and the same? Members of the rational choice school would agree with one or both of the following responses. First, these assumptions accurately describe how most persons approach the world; clearly, Mother Teresa is the exception, not the rule. Most people most of the time act in a manner that is far from altruistic. Second, the empirical accuracy of assumptions is not especially important; a theory should be judged not by its assumptions but by what it does with those assumptions. "Theoretical models should be tested by the accuracy of their predictions rather than by the reality of their assumptions" (Downs 1957, 21, citing Milton Friedman). Because rational choice theory begins with a small set of statements that are assumed to be true, it can use deductive logic to derive a host of powerful interpretations of politics. "The crucial characteristic is the generation of interesting and non-obvious statements about politics from a set of *a priori* and a system of logic" (Laver 1981, 11). Rational choice theory argues that it is usually accurate and always useful for analysis to assume that all persons act rationally to maximize their self-interest.

William Riker's *Theory of Political Coalitions* exemplifies the wide scope of rational choice theory. Riker examines the formation of alliances among political actors, addressing organizations like political parties and governments as if they were individuals calculating rationally to maximize their interests. According to him, the "size principle" accounts for the formation of all types of coalitions and alliances: "*In social situations similar to n-person, zero-sum games with side-payments, participants create coalitions just as large as they believe will ensure winning and no larger*" (Riker 1962, 32–33, emphasis in original). This abstract and forbidding statement has powerful implications. It tells us to analyze politics as if it were a competitive game; doing so allows us to apply a mode of reasoning known as the mathematical theory of games. From the assumptions of rational choice theory and the application of this form of mathematical reasoning, Riker derives the size principle: Where there are any number of competitors and definite winners and losers and where inducements can be offered to form alliances, a coalition of the smallest possible size will form. Because this is a mathematical and, therefore, abstract truth, he suggests, this solution will always occur—everywhere—if the assumptions are accurate and the derivation is properly drawn. Consider the example of a legislature composed of 300 members and 5 parties. According to Riker's thinking, here, as in all such cases, the relative size of the parties will determine the formation of a governing cabinet. The smallest number of parties that controls more than 150 seats will coalesce. He contends that political alliances do not respond to calculations based on political ideologies and principles, to differences in the styles of politics that may vary across cultures, or to the particular political comings and goings of a parliament or party convention. Rather, political parties seek to control governing offices. As rational maximizers of their own self-interest, they strive to share the spoils with as few partners as possible. And he believes that to predict the outcome of cabinet negotiations, that is all you need to know. Riker and other rational choice theorists display exceptional intellectual power and daring.

How Political Groups Form
and Collective Action Takes Place

The problem of collective action stands as a classic question for this research school. Assuming that individuals rationally pursue their self-interest, how will large numbers ever join together to act as one? Won't each person be tempted to take a "free ride," leaving the work for others? If everyone does this, how do people ever act together?

Two centuries ago, the philosopher David Hume illustrated the problem of joint action in a world of rational, self-interested persons:

> Two neighbors may agree to drain a meadow which they possess in common, because it is easy for them to know each other's mind; and each must perceive that the immediate consequence of his failing in his part is abandoning the entire project. But it is very difficult, and indeed impossible, that a thousand persons should agree on any such action; it being difficult for them to concern so complicated a design, and still more difficult for them to execute it; while each seeks a pretext to free himself of the trouble and expense and would lay the whole burden on others. Political society easily remedies both these inconveniences. Magistrates . . . prevent . . . failure because they find no interest in it; either immediate or remote. Thus bridges are built, harbors are opened, ramparts are raised, canals formed, fleets equipped, and armies disciplined, everywhere by the care of government (cited in Hendel 1953, 101).

The pursuit of individual rationality is seen to inhibit the collective good, hurting the individuals as well; acting in what they perceive to be their own interest, individuals actually harm themselves. Hume's solution to this dilemma recalls the answer offered by Thomas Hobbes more than a century earlier: Only the force and majesty of government can induce individuals to act together, helping each other and furthering their self-interest at the same time. In the absence of force, collective action will not occur.

A related way to view this issue is to think of the supply of public goods, those items characterized by jointness of supply (they can be produced only by a group of persons working together) and jointness of consumption (once available, no one can be kept from using them). Like a cleared meadow, national defense is a public good. Once provided, no one who lives in the nation can be excluded from its benefit. But to provide it, large numbers of persons must act together. Clean air is also an example of a public good, as are the formation of interest groups and participation in national elections in a democracy. Rational choice theorists believe that, in pursuing their own self-interest, individuals always have strong incentives to free ride, to take advantage of others' efforts—allowing them to volunteer for the army, to clean the air, to form a trade union, or to go to the polls. Doing so enables each person to maximize his or her benefits while minimizing the costs. Further, these theorists claim that no one seeks the common good in and of itself (or, to rephrase this claim slightly, so few people do that it is not useful to analyze the world as if this were a real possibility—there are very few persons like Mother Teresa). Let me cite Laver on this point: "While we assume that rational men will desire public goods, we do not need to assume that they will desire them intrinsically" (1981, 37). And because each of us will perform the same calculation, there is no reason to think that collective action will ever occur or that public goods will ever be produced.

Rational choice theory seeks solutions to the problem of collective action when it explains those elements of politics that involve more than simple calculations and applications of individual interest. Hobbes's answer, specifying that public goods are provided in response to the threat or application of government power, is useful here. An alternative solution is to turn public goods into private goods—by paying a private hauling company to pick up the trash, for example. This obviates the need to force or induce persons to take care of such a problem on their own. Another solution emphasizes the size of the group. Where there are relatively few persons involved and the contribution of each person is necessary for the production of the public good, each knows that his or her contribution is vital to the outcome. Hence, no one has any incentive to free ride. Still other solutions involve instances in which public goods are supplied as a by-product of individuals pursuing their self-interest. Military service is a prime example. Persons able to obtain higher salaries in the armed forces than in the civilian market are apt to enlist, thereby providing a public good while helping themselves. And selective incentives—offering particular benefits to particular people—can replace the draft as a recruiting tool. Similarly, making it easier for union members to get jobs or health and vacation benefits enhances the likelihood that unions will form (Olson 1968). These examples show that applying deductive reasoning to a limited set of assumptions may yield solutions to the problem of collective action.

The Problem of Turnout

Rational choice theorists analyze turnout in national elections as an instance of the problem of collective action. And by returning to the question of turnout, we can get a closer look at their school of analysis. These theorists ask why persons vote, not why they do not vote. Because few if any voters obtain personal benefits by going to the polls, it seems likely that few rational seekers of self-interest will vote. But many, in fact, do. Therefore, these political scientists must seek an explanation of turnout without violating the assumptions of their theory.

In principle, the approach provides a straightforward answer to the calculus of voting. To cite Anthony Downs, "Every rational man decides to vote just as he makes all other decisions; if the returns outweigh the costs he votes; if not, he abstains" (1957, 260). The problem is that it is difficult to specify the personal benefits that most persons obtain by voting, while it is relatively easy to list the costs. Although officeholders and their dependents can easily see how they will directly prosper or suffer from the outcome of elections, no one else can so readily relate the outcome of elections to his or her own gain or loss. Why then do we bother to vote?

Rational action theorists have proposed that there *are* personal benefits that are maximized and costs that are minimized when individuals go to the polls. As Downs says: "If voting costs exist, pursuit of short-run rationality can conceivably cause democracy to break down. However improbable this outcome may seem, it is so disastrous that every citizen is willing to bear at least some cost in order to insure himself against it. The more probable it appears, the more cost he is willing to bear" (1957, 286). Riker and Peter Ordeshook (1968), whose argument is used by Wolfinger and Rosenstone, posit that voters "derive positive satisfactions from complying with the ethic of voting, affirming allegiance to the political system, affirming partisan preference" (cited in Laver 1981, 105). To analyze turnout, Downs, Riker, and Ordeshook relax the assumption that individuals do not intrinsically value social goods.

This solution violates one of the approach's guiding assumptions. And Downs's specification does not solve the free-rider problem. As Laver notes, "Each voter cannot insure *himself or herself*, but can insure the *whole group*, against the collapse of competition, because competition is a public good. It will always be rational for any individual to stay in bed, and let the rest of society insure against collapse" (1981, 105, emphases in original). Each and all individuals, therefore, will not vote.

Members of the rational choice school offer other explanations for the obvious fact that many people do, indeed, vote. Laver's own solution posits that the costs of voting are very small. After all, we expend very little time, energy, and shoeleather when we go to the polls. "If this is the case, then even a tiny probability of influencing the result may offset any costs in attempting to do so" (Laver 1981, 107). It follows that differences in the costs that pertain to the act of voting—whether a person loses salary, the actual distance to the polls, the state of the weather—affect the decision to vote or not to vote. Similarly, John Ferejohn and Morris Fiorina expand the range of rational choice solutions to the vote calculus and replace the principle of utility maximization with the criterion of "minimax regret." They suggest that individuals act to minimize their maximum regret. Thus, voters do not consider the probabilities of a matrix of outcomes but the possibility of an outcome that they do not at all desire—a matrix of regrets. They vote when casting a ballot gives them reason to suppose that they are doing something, even something minute, to avoid this dreaded outcome. Furthermore, Ferejohn and Fiorina reason that utility maximizers need many incentives to go to the polls, "whereas minimax regret decision makers need little incentive to participate. And one should remember that most people do vote. A voter would reason, 'My God, what if I didn't vote and my preferred candidate lost by one vote? I'd feel like killing myself' " (1974, 535). In this perspective, voting is seen as an easy way to avoid a terrible situation. Ferejohn and Fiorina associate variations in turnout in an electorate with differences in the presence of certain calculators among that electorate. They predict that the more persons there are who operate in terms of minimax regret, the higher the turnout rate will be.

Turnout continues to bedevil rational action theorists. Ordeshook, a leading exponent of the approach, summarizes several criticisms of Ferejohn and Fiorina's effort: "This criterion, however, can yield silly predictions. For example, if every citizen believes that having a fatal accident on the way to the polls is a conceivable possibility (the issue of how remote is irrelevant), then no one should vote" (1986, 486). In "The Selfish Voter Paradox and the Thrown-Away Vote Argument," Paul Meehl, a critic of rational choice theory, underlines the difficulties faced by those who would tie the decision to vote to the calculation that casting a ballot makes a voter better off than not doing so:

> Recently, there has been growing an uncomfortable awareness that such "economic" theories have major trouble dealing with a big brute fact, to wit, that the empirical probability of an individual voter's behavior determining the outcome of a large scale (e.g., U.S. presidential) election is negligible. Riker and Ordeshook estimate it as $p = 10^{-8}$, and my rough calculations indicate that my chances of determining who becomes President are about the same order of magnitude as my chances of being killed driving to the polls (1977, 11).

Ordeshook describes the current state of rational choice research on turnout. Because it is difficult to measure the psychic benefits and costs of voting, he says, we come close to saying that people vote because they believe it is better for them to vote than not to vote. This, in turn, seems to be a tautology. "Do people vote merely because they are socialized to do so?" he asks (Ordeshook 1986, 50). Rational action theorists cannot explain the decision to vote until they resolve the question of how to analyze the calculations of particular voters.

Rational choice theory offers a complete perspective on political analysis. Building on a carefully defined set of assumptions about individuals and their goals and using deductive logic, political scientists from this school offer solutions to a wide range of political phenomena. Notice, too, that rational action theorists emphasize the power of deductive logic rather than empirical evidence as they test and substantiate their hypotheses. Whether you accept this approach or not, you will rethink many of your long-held and deeply entrenched views of politics as you read the work of such theorists.

POLITICAL ATTITUDES AND POLITICAL BEHAVIOR

A second research school examines variations in attitudes, motives, and other psychological characteristics in order to explain political behavior. Since the beginning of the twentieth century—first in the work of Arthur Bentley (1909) and then most prominently in Harold Lasswell's studies (1962a, 1962b)—political scientists seeking to couch their explanations of political phenomena in the language of motives and purposeful action have been drawn to the work of psychologists. Like rational action studies, these analyses focus on the individual. Here, however, research seeks to posit types and clusters of attitudes. The political scientists who use this approach deny the claim that all persons seek to maximize their short-run self-interest. Instead, they contend, individuals have different sets of attitudes, and even in the same circumstance, they will behave in different ways. Political behavior varies, therefore, because individuals are motivated by different sets of goals and have diverse attitudes about politics.

This research school emphasizes several basic ideas:

1. Attitudes contain three elements: affective or emotional content; cognition, involving what a person knows or believes to be true; and the intention to act in a particular way.
2. Attitudes are distinct from and precede action. Consequently, they may be used to explain behavior.
3. It is important to organize attitudes into clusters of beliefs and thereby uncover the underlying principles.
4. It is also important to uncover the components of attitudes and to relate them to behavior.
5. Studies of political attitudes and behavior feature carefully designed empirical work and hypotheses drawn from rather loosely bound theories. Unlike rational action theory, they do not use deductive arguments and the proofs of mathematical reasoning.

Analysts of political attitudes generally agree on how to obtain data. They rely heavily on sample surveys of populations, devoting much attention to the quality of the data obtained in public opinion polls. They examine the reliability and the validity of the questions asked and answers received in such surveys; after all, it may not be easy to use the answers provided in telephone conversations as the means of "getting into the heads" of respondents in the mass surveys. They also struggle to make sure that the surveys draw proper samples of the population that will allow researchers to generalize from the sample surveyed to the population as a whole. The assessment of the quality of data obtained from public opinion polls is an ongoing theme of this research.

Political scientists in this research school also agree on how to analyze their data and on the proper standards of analysis. The study of political attitudes and behavior has moved from simple graphs and cross-tabulations, through various techniques of correlational analyses and other tests for bivariate relationships, to multiple regression and more sophisticated methods—all aimed at specifying the relative importance of the explanatory variables and the relationships among them. Equally important, these scholars share the same definition for explanation, which is tied to the ability to demonstrate a powerful empirical relationship. Simple correlations no longer suffice. The elements of regression analysis measure the relative impact of each variable on vote choice while controlling for the influence of the other explanatory variables. And the R^2 statistic identifies the proportion of the variance in the dependent variable that can be accounted for by the explanatory variables.

Studies of vote choice, especially in U.S. elections, and of political culture—the set of values and beliefs about politics that characterize members of a society—exemplify the approach that does political science by relating political attitudes and political behavior. You will encounter many of these studies in your explorations of political science; it will be useful, therefore, to examine their basic claims to knowledge more closely.

The Michigan Model of Electoral Behavior

Studies of vote choice in the United States have long centered on the analysis of the individual's attitudes toward the parties and the candidates. As you have seen in the work of Wolfinger and Rosenstone and of Powell, a guiding hypothesis relates psychological identification with a political party to support for that party at the polls. This variable first appeared in a book by Angus Campbell, Philip E. Converse, Warren E. Miller, and Donald E. Stokes, entitled *The American Voter* (1960). This classic study of electoral behavior in the United States introduced what is now known as the Michigan model of electoral behavior, named for the university at which the basic work was done.

According to the Michigan model, party identification guides the perception and evaluation of political information and behavior: "Generally this tie is a psychological identification, which can persist without legal recognition or evidence of formal membership and even without a consistent record of party support. Most Americans have this sense of attachment with one party or another. And for the individual who does, the strength and direction of party identification are facts of central importance in accounting for attitudes and behavior" (Campbell et al. 1960, 121).

As you will see in the next chapter, this approach, long the dominant mode of studying electoral behavior in the United States, has come under attack in recent years. And some new work adds attitudes toward the candidates to the center of the analysis. For example, Stanley Kelley, Jr., and Thad Mirer offer "the voter's decision rule":

The voter canvasses his likes and dislikes of the leading candidates and major parties involved in an election. Weighing each like and dislike equally, he votes for the candidate toward whom he has the greatest net number of favorable attitudes, if there is such a candidate. If no candidate has such an advantage, the voter votes consistently with his party affiliation, if he has one. If his attitudes do not incline him toward one candidate more than toward another, and if he does not identify with one of the major parties, the voter reaches a null decision (1974, 574).

Here, too, attitudes define perceptions and evaluations and therefore condition behavior. Researchers examine responses to survey questions from a representative sample of the U.S. population to identify such attitudes toward the parties and the candidates. These studies exemplify the way most scholars study electoral behavior in the United States.

Political Culture

Gabriel Almond and Sidney Verba's study, *The Civic Culture* (1963), examines political attitudes in order to explain the stability of democracies. Analyzing responses to surveys taken of large samples in the United States, Britain, West Germany, Italy, and Mexico, the authors categorize the distinctive sets of national responses into political cultures. They examine the presence and effects of the subjective competence of citizens—a concept very close to political efficacy, which, as you have already seen, is used by Wolfinger and Rosenstone and by Powell: "Compared with citizens whose subjective competence is low, the self-confident citizen is likely to be the active citizen: to follow politics, to discuss politics, to be a more active partisan. He is also more likely to be satisfied with his role as a participant and, subject to certain exceptions discussed above, likely to be more favorably disposed toward the performance of his political system and to have a generally more positive orientation to it" (Almond and Verba 1963, 257). Relative to the other three countries, maintain Almond and Verba, the United States and Britain have a higher proportion of such citizens. Both nations are characterized by a civic culture, a set of attitudes that fosters political participation and the stability of democracies. On the other hand, in Italy and Mexico, high levels of alienation inhibit participation and democracy, and high levels of political detachment weaken the effect of a strong sense of subject competence in Germany. Inspired by Almond and Verba, students of political culture have sought to relate variations in the presence of particular attitudes among citizens of a particular democracy to the aggregate characteristics of politics.

Relating Complex Attitudes to Political Behavior

Current research seeks to uncover more complex relationships among attitudes and behavior by introducing new concepts and variables and novel hypotheses. Three characteristics of attitudes are hypothesized to influence the likelihood that they will affect subsequent behavior: (1) Attitudes based on direct, personal experience are more important than those that have been formed outside an individual encounter; (2) The most clearly defined attitudes have a greater impact than those that are imprecise; (3) The more accessible (that is, the more easily remembered) the attitude is, the greater its effect on behavior is. Furthermore, factors related to personality types and social circumstances modify the impact of attitudes on behavior. For example, persons with high self-esteem are especially likely to act on their beliefs, and persons not given to helping others may do so when surrounded by people who expect such behavior. The effort to move beyond the simple association of attitude and behavior has added new concepts, variables, and hypotheses, increasing the complexity of the underlying theory.

Russell Fazio (1986) offers a model of the links between attitudes and behavior. The first step is labeled "object-evaluation association"—the first glimmer of a feeling, of knowledge, and of the intention to act. Over time, direct and emotional experience with the object moves it along a scale, as do frequently reading and hearing about the object. "Ease of access" is followed by "selective perception" of all subsequent information related to the object; next come "immediate perceptions of the object" and then "definitions of the event and the situation." When all factors are present, attitudes affect behavior. Put differently, Fazio asserts that when an attitude is stronger and the person's access to it is easier, it is more likely to influence how he or she sees and evaluates the world and to affect his or her behavior.

Fazio's hypotheses come from surveys of college students and from laboratory experiments, as well as a study of several hundred voters in Bloomington, Indiana. In June 1984, a group of 245 potential voters was questioned. Fazio sought to ascertain their attitudes toward the presidential candidates by asking them to respond to two statements: "A good president for the next four years would be Ronald Reagan [Walter Mondale]." The speed with which the respondents replied tapped the accessibility of their attitudes toward each candidate. The next phase of the experiment occurred in October, after the first presidential debates. The same respondents were mailed questionnaires, asking them to judge the performance of each candidate. This analysis was designed to investigate the degree of selective perception. A month later, they were asked how they intended to vote in the election. Fazio's study demonstrates that attitude accessibility (as measured by the speed of response) affects both the perceptions of the objects (here, Reagan's and Mondale's performances in the debates) and the consistency in the relationship between attitude and behavior (in this case, the decision to support Reagan or Mondale). "For both the entire sample and the subsample including only the voters, respondents whose attitudes toward Reagan were highly accessible displayed significantly greater attitude-behavior consistency than those whose attitudes were relatively less accessible. Indeed, among the voters in the high accessibility group, nearly 80% of the variance in voting behavior, as compared with 44% among low accessibility voters, was predicted by attitude toward Reagan" (Fazio and Williams 1986, 510). In addition, the more readily accessible the attitude was when first measured, the more the respondents believed that their preferred candidate won the debates and the more certain they were to vote for him. Indeed, the higher the initial level of attitude accessibility was, the more likely the respondents were to believe that the candidate's running mate won the debate between the vice presidential nominees (George Bush and Geraldine Ferraro). Fazio's research exemplifies the effort to link attitudes and behavior in order to ground explanations of politics in the psychological dispositions of the actors.

He and other political scientists from this research school agree on fundamental questions and methods, even when they differ over which hypotheses to test. Explanations of political phenomena, they insist, demand motives, dispositions, and answers to why persons behave as they do, together with information about the mental states of the actors. These political scientists question their subjects through surveys and intensive studies, then organize their data into quantitative analyses. They use the ability to account for variance in the dependent variable as the definition of explanation. And multivariate regression analyses are employed to assess the relative influence of different explanatory variables on the phenomenon to be explained. In their work, evidence replaces deductive logic as a basis for claims to knowledge.

APPROACHES FROM ANTHROPOLOGY

Some political scientists assume the intellectual stance of anthropologists. Organizing research at the group or structural level, they study politics in defined settings like villages, legislatures, and the decisionmaking bodies of political parties. This research school directs attention to the ways in which members of a particular community perceive and interact with each other. It offers a distinctive methodology for research but very few general concepts, hypotheses, and theories.

Indeed, some proponents of this research school deny that there can be theoretical systems with wide scope in the social sciences.

Anthropologists maintain that behavior, attitudes, and values must be understood in the context of the culture in which they occur. They deny that it is always useful to define self-interest the way rational action theory does, by associating it with economic benefits. In the presidential address to the Society for Cross-Cultural Research, Marc Howard Ross stresses this point:

> Humans do not just act; they also process actions, and this processing can have important effects on subsequent behavior. . . .
> Economic action, while often central to human behavior, rarely explains it by itself. Common economic situations can create constraints, but often they do not result in common actions. Economic conditions are filtered through perceptions and ideas about action possibilities. Consciousness is a cultural product only partially shaped by economic factors (1988b, 117).

According to this approach, the meanings of rationality and self-interest depend on the cultures in which persons live. All forms of social action must be interpreted in light of the surrounding structures and culture.

Anthropologists assume the existence of a community, composed not of individuals per se but of structured relationships.

> The word "structure" implies something composed of interdependent parts, and parts of a social structure are not individuals but activities or institutions. A society is not an agglomeration of persons but a system of social relations. . . . Many excellent monographs have examined different institutions among different peoples and have shown how they determine and are determined by the other institutions of their society, how, in a word, their activities and beliefs are consistent with each other (Pitt-Rivers 1971, xxv–xxvi).

The persistence of these patterns allows people to understand what is going on around them, to give meaning to their actions, and to report these meanings to the observer.

Analyses that draw on the perspectives and methods of anthropology take us beyond Western cultures to investigate small-scale and nonindustrial societies. These studies insist that we should be sensitive to problems of cross-cultural generalizations.

Consider once again the relationship between turnout and political participation. Where most people take part in politics by voting, there is good reason to examine turnout as an instance of the general concept of political participation, perhaps even to substitute the analysis of who casts a ballot for the analysis of who takes part in politics. But there are, of course, other ways to engage in politics. How then should you study political participation where there are no elections? To answer this question, you need two things: a method of research that enables you to study less obvious forms of political participation and an abstract definition of political participation that does not equate the concept with voting.

If motives are best ascertained by observing behavior over a long period of time—interpreting the meaning of actions in the context of surrounding beliefs and expectations—then anthropologists immerse themselves in the communities they study. The result of this research is known as an ethnography. Simple responses to survey questions will not do: Political efficacy means more than the response to the question, "People like me can influence government policy," to note Powell's and Wolfinger and Rosenstone's operationalization of this concept. To determine whether people believe themselves to have subjective political competence, you must understand the meaning of political participation to them and in the community in which they live. You need to observe them and their culture over a long period of time. You must ask them and then ask them again. Hence, in order to know how to analyze voting, lobbying, demonstrating, and other forms of political participation, you need a detailed knowledge of the community's culture.

Clifford Geertz, a leading exponent of this form of research, insists that analysis seeks to understand the meaning of actions. "The thing to ask is what their import is: what it is, ridicule or challenge, irony or anger, snobbery or pride, that, in their occurrence and through their agency, is getting said" (Geertz 1973, 10). Going into the field—observing, questioning, speculating—anthropologists seek to make sense of what other people do. In Geertz's words, "Our data are really our own constructions of other people's constructions of what they and their compatriots are up to" (1973, 9). As anthropologists work, they detail the perceptions, actions, and structures that compose the community:

> Ethnography is thick description. What the ethnographer is faced with—except when (as, of course, he must do) he is pursuing the more automatized routines of data collection—is a multiplicity of complex conceptual structures, many of them superimposed upon or knotted into one another, which are at once strange, irregular, and inexplicit, and which he must contrive somehow first to grasp and then to render. . . . Doing ethnography is like trying to read (in the sense of "construct a reading of") a manuscript—foreign, faded, full of ellipses, incoherencies, suspicious emendations, and tendentious commentaries, but written not

in conventionalized graphs of sound but in transient examples of shaped behavior (Geertz 1973, 9-10).

The ethnographer's strength, argues Geertz, rests not on an ability to gather facts about strange places "but on the degree to which he is able to clarify what goes on in such places, to reduce the puzzlement . . . to which unfamiliar acts emerging out of unknown backgrounds naturally give rise" (1973, 16). Anthropologists seek to find their way among strangers, to learn how these humans live their lives.

In "Political Organization and Political Participation," Ross solves the problem of providing an abstract definition of political participation. Expanding the concept, he defines it as "efforts on the part of members of a community to influence, either directly or indirectly, the authoritative allocation of values in their community" (Ross 1988a, 74). Voting in elections is one indicator of political participation; so, too, is speaking at a general village meeting. Ross also divides participation into range and involvement. Range refers to the areas of life affected by authoritative power and involvement. The abstract definition of involvement is "whether participation in decision making is the province of a small number of people or whether a broad portion of the community becomes active either directly or indirectly" (Ross 1988a, 74-75). He then applies the rules of operationalizations to these concepts. In addition, he separates the concept of involvement into four levels: It is "widespread" when the forums for decisionmaking "are open to all adults and involvement seems relatively great." The lowest level ("low or nonexistent") is present "where leaders make most decisions and involvement of the average person is highly limited or absent" (Ross 1988a, 78). As anthropologists analyze diverse cultures, they force political scientists to expand and carefully define critical concepts of political science.

Cross-cultural Analyses:
How Can We Generalize from Particular Cases?

Geertz and Ross move the results of ethnographic research in different directions, taking opposing stands on whether or how we may generalize from a particular field study. Geertz maintains that we should seek to better understand the particular community. Reminding us of the limited nature of each and every ethnography, he sharply circumscribes our ability to test general hypotheses and draw wide-ranging theoretical conclusions from our research. Ross, however, summarizes ethnographies into numerically ordered data, enabling him to relate the particular analyses to more general theories of politics.

Note that Geertz attaches inherent limitations to any and all analyses. In the passage cited above, he equates ethnographies with the effort to "construct a reading of" a manuscript. Hence, he suggests that the ethnographer seeks a plausible reading of a situation, not the only interpretation or the "right" analysis. Research seeks to understand the meaning of social action, knowing that there are always multiple meanings. As a result, he urges us to be very cautious as we try to generalize beyond the specific community.

Note, as well, that Geertz directs attention to the particulars of each community. The standard of "thick description" allows us to sort a good account from a bad one. "It is not against a body of uninterpreted data, radically thinned descriptions, that we must measure the cogency of our explications. . . . It is not worth it, as Thoreau said, to go round the world to count the cats in Zanzibar" (Geertz 1973, 16). He presents the same point in a more abstract formulation: "The important thing about the anthropologist's findings is their complex specificness, their circumstantiality" (1973, 23). In place after place in his essay, he reaffirms his belief that anthropologists must give us specific descriptions of the complexities of social life.

Geertz's essay displays a persistent tension. On one hand, he insists that research elucidate the specific, rather than attempt to formulate general hypotheses and theories. "Culture analysis is (or should be) guessing at meanings, assessing the guesses, and drawing explanatory conclusions from the better guesses, not discovering the Continent of Meaning and mapping out its bodiless landscape" (Geertz 1973, 20). Theories should not "codify abstract regularities"; they should enable us "to make thick description possible, not to generalize across cases but to generalize within them" (1973, 26). On the other hand, Geertz shies away from concluding that general concepts may not be applied to particular cases. He notes that thick descriptions allow us to give meaning to "the mega-concepts with which contemporary social science is afflicted—legitimacy, modernization, integration, conflict, structure" (1973, 23). Here, his ambivalence shines through when he labels abstract concepts "afflictions." In a more positive formulation, he maintains that "the aim is to draw large conclusions from small, but very densely textured facts; to support broad assertions about the role of culture in the construction of collective life by engaging them exactly with complex specifics" (1973, 28). Overall, Geertz insists on the need for thick description and general concepts and maintains that we may offer no more than generalizations about specific communities.

Ross, however, illustrates a variety of political anthropology that generalizes from ethnographies and employs data from these studies to test theories of politics. Using George Murdock and Peter White's standard cross-cultural sample, which reports on the results of ninety ethnographies from nonindustrial societies, Ross expands the abstract and operational definitions of political participation and tests hypotheses drawn from alternative theories of this phenomenon, some of which you have already seen used in analyses of turnout. One set involves the "level of resources." For example, he says, "The socioeconomic or mobilization hypothesis connects the rise of political involvement to the spread of individual resources, such as education and wealth" (Ross 1988a, 75). Ross cites others who tie variations in individual participation with variations in social status and differences in rates of participation across societies with variations in " 'societal complexity,' such as that associated with high levels of industrialization" (1988a, 75). He offers another hypothesis: "A second form of the level of resources argument regards participation as a product of psychocultural forces in a society and connects early learning experiences to later life orientations" (1988a, 75). He suggests that persons with "participatory personalities" are more likely to take part in politics, and he also tests hypotheses that rest on the characteristics of social and political institutions: "Political action, in this view, is part of a broader complex of institutional patterns which can favor or inhibit the impact of particular individuals and groups in a society. Three features of preindustrial social organization are particularly likely to be related to range and involvement: the concentration of power and authority, the strength of cross-cutting ties, and the importance of fraternal interest groups in a society" (1988a, 75–76). Thus, you can see that Ross's research applies hypotheses used to explain electoral turnout in industrial democracies to political participation in nonindustrial societies.

Very much unlike Geertz, Ross uses the techniques of multivariate analysis on the data drawn from the ethnographies. First, he codes the reports into operational measures of rival explanatory variables. Then, he tests for their relative explanatory power. His results demonstrate that political involvement is a "direct function of political organization and only indirectly related to socioeconomic complexity" (Ross 1988a, 79). Ross's findings also deny that education, wealth, and other measures of social status, as well as particular psychological characteristics, affect the likelihood that a person will be involved in politics.

> A starting point in understanding our results comes from Verba, Nie, and Kim, who also identify political organization as central in their explanation of cross-system differences in participation. While individual resources . . . can be crucial determinants of political action, they show that these variables make much more of a difference in some countries . . . than in others . . . as institutional arrangements can enhance, have no effect

upon, or inhibit the impact of individual differences on political participation (1988a, 82).

His analysis further weakens the general utility of Wolfinger and Rosenstone's explanation of turnout and strengthens both Powell's and Jackman's contention that variations in the characteristics of political institutions have the greatest influence on cross-national variations in political participation.

Questions on generalization and the proper place of theory divide political anthropologists. Geertz maintains that the abstract concepts of political science may be used to help develop thick descriptions of particular communities. Ross uses ethnographies to measure abstract concepts and test hypotheses. He denies Geertz's view that the goal of research is a better understanding of the particular. In turn, Geertz denies Ross's ability to generalize from the results of ethnographies to measures of abstract variables. Finally, Ross pulls studies using the research methods of anthropology toward other forms of political science, but Geertz suggests that the social sciences stand apart from the other sciences.

To summarize this research school, several characteristics should be highlighted. First, research in political anthropology involves fieldwork. Scholars go to the community they choose to study and spend years observing and talking with its members. As they study the intricacies of the community's life, they learn how to observe the structures and culture present there and develop a detailed picture of a particular place. A persistent question is whether it is appropriate to generalize from the particular study to other cases. Some anthropologists deny our right to generalize, insisting that each community is unique. Instead, they direct us to describe, richly and precisely, the particular culture and place. Others maintain that taking into account material obtained from diverse and frequently overlooked societies allows us to develop especially powerful hypotheses. Overall, political anthropologists do not offer novel concepts and hypotheses. Rather, they raise questions and suggest findings that force us to rethink the orthodox understandings of politics and the modes of doing political science.

MARX'S THEORY

Karl Marx's theory of social science has changed the world. Just think of the political activists and government leaders who strode onto the stage of history following Marx's lines and directions and struggling to fulfill his dreams and predictions. Students of Marx's analyses of

European capitalism formed the political movements, unions, political parties, and revolutionary cells of the Socialist and Communist parties. And their colleagues organized parallel movements in Africa, the Americas, and Asia. Across the world, these political activists battled to apply the tenets of Marx's social science.

Writing more than a century ago, sometimes in collaboration with Friedrich Engels, Karl Marx offers theoretically compelling analyses of extraordinary scope. He works from a carefully defined set of assumptions to present explanatory hypotheses and predictions of a broad array of phenomena. Furthermore, he claims to offer an accurate reading of reality, not just another interpretation. The questions he addresses cover, among other things: the rise of industrial economies; patterns of industrialization; the relationship among economic, social, and political structures; the conditions under which revolution will occur in capitalist societies; the place of class and class conflict in capitalism; the formation of political organizations; and conflict and cooperation among nations. Marx insists that social science include normative assessments and *praxis*—calls to action based on the theoretical understanding of issues and events. In his criticism of German philosophy, he declares that "the philosophers have only *interpreted* the world, in various ways; the point, however, is to *change* it" (from *Theses on Feuerbach,* cited in Tucker 1978, 145, emphasis in original). Marx's studies include initial forays into the principles of social life and human behavior (set out, for example, in *The German Ideology* and *A Contribution to the Critique of Political Economy*); detailed analyses of political events (such as *The Class Struggles in France* and *The Eighteenth Brumaire of Louis Bonaparte*); and a massive study of capitalism (summarized in *Capital*). The range of cases covered, the explanatory power, and the call to action have given his analysis an extraordinary appeal not only to political activists but to scholars, as well.

The best way to understand Marx's approach to social science is to read his work carefully and to reread it many times. This is especially true because there are so many interpretations of his theories. My goal in this volume is to present a reading of Marx that emphasizes the theoretical power of his argument, not an overview of his life's work. You must master Marx on your own.

Social Bonds Condition Individual Life

Marx presents a set of universally applicable principles of social, economic, and political life. Like the anthropologists, he focuses attention on the structural level of analysis—on the communities and structures that provide the context and determinants of how people behave. However, Marx stresses that economic patterns provide the bedrock upon which society and politics rest. Throughout this section, I will frequently let Marx speak for himself.

First of all, he maintains that individuals live their lives in relations with others.

> To speak precisely and in ordinary language, the members of civil society are not atoms. The characteristic quality of an atom is to have no qualities, and consequently no relations determined by its own nature with other human beings outside itself. . . . The individual finds himself forced by every one of his senses to believe in the existence of the world and of other individuals . . . . Every one of his activities and qualities, every one of his aspirations, becomes a need, a want which transforms his egoism into a desire for things and human beings outside himself. . . . It is, therefore, natural necessity, it is the essential qualities of man, however alienated the form in which they appear, it is interest, which hold together the members of civil society, whose real bond is constituted by civil and not by political life (from *The Holy Family*, cited in Bottomore and Rubel 1964, 219–220).

According to Marx, it is not useful to analyze politics as if only individuals exist, as rational choice theory and the research school of political attitudes and behavior would have it. People are naturally and necessarily social, Marx tells us, and social ties necessarily bind individuals together.

Marxist theory also contends that meaningful analysis takes place at the structural level. There are two critical points here. First, the particular components of a society interrelate with each other. And second, the economic structure carries primary weight, determining the characteristics of the other structures. Indeed, politics is a second-level derivative of the economic structure:

> What is society, whatever its form may be? The product of men's reciprocal activity. Are men free to choose this or that form of society by themselves? By no means. Assume a particular state of development in the productive forces of man and you will get a particular form of commerce and consumption. Assume particular stages of development, commerce, and consumption and you will have a corresponding social order, a corresponding organization of the family and of the ranks and the classes, in a word a corresponding civil society. Presuppose a particular civil society and you will get particular political conditions which are only the official expression of civil society. . . .
>
> The mode of production of material life conditions the social, political, and intellectual life process in general. It is not the consciousness of men that determines their being, but on the contrary, their social being

determines their consciousness (from *Preface to a Contribution to a Critique of Political Economy*, cited in Smelser 1973, 3–5).

Therefore, Marx believes that change in the economic structure leads to revolution, which he defines as the change from one type of society to another. He also posits a process model, which enables him to analyze variation in the development of societies. This model is characterized by five elements: a general theme; clear entrance and exit points for each stage; the claim that no unit may skip a stage; the claim that each and every unit must go through each stage; and the claim that if a unit stops, its behavior will not be ideal. Revolution occurs through the transition from one stage to the next. Marx's process model examines whole societies as they move through the distinct stages of development:

> At a certain stage of their development, the material productive forces of society come in conflict with the existing relations of production, or—what is but a legal expression for the same thing—the property relations within which they have been at work hitherto. From forms of development of the productive forces these relations turn into their fetters. Then begins an epoch of social revolution. With the change of the economic foundation the entire immense superstructure is more or less rapidly transformed. . . . In broad outlines Asiatic, ancient, feudal, and modern bourgeois modes of production can be designated as progressive epochs in the economic formation of society. The bourgeois relations of production are the last antagonistic form of the social process of production—antagonistic not in the sense of individual antagonism but of one arising from the social conditions of life of the individuals; at the same time the productive forces developing in the womb of bourgeois society create the material conditions for the solution of that antagonism. This social formation brings, therefore, the prehistory of human society to a close (from *Preface to a Contribution to a Critique of Political Economy*, cited in Smelser 1973, 3–5).

Marx also states that individuals find their places in the class structures of their societies. Their goals and behavior derive from and are explained by their positions in the economic, social, and political structure, especially how they stand in relation to the means of production. Human nature, therefore, is that of a creative laborer. In *The German Ideology*, he writes: "As individuals express their life, so they are. What they are, therefore, coincides with their production, both with what they produce and how they produce. The nature of individuals thus depends on the material conditions determining their production" (Marx and Engels 1963, 7). Marx assumes the existence of an essential definition of the human being and ties that essence to how a person labors—his or her place in the means of production—and to other persons who share that same position. These ties define the individual's goals.

In summary, Marx maintains that societies should be analyzed as patterns of interacting structures in which economic structures determine all other forms of behavior. Societies move along a scale of development, powered by contradictions between needs of production and the organization of social and political life. And individuals are defined by the way they work.

What Justifies the Theory?

How does Marx know what he knows? How does he substantiate these broad claims? Essentially he reasons from a small number of axioms, and he begins by answering the question of how humans sustain their lives. What must they do in order to go on living and to create new human beings?

> The first premise of all human existence, and therefore of all history, [is] the premise namely that men be in a position to live in order to be able to "make history."
>
> The second fundamental point is that as soon as a need is satisfied (which implies the action of satisfying and the acquisition of an instrument), new needs are made; and this production of new needs is the first historical act. . . .
>
> The third circumstance which, from the very first, enters into historical development, is that men, who daily remake their own life [sic], begin to make other men, to propagate their kind: the relation between man and wife, parents and children, the family. . . .
>
> The production of life, both of one's own in labor and of fresh life in procreation, now appears as a double relationship: on the one hand as a natural, on the other as a social relationship. By social we understand the cooperation of several individuals. . . . It follows from this that a certain mode of production, or industrial stage, is always combined with a certain mode of cooperation, or social stage, and this mode of cooperation is itself a "productive force." Further, that the multitude of productive forces accessible to men determines the nature of society, hence that "the history of humanity" must always be studied and treated in relation to the history of industry and exchange. . . .
>
> With increased productivity, the increase of needs, and what is fundamental to both of these, the increase of population . . . there develops the division of labor (Marx and Engels 1963, 16–20).

Marx elaborates these points earlier in the same work:

The nature of individuals thus depends on the material conditions determining their production. . . .

This production only makes its appearance with the increase of population. In its turn this presupposes the intercourse of individuals with one another. The form of this intercourse is again determined by production.

The relations of different nations among themselves depend upon the extent to which each has developed its productive forces, the division of labor, and internal intercourse. But not only the relation of one nation to others, but also the whole internal structure of the nation itself depends on the stage of development reached by its production and its internal intercourse (Marx and Engels 1963, 7–8).

Marx instructs us to start at the beginning, namely, to ask what must be done to keep a person alive. His answer is that a person must obtain food, shelter, and clothing. But to meet these needs, each individual must have the assistance of others. Similarly, there can be no children without the social and physical assistance of others. Because the need for others is a requisite of staying alive, social ties define each person. How one meets those needs—how one labors—explains how one interacts with others. Put differently, how people work explains the social and political characteristics of their society.

Marx's own primary interest was explaining, predicting, and helping to establish the conditions that would fundamentally alter the capitalist world in which he lived, transforming it into a better, more just, and equal world. He places his theory of revolution under capitalism into a more general theory of revolution in all societies. His process model details stages of social and economic development and revolutionary transformation: Asiatic, ancient, feudal, and capitalist, Socialist, and Communist. Revolution occurs, he tell us, when the existing stage of development loses its productive force. Marx proudly and happily combined normative and analytical concerns.

The Concept of Class in Marx's Net of Analysis

The concept of class is at the core of Marx's theory. It provides the key to the analysis of how individuals are tied to each other and how conflict between classes leads to revolution. In his view, no other conflict, no matter how bloody, can effect a revolution. All critical hypotheses in Marx's theory use the concept of class, and he highlights a complex interaction between class position and a person's attitudes, values, and action.

Under capitalism, he says, everyone learns and accepts the culture of the capitalist class. In *The German Ideology,* he writes:

> The ideas of the ruling class are in every epoch the ruling ideas: i.e., the class which is the ruling material force of society is at the same time its ruling intellectual force. The class which has the means of material production at its disposal has control at the same time over the means of mental production, so that thereby, generally speaking, the ideas of those who lack the means of mental production are subject to it. The ruling ideas are nothing more than the ideal expression of the dominant material relationships . . . hence of the relationships which make the one class the ruling one, therefore, the ideas of its dominance (cited in Tucker 1978, 172).

In other words, as you attend school, read the newspapers, pay attention to the other media, and go to church, you learn the values that sustain capitalism.

But no matter what the capitalists teach the workers, how they work is the best and really only determinant of their values and culture. Workers see each other at work, go to and from the factory together, and come to understand that they are like each other. Equally important, they realize that their interests are fundamentally different from those of the capitalists. Because intellectual understanding comes from one's place in the world of labor, Marx argues that workers must develop these ideas. Note that he maintains that his ideas are in accord with reality; as a result, workers will necessarily come to see the world as it actually exists. Socialist activists can speed this process by teaching the workers the tenets of Marxism, but they do not make it happen. Here and in many other places, Marx insists that what is real will be understood.

More generally, as economic development occurs, social relations change, and ties among members of the same social class form. Changes in the division of labor and alterations in the manner of production necessarily alter the values and actions of individuals. "Connected with this a class is called forth, which has to bear the burdens of society without enjoying its advantages, which ousted from society, is forced into the most decided antagonism to all other classes; a class which forms the majority of all members of society, and from which emanates the consciousness of the necessity of a fundamental revolution, the communist consciousness" (from *The German Ideology*, cited in Tucker 1978, 192–193). Changes in the modes of production bring forth a revolutionary class, which shakes off the restraining vision of the outdated values.

How does Marx define the class concept? Nowhere in his writings does he offer a formal definition and operationalization of the concept. Rather, his meaning can be taken from various implications and statements he makes. For example, he states that social classes derive from the different places in the division of labor and that membership in a class is defined by one's relationship to the means of production. The development of capitalism divides labor into two classes: Capitalists own the means of production, and members of the proletariat sell their labor power to those who own the means of production. Classes, however, are more than economic categories. They are social and political communities, which form the cleavages of industrial societies. Marx illustrates this point by showing how the "small-holding peasants" in France were not a class:

> In so far as millions of families live under economic conditions of existence that divide their mode of life, their interests and their culture from those of the other classes, they form a class. In so far as there is merely a local interconnection among these small peasants, and the identity of their interests begets no unity, no national union, and no political organisation, they do not form a class (from "The Historical Specifics of the Class Struggle" in *The Eighteenth Brumaire of Louis Bonaparte*, cited in Tucker 1978, 608).

Thus, under capitalism, industrial workers form a social class in which objective economic position determines social ties, subjective identity, political interests, and political behavior. The proletariat is the productive class, and the existing social, cultural, and political structures exploit and limit the productive contribution of industrial workers. The proletariat, therefore, is a class engaged in revolutionary political action.

Furthermore, Marx states that where there are social classes, there is class conflict. Different locations in the division of labor are associated with conflicting interests. In turn, the opposing interests produce conflict between the social classes. Consequently, only where there is no division of labor are there no social classes and no class conflict. The absence of a division of labor defines the future Communist society: "In communist society, where nobody has one exclusive sphere of activity, but each can become accomplished in any branch he wishes, society regulates general production and thus makes it possible for me to do one thing today and another tomorrow, to hunt in the morning, fish in the afternoon, rear cattle in the evening, criticise after dinner, just as I have in mind, without ever becoming hunter, fisherman, shepherd or critic (from *The German Ideology*, cited in Tucker 1978, 160). All other societies are necessarily characterized by a division of labor, classes, and class conflict, and he predicts that all will end in revolution.

According to Marxist theory, the conflict between the working class and the capitalists defines production, social life, and politics. Capitalism requires the accumulation of capital—resources to be invested into production that come from the profits of the surplus-value of production. (Surplus-value is the difference between the value workers produce from their labor and the wages they receive.) Therefore, capitalists strive to extract surplus-value from the proletariat. By extension, competition among the capitalists demands that they extract increasing amounts of surplus-value from that group, lest they be driven out of business. In turn, this competition among the capitalists leads to growth in the size of the proletariat, mechanization of the labor process, expansion of the workplace, alienation and immiseration of the workers, political organization of the workers, crises of capitalism, internationalization of capitalism, conflict between workers and the capitalists, and revolution.

> Expropriation is accomplished by the action of the immanent laws of capitalistic production itself, by the centralization of capital. One capitalist always kills many. Hand in hand with this centralization, or this expropriation of many capitalists by a few, develop, on an ever-extending scale, the cooperative form of the labor-process, the conscious technical application of science, the methodical cultivation of the soil, the transformation of the instruments of labor into instruments of labor only usable in common . . . the entanglement of all peoples in the net of the world-market, and with this, the international character of the capitalistic regime. Along with the constantly diminishing number of the magnates of capital, who usurp and monopolize all advantages of this process of transformation, grows the mass of misery, oppression, slavery, degradation, exploitation, but with this too grows the revolt of the working-class, a class always increasing in numbers, and disciplined, united, organized by the very mechanism of the process of capitalist production itself. The monopoly of capital becomes a fetter upon the mode of production, which has sprung up and flourished along with, and under, it. Centralization of the means of production and socialization of labor at last reach a point where they become incompatible with their capitalist integument. This integument is burst asunder. The knell of capitalist private property sounds. The expropriators are expropriated (Marx 1906, 836–837).

In sum, Marx believes that capitalist development entails competition among the capitalists, which increases the exploitation of the proletariat. As a result, the revolutionary consciousness, organization, and action of the working class grows, and revolutionary conflict between capitalist and proletariat follows. He thus weaves precise hypotheses into a tapestry depicting the revolutionary transformation of capitalism.

Political scientists seeking to apply and test Marx's theory have devoted particular attention to the politicization of social classes. They study, among other things, the formation of Socialist parties and labor unions; the effect of class position on vote choice; the likelihood of strikes and revolutionary outbreaks; and how the patterns of capitalist accumulation affect government policy. They use Marx's concepts and hypotheses to provide descriptively rich and theoretically significant analyses of capitalist politics. (Marx's influence on Piven and Cloward's work should be evident.) His approach provides concepts, variables, and hypotheses in a distinct language of analysis, claiming to lay bare the determinants of politics in capitalist societies. At the same time, it contains a call to political action: It is good and proper to enhance the power of the working class and to act to bring about the revolution. Marx's theory claims to have uncovered both the determinants of revolutionary change and the means to hasten that process.

WEBER'S SOCIAL SCIENCE

Max Weber was a founding father of contemporary social science. Writing a generation after Marx, he denied many of Marx's favorite hypotheses, unraveled his theoretical net, and promoted liberal democratic politics rather than Socialist and revolutionary politics. Weber's own research was prodigious. Beginning with a study of agricultural workers in the eastern portions of Germany, he went on to analyze ancient Israel, ancient India, ancient China, Roman law, the history of the city, and the philosophy of music. His most famous single work, *The Protestant Ethic and the Spirit of Capitalism* (1958), contests Marx's analysis of the rise of capitalism. Indeed, it is appropriate to see much of Weber's work as a direct confrontation with Marx. Weber denies the possibility of complete theories of politics that offer solutions to all problems. In their place, he offers "shafts of light"—criticisms, methodological strictures, a detailed philosophy of social science, and searching questions about the meaning of science. In contrast to Marx's laws and certainties, Weber offers new questions, guides to research single hypotheses, and limited knowledge.

Reading Weber forces us to rethink many of our simple expectations about how to study the social and political world. He denies our ability to see completely and clearly and, therefore, to describe completely and clearly the world around us.:

> As soon as we attempt to reflect about the way in which life confronts us in immediate concrete situations, it presents an infinite multiplicity of successively and coexistently emerging and disappearing events both "within" and "outside" ourselves. The absolute infinitude of this mul-

tiplicity is seen to remain undiminished even when our attention is focused upon a single "object," for instance, a concrete act of exchange, as soon as we seriously attempt an exhaustive description of all the individual components of this "individual phenomena," to say nothing of explaining it causally (from *The Methodology of the Social Sciences*, cited in Eldridge 1980, 11).

It follows that if complete description is impossible, so, too, is full explanation. Consequently, Weber asserts that any effort to claim that our theories are in complete accord with reality must fail.

Weber on Marx's Concept of Class

Weber's fundamental disagreement with Marx should begin to be evident from just this statement alone. To help you understand the depths of their differences, we need to look directly at Weber's criticism of the Marxist concept of class.

That concept, he says, contains empirical and theoretical flaws. First, the relationships between class and other social, economic, and political variables are conditional, best described as statistical rather than universal generalizations, and are indeterminate in their causal flow. Class is but one possible basis of political action. "In our terminology, 'classes' are not communities; they merely represent possible and frequent bases for communal action." In Weber's conceptual language, class is an objective economic category, defined by place in the commodity or labor markets and by the possession of goods and opportunities for income: "Class situation is in this sense ultimately market situation" (cited in Eisenstadt 1968, 170–171). Class position entails no necessarily shared interests and may or may not lead to common action. When it does, it is "linked to the general cultural conditions, especially of an intellectual sort" and the extent to which persons view their position as a consequence of their class (Weber, cited in Eisenstadt 1968, 173). "Thus every class may be the carrier of any one of the possibly innumerable forms of 'class action,' but this is not necessarily so" (Weber, cited in Eisenstadt 1968, 174). Therefore, argues Weber, Marx's concept of class is poorly defined and is used in hypotheses that are empirically false.

In the essay, "Socialism," written in 1918 (cited in Eldridge 1980, 191–219), Weber directly negates predictions taken from Marx's theory. He denies that the workers are getting poorer, that there is an ever-increasing number of permanently unemployed, and that capitalism is necessarily characterized by ruthless competition among the capitalists. Weber states that classic socialism's hope for economic crises "has been essentially given up today. For while the danger of a crisis admittedly has not disappeared, its relative importance has diminished now that businessmen have progressed from ruthless competition to syndication" (cited in Eldridge 1980, 207–208). Hence, Weber maintains, Marx's theory as such is false. It is interesting and useful in providing partial explanations, but it fails as a true and complete theory of capitalism.

Weber's criticism of Marx underlines his rejection of all efforts to develop complete explanations of social phenomena:

> We will only point out here that naturally all specifically Marxian "laws" and developmental constructs, in so far as they are theoretically sound, are ideal types. The eminent, indeed, heuristic significance of these ideal types when they are used for the assessment of reality is known to everyone who has ever employed Marxian concepts and hypotheses. Similarly, their perniciousness, as soon as they are thought of as empirically valid or as real (i. e., truly metaphysical) "effective forces," "tendencies," etc., is likewise known to those who have used them (from *The Methodology of the Social Sciences*, cited in Eldridge 1980, 228).

I will return in a moment to the meaning of "ideal-type." First, however, I want to emphasize that Weber does not deny our ability to describe or explain the political world. Rather, he insists that description and explanation must always be partial. Description is not easier than explanation; both are difficult. But as analysts, we strive to do as much as we can, knowing that we can never be certain of our descriptions and explanations. Weber does not advance laws and theories of politics. Instead, seeking to adapt his thinking to what he perceives to be the nature of social and political reality, he develops a distinctive methodology for social science.

Weber's Guide to Social Science

In his new methodology, Weber posits three components. The first is social action—those actions and interactions of humans that are oriented to the actions of other persons. "Action is social in so far as, by virtue of the subjective meaning attached to it by the acting individual (or individuals), it takes account of the behaviour of others and is thereby oriented in its course" (Weber, cited in Eisenstadt 1968, 3). The second component is social facts—those actions and interactions of humans that have the characteristics of natural events, like population patterns and migration flows. "For example, a mere collision of two cyclists may be compared to a natural event. On the other hand, their attempt to avoid hitting each other, or whatever insults, blows, or friendly discussion might follow the collision would constitute 'social action'" (Weber, cited in Eisenstadt 1968, 5). Finally, there is social structure—

the social interactions of a plurality of persons, which take on effects of their own. Because social action necessarily reflects a person's goals and perceptions, the explanation of social action must involve the analysis of the other's mind. At the same time, social action is conditioned and characterized by the interaction of large numbers of people, and these, too, require separate analysis. Hence, a proper and adequate study of social phenomena, among them political behavior and institutions, entails analysis at both the individual and structural levels.

Weber maintains that social phenomena are distinct from other phenomena because those who engage in social action give it meaning. Therefore, he insists, the analysis of social phenomena must include the effort to understand the motives, perceptions, and goals of the actors. "Subjective understanding is the specific characterisation of sociological knowledge" (Weber, cited in Parsons 1964, 104). You should notice the impact that Weber's thinking has had on Geertz. Indeed, Geertz draws a direct line from Weber to the analysis of culture and thick description. "Believing, with Max Weber, that man is an animal suspended in webs of significance he himself has spun, I take culture to be those webs, and the analysis of it to be therefore not an experimental science in search of law but an interpretive one in search of meaning" (Geertz 1973, 5). The explanation of social action requires interpreting the meaning that the actors give their actions.

How can we claim to understand the motives of the actors sufficiently to explain their behavior? How do we explain social phenomena? Weber's method combines two elements: *verstehen*—the analytic act of empathetic understanding, which works by positing a plausible context for the social action—and the empirical verification of the posited motive against subsequent action. "More generally, verification of subjective interpretation by comparison with the concrete course of events is, as in the case of all hypotheses, indispensable" (Weber, cited in Parsons 1964, 97). Sometimes, this can be done through psychological tests. But it usually requires comparing large numbers of cases, searching for the absence or presence of alternative explanatory factors. The explanation of a particular event, a concrete course of action, requires the location of a motive. And verification of the motive requires empirical evidence.

To explain a pattern of events, "a correct causal interpretation of typical action," Weber insists that an adequate motive must be verified as present and that it be shown that its presence is frequently associated with the resulting behavior (cited in Parsons 1964, 99). The explanation of social patterns must be causally adequate, that is, "according to established generalizations from experience, there is a probability that it will always actually occur in the same way" (Weber, cited in Parsons

1964, 99). No matter how high the correlation between two variables, without a verified motive, the relationship "is still an incomprehensible statistical uniformity" (Weber, cited in Parsons 1964, 99). And no matter how plausible the interpretation of a social phenomenon, it may be said to explain it "only in so far as there is some kind of proof for the existence of a probability that action in fact normally takes the course which has been said to be meaningful. For this there must be some degree of determinable frequency of approximation to an average or pure type" (Weber, cited in Parsons 1964, 99). The strong efforts of Wolfinger and Rosenstone and of Powell to provide data on the attitudes and motives of voters provides evidence of the extent to which contemporary political science has taken Weber's strictures to heart. Geertz, it would seem, heeds Weber's call for empathetic understanding but ignores the need for statistical generalizations. Weber maintains that both motives and statistical uniformities are required to explain social patterns.

How can political scientists establish the motives of persons they cannot observe? Indeed, how can they hope to explain the actions of persons no longer alive? Most political scientists—like Powell, Wolfinger, Rosenstone, Almond, and Verba—do not try, choosing, instead, to focus their efforts on those whom they can observe through survey data. Others mistakenly derive motives from behavior, engaging in a tautological effort. Weber offers a novel solution to this perplexing problem.

He posits a typology of orientation to social action that may be applied to persons in all societies and all periods. First, Weber distinguishes between the means and ends of actions and between rational and nonrational behavior. This produces a typology with four cells: traditional, emotional, absolute value rational, and instrumental value rational. A traditional orientation to action characterizes those who simply adopt, without thinking, life patterns from parents and community. Those who have an emotional orientation to action leap at their values, again without making a reasoned judgment. The last two orientations involve the use of reason. The absolute value rational orientation typifies persons who make emotional commitments to their ultimate goals but reason carefully how to reach those ends. Finally, persons who calculate their interests, reasoning about the ultimate purpose of their lives as well as calculating how best to reach their goals, are categorized as instrumental value rational types (Weber, cited in Eisenstadt 1968, 6). Weber maintains that these and only these four types characterize all persons wherever they are and whenever they live. Each person is more strongly characterized by one of these orientations than by any of the others. This typology allows Weber to analyze goals and values. He does not assume that all persons share the same goals, as rational action theory does. Nor does he assume that persons of the same class or community share the same orientation to action. At the same time, he claims the ability to analyze goals and values without using surveys, personal interviews, or the anthropologist's techniques of ethnographic research.

To analyze social structures, Weber expands on the technique of ideal-types—analytic constructs that are models of phenomena containing a set of logically related characteristics. These are abstractions, not mirrors but approximations of reality devised to assist analysis. "In *all* cases, rational or irrational, sociological analysis both abstracts from reality and at the same time helps us to understand it, in that it shows with what degree of approximation a concrete historical phenomenon may be in one aspect 'feudal,' in another 'patrimonial,' in another 'bureaucratic,' and in still another 'charismatic' " (Weber, cited in Parsons 1964, 110, emphasis in original). Unlike Marx, Weber does not posit social and political laws. Instead, he proposes abstractions and compares concrete events to these ideal-types. Each ideal-type aids analysis, but it is not a replication of the "world out there." It can only observe a part of reality, and it can never do so completely.

Weber offers a typology of authority structures to analyze political institutions, which he defines as legitimate arrangements of power among large numbers of persons. Hence, the basis on which authority is claimed and granted is the key to their analysis. He proposes three ideal-types based on the claims to legitimacy: charismatic, traditional, and rational-legal.

> Legitimacy may be ascribed to an order by those subject to it in the following ways:-
> (a) By tradition; a belief in the legitimacy of what has always existed; (b) by virtue of affectual attitudes, especially emotional, legitimising the validity of what is newly revealed or a model to imitate; (c) by virtue of a rational belief in its absolute value, thus lending it the validity of an absolute and final commitment; (d) because it has been established in a manner which is recognized to be legal (Weber, cited in Eisenstadt 1968, 12).

This typology is meant to apply to all polities over time and space.

He also suggests that variations in the bases of legitimacy are directly associated with variations in a political structure's other characteristics. For example, Weber hypothesizes:

> The corporate group which is subject to charismatic authority is based on an emotional form of communal relationship. The administrative staff

of a charismatic leader does not consist of "officials". . . . It is not chosen on the basis of social privilege nor from the point of view of domestic or personal dependency. It is rather chosen in terms of the charismatic qualities of its members. . . .

Charismatic authority is thus specifically outside the realm of everyday routine and the profane sphere. In this respect it is sharply opposed both to rational, and particularly bureaucratic, authority, and to traditional authority (Weber, cited in Eisenstadt 1968, 50–51).

Weber maintains that variations in the presence of particular authority structures have direct consequences for other structures: "Pure charisma is specifically foreign to economic considerations" (cited in Eisenstadt 1968, 52). The rise of charismatic movements in turn results from and brings enormous transformations: "In traditionally stereotyped periods, charisma is the greatest revolutionary force" (Weber, cited in Eisenstadt 1968, 53). Furthermore, political phenomena are not simply determined by other more supposedly fundamental structures; they carry independent explanatory power of their own.

Weber maintains that capitalist democratic society is characterized by the spread of instrumental rational orientations to action and rational legal-authority structures. Both are personified by the official. In "Socialism," which I cited earlier, he maintains that Marx misunderstood the fundamental characteristic of the contemporary world:

> Parallel to these very complex processes, however, there appears a rapid rise in the number of clerks, i.e. in private bureaucracy—its growth rate is statistically much greater than that of the workers—and their interests certainly do not lie with one accord in the direction of a proletarian dictatorship (Weber, cited in Eldridge 1980, 207).
>
> Public and trust concerns, however, are strongly and quite exclusively dominated by the official, not the worker. . . . It is the dictatorship of the official, not of the worker, which, for the present, at any rate is on the advance (Weber, cited in Eldridge 1980, 209).

Weber maintains that Marx exaggerated the importance of class in capitalist society. In its place, he notes the growth in the number of persons calculating their means and ends and of bureaucracies, the institutionalization of rationality in social structures.

The typologies of social action and political structures suggest how Weber relates the individual and group levels of analysis. People in particular political structures usually have the same orientations to social action. And just as social structure does not determine social action, the latter does not explain the former. Each is a separate sphere, but each is related to the other. He therefore stresses that analyses of politics demand that we show how the levels interact.

Weber on the Meaning of Social Science

Weber's work contains a recurrent tension: We strive with all our might to know the world, yet we can never know it completely. In his classic essay, "Science as a Vocation," he develops several consequences of this apparent contradiction. One set of his arguments deals with the nature of scientific knowledge. First, he notes that each effort to analyze the world is necessarily specialized, produced by and also limited by the scholar's tools and theories. Second, each scientist must know that his or her work will be surpassed. "In science, each of us knows that what he has accomplished will be antiquated in ten, twenty, or fifty years. That is the fate to which science is subjected; it is the very *meaning* of scientific work. . . . We cannot work without hoping that others will advance further than we have. . . . In principle, this progress goes on *ad infinitum*" (Weber, cited in Gerth and Mills 1958, 138). Third, scientific knowledge means that we can master the world through rational processes. "There are no mysterious incalculable forces that come into play, but rather that one can, in principle, master all things by calculation" (Weber, cited in Gerth and Mills 1958, 139). (Recall that Gellner establishes this point as one of the critical assumptions of science.) In principle, Weber maintains, science provides the means to analyze the world.

What meaning does this science have? he asks. How does the "disenchantment of the world" affect the meaning of our life in the world? Citing Lev Tolstoi, Weber maintains,

> For civilized man death has no meaning. It has none because the individual life of civilized man, placed into an infinite "progress," according to its own imminent meaning should never come to an end; for there is always a further step ahead of one who stands in the march of progress. And no man who comes to die stands upon the peak which lies in infinity. Abraham . . . died "old and satiated with life" because he stood in the organic cycle of life; because his life in terms of its meaning and on the eve of his days, had given to him what life had to offer; because for him there remained no puzzles he might wish to solve; and therefore he could have had "enough" of life. Whereas civilized man, placed in the midst of the continuous enrichment of culture . . . may become "tired of life," but not "satiated with life." He catches only the most minute part of what the life of the spirit has to bring forth ever anew, and what he seizes is always something provisional and not definitive, and therefore death for him is a meaningless occurrence. And because death is meaningless, civilized life as such is meaningless (Weber, cited in Gerth and Mills 1958, 138–139).

Science can only provide partial and temporary answers to our questions. It cannot answer "the only question important for us: 'What shall we do and how shall we live?'" (Weber, cited in Gerth and Mills 1958, 143). Science cannot answer fundamental questions, but it can answer questions within its frame of reference. Modern man has no choice, implies Weber, but to go on asking and answering the questions of science. At the same time, he has no choice but to struggle with the meaning of life.

Several themes of Weber's work have had an extraordinary impact on contemporary political science. From him, we get the uncompromising claim that in order to explain we must posit and verify the presence of distinct motives. He counsels as well against viewing politics as dependent on other supposedly more basic phenomena. Weber insists that both individual and structural levels of analysis be included in all studies and maintains that each analysis can offer no more than a partial answer. More fundamentally, he instructs us that scholarship can do no more than suggest limited answers to analytic questions; it can offer no guides to the ultimate meaning of life. Reading Weber forces us to confront the basic questions of claims to knowledge.

THE NEXT STEP

The theoretical approaches discussed in this chapter are characterized by strong similarities and marked differences.

- Rational action theory and political psychology stress analysis at the level of the individual.
- Marx's analysis and political anthropology subsume the individual in the surrounding social structure.
- Weber insists on the independence of each level of analysis. Good social science, he maintains, requires the analysis of both social structure and social action.
- Where rational choice theorists posit that all individuals are rational maximizers of their subjective utility and will respond in the same way to the same circumstances, political psychologists search for types of attitudes and motives, and Weber posits four types of orientation to action.
- Where Marx insists that the mode of production is the fundamental element of social structure, political anthropologists examine the interaction of the various elements of a community, and Weber offers a typology of authority structures.

- Marx and rational action theorists reason deductively from a set of axioms. They usually use empirical evidence to illustrate rather than to substantiate or test their propositions.
- Both Marxist political scientists and rational choice theorists assume that all persons are rational maximizers of their interests, but they disagree over the source of those interests. Marx maintains that they come from the individual's class, denying that they are only personal.
- Geertz's call for thick descriptions reappears in the work of many who follow Marx and Weber, as well. It is never present in the scholarship of rational choice theorists or those who work on the relationship between political attitudes and behavior.
- Statistical standards of explanation, in the sense of the ability to account for variation in the dependent variable, characterize the study of political attitudes and behavior and sometimes appear in the work of Marxists, Weberians, and rational choice theorists. Here, analysis requires information organized as quantitative data.
- Where the standard of thick description applies, studies present detailed descriptions and discursive narratives.

Any piece of analysis in political science may use one or more of the approaches of these research schools, although rational choice theorists and Marxists are more inclined than others to stay within the intellectual boundaries of their own approach.

In political science, as in all other disciplines, research schools teach us how to observe the world. Without the concepts, hypotheses, theories, and methods, there is nothing "out there." But in this field, no single theory or research school defines the discipline. As a result, analyses of particular subjects almost always involve a clash between different theoretical approaches. In the next chapter, we will look more closely at how the various theories and models address classic topics of political research. Sometimes, they will speak past each other. At other times, they will offer contradictory claims. As we proceed, you should consider how to assess the different claims and decide which ones to deny and which to accept.

CHAPTER 4

How Research Schools Structure Analysis and Produce Conflicting Visions of Politics

Differences in how to do political science derive from variations among the research schools in the field. The alternative studies of turnout, which you examined in Chapter 2, and the analyses of revolution, political groups and collective action, electoral choice, and demonstrations and political violence, to which we will now turn, vary significantly in the extent to which they reflect one or more of the research schools. Recall that Piven and Cloward closely tie their work to Marx and that Riker's theory of political coalitions flows directly from the principles of rational action theory. Jackman combines rational choice theory with structural variables, and *Who Votes?* is even more eclectic, relying primarily on the approach of political attitudes and behavior but also drawing hypotheses from rational choice theory. Powell, as you know, insists on testing hypotheses that include variables on both the individual and structural levels of analysis. Note, too, that Ross purposefully tests hypotheses drawn from competing theories of political participation and combines the reports of anthropologists and rather sophisticated data analysis. Clearly, then, different approaches to the study of a topic produce alternative analyses.

Different approaches, of course, invite different questions and offer different analyses of the same topic. Rational action theorists ask why political groups form. Marxists probe what accounts for variations in the characteristics of political groups based on social classes. Those who study political attitudes and behavior want to know why individuals act as they do, as T. R. Gurr probes in *Why Men Rebel* (1970). And rational choice theorists seek to specify the conditions that induce persons to calculate that taking to the streets will maximize their personal benefits. Similarly, most students of electoral behavior in the United States ask about the motives for voting for a particular party or candidate, and structural analysts examine the relationship between social and electoral divisions in an electorate.

Even when scholars pose the same questions, theoretical divergences produce different answers. You will not be surprised to learn that Marx and Weber offer diametrically opposed explanations for the rise of the West's distinctive civilization. Research schools also may differ in the methods of analysis they employ. Rational choice theorists, for example, use deductive logic to substantiate their claims and typically examine empirical evidence to illustrate but not test their arguments. Many Marxists, facing a host of problems for their theory, have reduced their reliance on the power of deductive logic and increased the emphasis on empirical precision.

But do not think that all is confusion. After all, despite the differences among the approaches to turnout, all studies of this issue share the same concepts and measures and observe the same levels of turnout in the United States and other democracies; three of the four (Powell, Jackman, and Piven and Cloward) use structural variables to explain turnout and agree on the importance of cross-national analysis to substantiate their hypotheses. And three of the four (Powell, Jackman, and Wolfinger and Rosenstone) use statistical tests to establish their empirical findings. Note, too, that Ross uses the same hypotheses and statistical methods in his analysis of political participation. Furthermore, regardless of their research school, most analysts of mass politics—vote choice, political protest and violence, turnout—substantiate their propositions with carefully designed empirical tests and the same statistical techniques that are used by scholars of political attitudes and behavior. Clearly, then, there are significant areas of theoretical and methodological agreement in political science.

As you review each topic, you will be struck by the presence of competing explanations for the same phenomena. Whether you find the controversies distracting or invigorating will depend on more than your personal taste. Remember that the primary goal is to explain political phenomena. Sometimes, we may learn from scholarly debates. Or, if analysts are speaking past each other, it may be difficult to judge their disagreements. You should consider whether the controversies surround more or less successful efforts to solve analytic puzzles and whether each of the competing claims makes a strong case. Consequently, you will also need to consider how to adjudicate among competing claims to explain political phenomena.

MARX AND WEBER ON REVOLUTION IN CAPITALIST SOCIETIES

In the previous chapter, I outlined Marx's and Weber's contrasting analyses of the contemporary world. Even though they agree that capitalism defines the societies of Western Europe and North America, they disagree on how best to analyze capitalist society, and they offer clashing predictions for its future. Marx argues that capitalism carries within itself "the seeds of its own destruction," and Weber maintains that capitalist society, left alone, is immune to revolution. Asking the same question, Marx and Weber provide diametrically opposed answers.

As you know, Marx combines a complex series of hypotheses to forecast the inevitable end of capitalism. Defining revolution as the change from one type of society to the next, he maintains that the inherent characteristics of capitalism determine its transformation into socialism. In his opinion, the internal logic of capitalism necessarily leads to class conflict and revolution. He also tells us there can be no capitalism without a subsequent transformation into socialism.

If revolution is a predetermined outcome of capitalist development, what is the role of voluntary human actions, such as strikes, demonstrations, electoral activities, and armed insurrection? At the beginning of the twentieth century, leaders of the German Socialist party, the dominant Marxist party of the era, based their answers to these questions on the prediction that the proletariat would necessarily become a majority of society. These Socialists reasoned that they should educate and organize the industrial workers into a mass political party and make sure that Germany became a democracy; by itself, victory at the polls would lead to the Socialist revolution. Note that this position denies the claim that revolution requires violence. Others derived from Marx the belief that the capitalists would not relinquish power without a fight. Therefore, they argued, the proletariat could not come to power without a mass uprising, involving strikes, demonstrations, and force. In the Tsarist Empire of Russia, V. I. Lenin insisted that without the leadership of professional revolutionaries, industrial workers would only develop "trade union consciousness" (Lenin 1943); only absolutely dedicated, secretive, and organized activists could channel economic demands into revolutionary action. These views underscore the centrality of the proletariat in Marx's theory of revolution in capitalist society. They also imply that competing hypotheses may be derived from his relatively tight web of concepts and hypotheses.

Weber depicts a very different capitalist society. In his view, private and public bureaucracies typify capitalist social organizations, and it is the clerks and other white-collar employees, not the capitalists and proletariat, that abound. The persistent calculations of means and ends and the rule of abstract laws that he cites entail the absence of fundamental moral commitments. As a set, these institutions, occupations, goals, and values define individual life under capitalism. Weber maintains that Marx misidentifies the concepts needed to analyze capitalism.

Furthermore, he argues, Marx misunderstands the dynamic qualities of capitalism. Weber sees the relationships among class and other social, economic, and political phenomena as conditional and indeterminate in their causal flow. The workers, he notes, are not becoming poorer, unemployment is not a necessary characteristic of capitalism, and there has, in fact, been a decrease—not an increase—of conflict among the capitalists. And as bureaucracies spread, behavior is increasingly guided by rules and the expectations of routines. "And where the bureaucratization of administration has been completely carried through, a form of power relation is established which is unshatterable. . . . Such a machine makes 'revolution' in the sense of the forceful creation of entirely new formations of authority, technically more and more impossible, especially when the apparatus controls the modern means of communication . . . and also by virtue of its internal rationalized structure" (Weber, cited in Parsons 1964, 75–77). Weber believes that the rise of bureaucracies leads to a hierarchical and authoritarian society—an "iron cage," in his metaphor, that rigidly controls and limits personal choices and opportunities. Therefore, capitalism contains the seeds of its petrification, not its destruction. It inevitably leads to a rigid society, bound by formal rules and individual calculations for personal gain. Under capitalism, we necessarily lose the ability to make and apply fundamental decisions about how to live our lives. Weber bemoans our iron cage of increasingly purposeless efficiency.

However, he holds out one possibility for the transformation of advanced industrial societies. You should be able to deduce this source of revolution from our discussion of his work in the previous chapter: The concept of charisma, applied to a political leader and movement, serves as the springboard for this analysis. Remember that Weber opposes charisma to the routines of everyday life. He sees charismatic orientations to action as emotional ones. In charismatic political movements, the leaders are perceived as extraordinary, in the literal sense of the word. They will command their followers to break established rules, and the people have the obligation to obey. Because they exist outside the logic of the organizations and orientations to action that typify capitalism, charismatic movements may emerge at any time. And because the bond between leader and followers is not limited by laws or traditions, the charismatic figure can demand anything of the flock. Only this kind of leader can impede the spread of rational orientations to action and bureaucracy, and only a successful charismatic movement can enable the members of society to confront questions of absolute values. According to Weber, the extraordinary power of charisma is the only source of revolution in a capitalist society characterized by bureaucratic structures and means-ends rational orientation to action.

Notice how Weber's analysis turns away from conditional statements and offers precise predictions. Here, he is doing more than criticizing Marx, offering "shafts of light," or discussing abstract methods of social science. In analyzing revolution in capitalist society, he necessarily offers strong claims to knowledge.

Notice, too, that Weber also succumbed to the temptation to translate these ideas into public policy. When he took part in the deliberations that resulted in the democratic constitution for the new German government that formed after World War I, Weber successfully struggled to introduce clauses that allowed for the direct election of a president and the right of the president to rule by emergency decree during national crises. In dread of the ever-growing bureaucracy, he sought to give the elected leader an ability to oppose it (Mommsen 1974). Ultimately, Adolf Hitler, an embodiment of the charismatic leader, used these clauses to undermine that democracy. The consequences of Weber's policy recommendations remind us that it is one thing to propose testable knowledge claims and quite another to make policy based on them.

Concern for the fate of Western civilization underpins these contrasting analyses. Building on a set of principles that emphasize the economic determinants of individual behavior and societal development, Marx claims to have uncovered the sources within capitalism that would inevitably lead to its transformation. Weber weaves together the power of authority and variations in values and interests as indicated by the orientations to action, arguing that capitalism itself contains no sources that will lead to revolution. On the contrary, he says, only a charismatic leader and movement—phenomena that lie outside the logic of capitalism—can effect a revolution. Clearly, although they address the same question, Marx and Weber use different theories and offer different answers to the issue of revolution in advanced industrial societies.

THE ANALYSIS OF POLITICAL GROUPS AND COLLECTIVE ACTION

Both rational choice theorists and those who use Marx's analysis grapple with the process by which political groups based on class ties form and by which collective action occurs. Both assume that individuals act to maximize their self-interest. Yet, they present diametrically opposed analyses of the processes that cause large-scale political movements to develop and compete.

Rational choice theorists pose serious problems for Marx and other structural analysts. They insist that it is not proper to solve the collective action problem by assumption alone. In *The Logic of Collective Action,* Mancur Olson, Jr., uncovers flaws in Marx's analysis of the formation of class in general and the political organizations affiliated with classes (such as labor unions, interest groups, and political parties) in particular. "The absence of the sort of class action Marx predicted is due in part to the predominance of rational utilitarian behavior. *For class-oriented action will not occur if the individuals that make up a class act rationally*" (1968, 105, emphasis in original).

In all cases of collective action involving large numbers of persons, he tells us, free riding is always the reasonable and expected choice of action. "The rational thing for a member of [a class] to do is to ignore his *class* interests and to spend his energies on his *personal* interests" (Olson 1968, 105, emphasis in original). At all stages of class action, it is never in the self-interest of a worker, for example, to join with other workers to form unions, vote, or demonstrate. "The crux of the matter, then, is that Marx's theory of social classes is inconsistent insofar as it assumes the rational, selfish pursuit of individual interests" (1968, 107–108). Marx's assumptions, Olson maintains, preclude Marx's conclusions.

Recall Marx's answer to these questions. He insists that some personal goals are identical to social ones. Individuals are not atoms; the need to survive necessitates ties to other persons and the subsequent understanding that one's needs are inherently bound to others' needs. It makes no sense to posit, as rational choice theorists do, the presence of significant individual goals that are not at the same time social goals. Furthermore, as you know, Marx maintains that all social ties are not equally binding. Human nature is defined by how one labors, and ties to workmates—those who share the same relationship to the means of production—outweigh all other bonds. Class interests, according to Marx, define the individual's personal interests. As a result, he argues that individuals pursuing their self-interest will form classes and engage in collective action.

You should not be surprised to learn that these two diverse approaches move analysis in very different directions. Beginning only with the existence of individuals and personal goals, rational action theorists seek to explain how any large national political group forms. They deduce explanatory conditions and offer empirical evidence to illustrate their propositions. But those who follow Marx detail the processes by which unions form, Socialist parties organize, and revolutionary collective action occurs. They examine the empirical evidence in order to spot the conditions that slow and speed the process, and, of course, they puzzle over the relative absence of revolutionary action on the part of the working class. Thus, each approach presents a different set of methods as well as concepts and hypotheses to solve a different set of problems.

Let's look more closely at Olson's own solution to the collective action problem. First, he distinguishes between large and small groups. Where there are relatively few persons involved, he notes, individuals easily form into groups. You should also recall from the previous chapter that rational choice theorists believe that it is relatively easy to monitor the contribution of each person in a small group; the free-rider problem applies only to large groups.

How does Olson solve the problem of the formation of labor unions and other examples of collective action among a large number of persons? True to the assumptions of his approach, he posits selective incentives (primarily involving economic interests) and coercion that will benefit or harm the individuals who join. "Only a *separate and 'selective' incentive* will stimulate a rational individual in a latent group to act in a group oriented way. In such circumstances group action can be obtained only through an incentive that operates, not indiscriminately, like the collective good upon the group as a whole, but rather *selectively* toward the individuals in the group"(Olson 1968, 51, emphasis in original). Inexpensive vacations and insurance policies provided exclusively to union members or hiring and promotion policies that favor those who join the unions are examples of selective benefits. Closed shops, which make it difficult for a firm to hire anyone who is not in the union, and the use of force against workers who would free ride illustrate coercion.

Olson stays within the logic of rational action theory and surveys histories of unions to illustrate his argument.

> In sum, compulsory unionism, far from being a modern innovation, goes back to the earliest days of organized labor, and existed even in the small, pre-national unions. Compulsory membership cannot, however, explain the creation of the first, small, local unions, as it can account for the viability of the later, larger national unions that the local unions ultimately created. . . . But it is possible for a small union to emerge without compulsion, and then, if it decides, to ensure its survival and increase its strength by making membership compulsory (Olson 1968, 69–70).

Because local unions involve relatively small numbers, Olson reasons, they readily solve the problem of collective action. Here, the empirical evidence illustrates the importance of selective incentives, particularly coercion, for the formation of national unions.

Thus, in using the logical power of rational choice theory and providing historical illustrations, Olson proposes that selective incentives induce individuals to decide that membership in a union or any other large political organization is in their personal interests. In the absence of these personal incentives, he argues, large-scale interest groups, unions, and political parties will not form. In other words, individual costs and benefits join with the consequences of group size to explain the formation of political groups.

Responses to Challenge: Rational Choice Theory

Sometimes, when we examine empirical evidence, we find a wide gap between what the theory tells us exists and what we can observe in the world. Just as rational action theorists expect relatively few citizens to vote, Olson predicts that very few will join large, national political organizations. Yet, there are many such political groups. Detailed studies of interest groups raise all kinds of problems for rational actor analyses of political groups.

I will elaborate this point by examining a study by Jack Walker, entitled "The Origins and Maintenance of Interest Groups in America" and published in the *American Political Science Review* in 1983. Walker examines only those groups formed by volunteers for the primary purpose of influencing government policy. He excludes labor unions, business corporations, agencies directly employed in the process of influencing government, and religious and other social membership groups but includes "all the voluntary associations in the United States which are open to membership and are concerned with some aspects of public policy at the national level" (Walker 1983, 391–392). During the past few decades, there has been a rapid and broad expansion of groups. Indeed, more interest groups formed between 1946 and 1980 than in the 100 previous years.

The results of Walker's mail survey provide little support for Olson's argument. Some 15 to 30 percent of these groups offer selective benefits as inducements to attract members, and "a relatively small number" can coerce persons to join (Walker 1983, 396–397). Walker points to the critical role of structural factors, such as "long-term improvements in educational levels," the "development of cheap, sophisticated methods of communication," a "period of social protest" that attracted new activists, and "massive new government programs," which have generated "voluntary associations among the service providers and consumers of the new programs." The critical factor is the funds provided by the government, private foundations, and private donors: "This study shows that during recent years, group leaders learned how to cope with the public goods dilemma not by inducing large numbers of new members to join their groups through the manipulation of selective benefits, but by locating important new sources of funds outside the immediate membership" (Walker 1983, 397). "Patrons of political action"—the government itself, foundations, and individual donors—provide the resources with which political groups open offices, hire lobbyists, develop membership lists, and pursue the activities that enable them to form and persist. Walker finds that growth in the number of interest groups frequently follows, rather than precedes, changes in government policy. The availability of funds is tied to the provisions of the tax code, laws concerning the costs of mailings, and rules about lobbying rights and registrations (1983, 402-403). Whether directly or indirectly, government action affects the formation and persistence of interest groups. In the analysis of collective action, Walker argues, we must examine direct empirical evidence on particular interest groups and not rely on deductive logic alone. At the same time, we should include structural variables and thereby move beyond the individual actors that populate the world of rational choice theory. Walker raises powerful questions about the way rational choice theory analyzes the formation of political groups.

Faced with such problems, many rational actor theorists relax some of Olson's assumptions, a technique already outlined in the preceding chapter. Arguing that Olson's assumptions of perfect information and economic self-interest are too restrictive, Terry Moe (1980; 1981) notes that individuals vary in their "perception of efficacy" and in their goals. The more efficacious people believe themselves to be, the more likely they are to calculate that their contributions will make a difference and to engage in collective action. Similarly, Moe adds "solidary" incentives—goals associated with friendship ties and social acceptance—and "purposive" incentives—those that come from moral and religious principles—to the list of goals rationally pursued by individuals. Expanding the number of goals, he says, increases the incentives that make it likely that a person will engage in collective action. Michael Hechter, in *The Principles of Group Solidarity* (1988), also moves beyond Olson's analysis by arguing that compliance is based on the extent to which the member's contributions and actions can be monitored and the extent to which he or she depends on the group for personal benefits. Like Olson, these and other scholars rely on deductive logic for theoretical power and provide empirical evidence to illustrate but not test their claims. Moe and Hechter exemplify the theorists who relax Olson's assumptions in order to explain the plethora of political groups.

Responses to Challenge: Marx's Theory

Political scientists who apply Marx's theory to the analysis of political groups and collective action face a different set of problems. Not only has the predicted workers' revolution in capitalism not occurred but scholars have had a difficult time finding evidence for many of his specific hypotheses about the formation of classes. Retaining the core assumption that capitalism defines the contemporary world, those who would apply Marx's theory have reworked the basic hypotheses and offered detailed empirical studies.

In *Working-Class Formation: Nineteenth Century Patterns in Western Europe and the United States* (1986), Ira Katznelson and Aristide R. Zolberg have gathered a collection of essays that break new ground in the study of mass politics. The authors share an approach that ties the general perspective of Marxist models to recent work in the field of social history, which allows them to heed Geertz's call for thick description. Here, the dependent variable includes informal and barely visible modes of resistance at the workplace in addition to strikes, demonstrations, boycotts, and electoral patterns. Pushing the definition of data well beyond sample surveys, they utilize memoirs, marriage patterns, pamphlets, popular magazines, reports of meetings, and changes in language. Like Piven and Cloward, these authors present much more than narrow histories of working-class politics in France, the United States, and Germany during the nineteenth century. They illustrate the approach that combines a structural level of analysis with detailed empirical studies of particular political organizations.

Katznelson's essay in that volume, "Working-Class Formation: Constructing Cases and Comparisons," and Jurgen Kocka's contribution, "Problems of Working-Class Formation in Germany: The Early Years, 1800–1875," detail the theoretical framework. The approach commences with the orthodox Marxist assumption that capitalist economic development provides the key to political development in general and the formation of working-class politics in particular. At the same time, it rejects the view that capitalism necessarily transforms industrial laborers into a class for themselves—conscious of their identity as workers, aware of their revolutionary potential, and engaged in political action to effect that revolution. Thus, these scholars seek to amend Marxist theory.

Katznelson and Kocka distinguish four levels of class analysis. The first is "experience distant," examining the "structure of capitalist economic development" and made specific to individual countries. The second explores how workers live, focusing on how they labor, their relations at the workplace, and where they reside (Katznelson 1986, 16). Next comes the level of perceptions, where classes share dispositions. Here, the task is to examine the ways by which workers interpreted their world (Katznelson 1986, 17). Modes and patterns of collective action constitute the fourth level, wherein "classes are organized and act through movements and organizations to affect society and the position of the class within it" (Katznelson 1986, 20). Katznelson and Kocka jettison Marx's deterministic claims about the formation of a politicized working class.

These scholars retain the basic claims of Marx's research school, but they substitute conditional relationships and detailed empirical evidence for the deterministic elements and deductive logic that Marx used. Katznelson and Kocka reject any claim that each level leads to the next one. To cite Kocka, "Under certain conditions those who share a common class position and [become aware and conscious of what they share] may, on the same basis, act collectively and perhaps organize, in conflict with other classes and perhaps the state" (1986, 282–283). Whether and how they do so are empirical questions. In other words, sometimes, those who work together also live near each other; sometimes, they do not. Sometimes, those who work together, who may live near each other, also think that they are like each other and share interests, but sometimes, they do not. Similarly, those who believe that they share interests may or may not join together in political action. And those who vote together may or may not demonstrate together. The influence of Weber's analysis on this effort to understand the politics of the working class is apparent here.

Each chapter in Katznelson and Zolberg's book is a detailed study of decisions made and applied in the process by which a nation's workers became organized. Martin Shefter's essay, "Trade Unions and Political Machines: The Organization and Disorganization of the American Working Class in the Late Nineteenth Century," assesses the formative years of the U.S. labor reform movement. He demonstrates the separation of "pure and simple" trade union activities from the political sphere, which was dominated by the middle classes and the Democratic and Republican parties. Mary Nolan's study, "Economic Crisis, State Policy, and Working-Class Formation in Germany, 1870–1900," joins Kocka's analysis to depict a very different world. She describes the well-organized national union movement formally linked to the Socialist party that drew large portions of the Protestant male working class into a relatively united movement espousing revolutionary claims. Taken together, these essays describe and seek to explain significant differences in the modes of collective action used by U.S. and German workers.

In summary, we can see that the rational action and Marxist research schools offer diverse analyses of political groups and collective action based on social classes. The former define the issue as just another example of the collective action problem and propose selective incentives that would lead a person to join a political organization. The political scientists in this camp respond to empirical challenges by modifying but not fundamentally changing their assumptions, concepts, and hypotheses. Those who would apply Marx's theory examine the formation of social classes in and of themselves; in their view, class is a unique form of political organization. But in the face of significant empirical challenges to Marx's hypotheses, many of these political scientists have modified their basic assumptions, concepts, and hypotheses.

THE ANALYSIS OF VOTE CHOICE

The analysis of voting has attracted more scholarly attention and research funding than any other subject of political science. In a review essay on electoral behavior, Herbert Asher highlights this: "When one asks where is the 'science' in political science, a common reply is to point the questioner to the field of voting behavior" (1983, 339). In important ways, the analysis of vote choice exemplifies the science of politics. Students of elections share research questions, concepts, and variables, as well as sources of data and techniques used to analyze this data. Within this community of scholars, the dominant approach is the Michigan model, whose basic tenets we examined in the previous chapter.

Contrasting theories characterize the analysis of electoral behavior. For the past three decades, the questions, assumptions, and methods of the Michigan school of electoral analysis have guided most studies of voting. An alternative perspective, typically used to study elections in European democracies, begins with the structural assumptions of Marx and Weber. Here, vote choice is believed to derive from the individual's place in the surrounding social and economic structure. As empirical challenges to this approach have appeared, some scholars have refined and defended their positions, some have introduced hypotheses drawn from rational action theory, and others have offered new analyses. Meanwhile, a lively theoretical debate accompanies the study of electoral behavior.

Because these political scientists use much the same research methods and examine much the same data, it will be relatively easy for you to see how their disputes unfold and how they defend their claims. You will not have the sense that these scholars are speaking past each other or that their disputes rest on such basic matters as the preference for deductive or inductive logics. Nor will you wonder whether more data will resolve the disputes. In this area of study, scholars agree that hypotheses should be derived from general theoretical propositions and tested with data drawn from properly constructed mass surveys. As we examine research on electoral behavior, observe how the various schools of analysis present and defend their claims to knowledge.

Defending and Refining the Michigan Model of U.S. Voting Behavior

As noted above, most research on electoral behavior in the United States draws on the precepts of the Michigan school, wherein vote choice is believed to stem most directly from the interaction of three sets of attitudinal variables. The first involves party identification, a concept you encountered in the preceding chapters. The other two—positions on the issues of the day and feelings about and evaluations of the candidates—are short-term characteristics. Consequently, the founders of this school—Angus Campbell, Philip E. Converse, Warren E. Miller, and Donald E. Stokes—expected party identification to influence the other two explanatory variables, as well as vote choice. Writing in *The American Voter,* the founding document, they contend that "the individual voter sees the several elements of national politics as more than a collection of discrete, unrelated objects. . . . A *candidate* is the nominee of his *party;* party and candidate are oriented to the same *issues* or *groups.* . . . As a means of achieving order, the transfer of cognitive attributes and affective values from one object to another undoubtedly plays an important role" (Campbell et al. 1960, 59, emphasis in the original). At the heart of this relationship is a psychological attachment to a party, the most stable of these attitudes. It serves "as a supplier of cues by which the individual may evaluate the elements of politics" (1960, 128). Campbell and his colleagues elaborate on this point: "Identification with a party raises a perceptual screen through which the individual tends to see what is favorable to his partisan orientation. The stronger the party bond, the more exaggerated the process of selection and perceptual distortion will be" (1960, 133). A loyal attitude toward a political party stands at the analytic center of this theory of voting behavior.

Campbell, Converse, Miller, and Stokes picture the determinants of vote choice as a funnel: "Most of the complex events in the funnel occur as a result of multiple prior causes. Each such event is, in turn, responsible for multiple effects as well, but our focus narrows as we approach the dependent behavior. We progressively eliminate those effects that do not continue to have relevance for the political act" (1960, 24). At the end of the funnel is a diamond-like relationship between vote choice and its proximate determinants. Explanatory arrows extend from party identification, issues, and candidate evaluations to vote choice and from party identification to the other two explanatory variables, as well. Further back stand variables without direct impact on vote choice, such as social class, religion, and region, which locate a person in the social structure. Vote choice, they say, is subject to both distant and proximate influences.

The model accounts for more than the decision to support a particular candidate in any one election. Theorists ask what determines the initial attachment to a political party, and their answer underlines the distance between the variables used in the Michigan model and the characteristics of the U.S. social structure. They find that it is not the individuals' class position, level of education, ethnicity, or religion but the processes of political socialization as they operate through the family that convey party identification to children. Persons whose parents shared strong political attachments have the strongest partisan identifications. Furthermore, where the same parties compete in election after election, exposure to political campaigns in and of itself strengthens party identification. In these cases, strength of party identification may be seen as a direct function of age. In turn, the stronger the partisan identification, the more likely a person is to support the candidates of that party in each and all votes, at a particular point in time and into the future. It follows, as well, that partisan identification can only grow in strength. The Michigan model obviously produces a rich harvest of explanatory hypotheses.

As you saw in the analysis of turnout, each variable is measured by responses in public opinion surveys taken just before or after an election. Measuring vote choice is a relatively straightforward process, using the person's answer to the question of how he or she voted or intended to vote. The operational definition of party identification remains the best-known indicator in all of political science. Therefore, researchers ask, "Generally speaking, do you think of yourself as a Democrat, Republican, or what? How strongly do you feel?" Here, the possibilities range from very strong to not so strong. The result is a seven-point scale: very strong Republican, strong Republican, not so strong Republican, Independent, not so strong Democrat, strong Democrat, and very strong Democrat. Operational definitions of an issue seek to measure the extent to which the respondents know and feel something about it, as well as the extent to which they perceive that one party is closer than the other to their position on that issue. The survey questions probe opinions on a broad array of issues (Campbell et al. 1960, especially 168–215). Evaluations of the candidates are obtained by seeking favorable and unfavorable references to them or by determining their place on a thermometer assumed to measure the respondents' feelings.

Recent research has located conceptual ambiguities and empirical anomalies in the Michigan model. The meaning of party identification, for example, is not sufficiently precise because it taps several attitudes at the same time. Herbert Weisberg summarizes some of these criticisms: "The empirical evidence is limited, but it does suggest that the usual unidimensional interpretation is incorrect. In particular, the usual strength of identification measure so confounds different components of partisan strength that past studies have not been able to study validly the nature of political independence" (1984, 475). He suggests that several questions be designed to reflect the different dimensions of party identification. You should also recall the hypotheses offered by Stanley Kelley and Thad Mirer, discussed in Chapter 3, that claim that evaluations of the candidates are more central to vote choice than party identification. Numerous other scholars have found evidence of declining levels of attachment to the Democratic and Republican parties across the electorates and drops in the strength of attachment as voters age. Such conceptual and empirical problems therefore raise questions for this model.

Some scholars have linked these problems to findings that indicate that voters are rational calculators, choosing the candidate or party closest to their perceived interests. This approach originates with Anthony Downs's *Economic Theory of Democracy* (1957) and V. O. Key's *Responsible Electorate* (1966). In both works, much emphasis is placed on economic issues. Another theorist, Morris Fiorina (1981), maintains that voters assess their "retrospective" successes during the tenure of the outgoing administration and that their "prospective" views of the contenders have an independent effect on whom they support at the polls. Donald Kinder and D. Roderick Kiewiet (1981) locate the presence of "sociotropic" voting—supporting the candidate most likely to help the economy as a whole, not only the individual. In this perspective, economic issues are believed to guide vote choice.

Others have found anomalies within the Michigan model. Applying statistical tests that examine the interaction among explanatory variables, John Jackson (1975), Benjamin Page and Calvin Jones (1972), and Philip Converse and Gregory Markus (1984) have shown that party identification responds to the voter's feelings about the candidates and views on particular issues. In a volume that extends the Michigan model, *The Changing American Voter* (1976), Nie, Verba, and John Petrocik locate extensive evidence of issue consistency among U.S. citizens in the 1960s and early 1970s. They join the many scholars who contend that the Michigan model was derived from an atypical period: In the 1950s, they argue, there were very few issues that were taken seriously and supported consistently by large numbers of citizens. Edward Carmines and James Stimson (1980) show that the nature of the issue, in and of itself and without regard to party loyalties or the candidates, affects the extent to which that issue influences the voting decision.

These findings draw attention to the assumptions that political scientists make about voters. For example, does the citizen's choice at the ballot reflect enduring psychological attachments, or does it respond to calculations on how best to advance his or her short-term personal interests? This echoes the debate between rational choice theorists and those who study political attitudes and behavior.

Today, the Michigan model, with party identification at its center, stands bent but unbowed. Proponents like Converse and Markus note that evaluations of the candidates were the most direct cause of vote choice in the 1976 presidential election. But they still insist on the fundamental analytic importance of party identification and maintain that their model completely explains the voting decision (Converse and Markus 1984, 150). Having noted the immediate explanatory power of the other variables, they reiterate the strength of the basic concept. "First, party identifications are much more stable in the intermediate term than other elements of the model. If the game were redefined as one of predicting a voting decision on the basis of political attitudes examined eight years earlier there would be no contest" (1984, 151). Second, the effects of party loyalty can be found at many stages in the analysis. "In short, then, while partisan predispositions are unlikely to dominate the process completely at given stages where the candidates are being assessed, these loyalties appear to make repeated inputs of substantial magnitude throughout the process" (1984, 151–152).

Many scholars other than Converse and his colleagues continue to employ the Michigan model. Weisberg, for example, does not use his criticisms of the model to argue for a new approach but for better measures of the classic variables. Indeed, his praise of the core concept highlights the widespread appreciation for this theoretical approach: "The new survey questions should lead to better measurement of the full concept of partisanship. Party identification has been the keystone of our understanding of voting behavior. With a little work to bolster its underpinnings, we may find that the concept is even richer and even more important than we realized" (Weisberg 1984, 475–476).

He and other scholars stand ready to modify—not abandon—the fundamental claims of the Michigan model. Indeed, almost all analyses of electoral behavior in the United States revolve around the basic concepts of party identification, attitudes on the issues, and feelings toward the candidates. Furthermore, Converse and Roy Pierce (1986) have responded to attacks on the basic model by arguing that it provides the best explanation of electoral behavior in France, as well as the United States, and, by implication, in all democracies.

For a long time, political scientists hesitated to apply the framework that centers on party identification to elections and voters in other democracies. Harking back to claims about the relative weakness of class ties in the United States, some scholars maintained that party identification emerges only in the absence of these more fundamental ties. "The possibility of class voting obviates the need for a decision guide. . . . In every European country there are class parties available to class-conscious voters. . . . Certainly, European elections and party systems have been interpreted in these terms. . . . Under these circumstances, it may not be surprising . . . that identification per se has failed to develop among Europeans" (Shively 1979, 1050). Many studies of European electorates treat partisan identification and vote choice as synonyms. They contend that, because voters frequently cast their ballots for party symbols or lists rather than single candidates, it makes little sense to distinguish a partisan loyalty from the decision to vote for a particular party. Even when David Butler joined with Donald Stokes (1974) in the first effort to apply the Michigan model to another national electorate—Great Britain's—they were very tentative. Their analysis sees the basic question as the explanation of party identification, not vote choice, and they use class as the primary determinant. Studies of European electorates frequently omit reference to party identification.

In *Political Representation in France* (1986), Converse and Pierce attempt to outflank critics by extending the Michigan model to France. Echoing previous analyses, they distinguish between long- and short-term explanatory forces. The voter's party identification, self-placement on a left-right scale, and attitudes toward Charles De Gaulle (the dominant political figure of the era) and the Catholic church fall into the former category. The voter's partisan sympathies, obtained by measuring responses to each party on a feeling thermometer, and his or her positions on major issues compose the short-term forces. Converse and Pierce reject the view that class determines electoral behavior in France. "The central fact about the relationship between social class and electoral behavior in France is the enormous discrepancy between the trivial impact of social class differentials and the expectations generated by the vocabulary, formulas, and interpretive frameworks employed by many if not most elite participants and observers" (Converse and Pierce 1986, 99). These political scientists apply the theoretical principles and methods of the school of electoral analysis that Converse helped to establish thirty years ago.

Results of multiple regression analyses underscore the overwhelming importance of the long-term forces, especially party identification, in accounting for electoral choice in France. Among those who voted in 1967, the four long-term factors account for almost 60 percent of the variance in vote choice at the first ballot, and the short-term forces add little to the explanatory power of the model. When Converse and Pierce exclude persons with no party identification (approximately 30 percent of the sample), the long-term forces account for two-thirds of the variance in vote choice. The analysis of voting on the second ballot in that election reaffirms this finding because almost all voters who were able to vote in the second round cast their ballots for the candidate who had been their choice the first round. Using the standards of voting analysis, Converse and Pierce demonstrate that attachment to a political party explains vote choice in the French elections of 1967.

Aware that some theorists deny that party identification can be applied outside the boundaries of the United States, Converse and Pierce maintain that party identification in France plays the same role that it does in Britain and the United States. In all three cases, they show that most persons with an attachment to a political party vote for that party in a particular election; they cite a high correlation between having a party identification and being involved in politics to a high degree in both the United States and France, and they provide evidence that, in these countries, persons with party identification usually retain that attachment over time (Converse and Pierce 1986, 96). In the process, the authors present an elaborate defense of the utility and applicability of the party identification concept in France.

Converse and Pierce also imply that the Michigan model adequately explains electoral behavior in all democracies, not just France and the United States. Remember that they tested the approach on French data because there was reason to suppose that it would not apply in France. Finding that party identification is the key to voting there consequently lends more powerful support to the general argument. They can reasonably maintain that the anomalies and conceptual ambiguities that we saw earlier are not major problems. And they and their colleagues can agree that better data, more developed studies, and more precisely worded measures of the critical variables will uncover more of the basic strengths of the Michigan model of electoral behavior.

The Decay of the Class Model of Electoral Behavior

Political scientists who analyze voting behavior in European democracies part company with those who specialize on the United States in two very important ways. First, the long-standing hypotheses in European-oriented literature derive from Marx, Weber, and others who focus on the structural level. Second, empirical anomalies and conceptual ambiguities have led many of these political scientists to abandon what was once the orthodox approach. They are not strongly committed to a single, guiding paradigm.

First, let's look at the orthodox approach to the analysis of voting in European democracies. In this approach, analysis typically locates the voter in the social structure, and vote choice is believed to respond to the individual's place in various social structures, particularly those of social class and religion. Because a person's primary loyalties are seen to belong to the social group, party identification as such does not exist. Psychological attachment to a political party is thought to arise only when it is seen as being tied to one's social cleavage; even then, it serves only to indicate these more substantial bonds. W. Phillips Shively's view, which I cited above, nicely illustrates this position. Psychological identification with a social group is assumed to be more fundamental and stable than party identification, and it is seen as the primary determinant of voting behavior. The influence of both Marx and Weber on this analytic tradition is clear.

Recent studies have unearthed much evidence that characteristics of the social structure do not tie voters into blocs persistently supporting the same political parties (Zuckerman 1982 and 1989). And numerous analysts have demonstrated the declining significance of class position on voting decisions. To cite Peter Pulzer's summary of what was once the orthodox wisdom, no longer may we proclaim that "class is the basis of British politics" (1967, 98). In Britain, class identification is neither very helpful in explaining vote choice at any one election nor very effective at convincing a person to vote for the same party in election after election (Zuckerman and Lichbach 1977; Franklin and Mughan 1978; Rogowski 1981). Ronald Inglehart (1977) has posited that more general "post materialist values" compete with and sometimes replace those associated with class positions. Recall, too, that Converse and Pierce deny the importance of class in French voting. Looking at the Netherlands, C. Van der Eijk and B. Niemoller summarize changes in this society that once was characterized by sharp religious and class cleavages: "One can doubt whether the traditionally popular research which aims to discover differences in social-structural and psychological characteristics between stable and changing voters makes much sense.

To exaggerate a little, every voter is a potential vote changer" (1985, 357). In their conclusion to the volume entitled *Electoral Change in Advanced Industrial Democracies,* Russell J. Dalton, Scott C. Flanagan, and Paul Allen Beck summarize their claims in this way:

> Electoral alignments are weakening, and party systems are experiencing increased fragmentation and electoral volatility. Moreover, the evidence suggests that the changes in all of these nations reflect more than short-term oscillations in party fortunes. This decomposition of electoral alignments often can be traced to shifts in the long-term bases of partisan support-party identification and social cleavages. Virtually everywhere among the industrialized democracies, the old order is changing (1984, 451).

In fact, numerous scholars have noted a weakening of the cleavage bases of European electorates.

Richard Rose and Ian McAllister's book, *Voters Begin to Choose: From Closed-Class to Open Elections in Britain* (1986), illustrates the effort to replace the orthodox, class-based model. Because of conceptual ambiguities in the meaning of class, Rose and McAllister operationalize class in different ways and offer multiple tests of the core hypothesis. They show that the Standard Index of Determination between any one measure of class and vote in 1983 was no higher than 18 (where the maximum score is 100). In 1964, the highest score was 25. When they examine factors indirectly related to class, the index remains low. Housing, car ownership, and union membership have the highest scores, 22, 15, and 14, respectively. Rose and McAllister then use another technique of multivariate analysis, the Automatic Interaction Detector algorithm (tree analysis), to show that class variables in combination do not explain voting patterns in Britain. The authors deny the view of a British electorate that is structured around class divisions. "More than five-sixths of the British electorate is 'mixed' in social position, having some stereotype working class characteristics and some stereotype middle class characteristics" (Rose and McAllister 1986, 99). No matter how it is measured, they say, class has very little effect on voting decisions in Britain.

Rose and McAllister offer a "model of lifetime learning"—the analytical heart of the book—to account for electoral choice in an "open" (as opposed to a "structured") British electorate. Their analysis uses five categories containing a total of eighteen explanatory variables: (1) preadult socialization: father's party, father's class, education, and religion; (2) socioeconomic interests: housing, union membership, nation, and current class; (3) political principles: socialism, welfare, racialism, and traditional morality; (4) current performance of parties: leaders, evaluation of governing party, evaluation of specific critical events, campaign and future expectation; and (5) current party identification. Theirs is a complex model of voting.

This model describes a reasoning electorate that learns as it grows older and makes voting decisions based on a changing and complex set of factors. Simple explanations are not deemed appropriate. Instead, Rose and McAllister enter the variables into the analysis according to a voter's "life-history": the socialization factors first, then social and economic interests, followed by political principles, and finally, evaluation of the current performance of the parties and party identification.

The results of empirical tests confirm their argument: "When tested across a decade of elections, the lifetime learning model gives a clear, coherent, and parsimonious account of the division between Conservative and Labour voters. At each election since October, 1974, it can account for four-fifths of the variance, an extraordinarily high proportion by comparison with conventional models of voting relying on a single set of influences" (Rose and McAllister 1986, 155). Furthermore, they note, political factors are more important in each of these elections (accounting for nearly two-thirds of the explained variation) than the variables associated with socialization processes and contemporary social and economic interests. In addition, Rose and McAllister reaffirm the declining significance of father's class and father's party as explainers of party support during the past twenty years. In their analysis, principled political views are the keys to vote choice.

Rose and McAllister also disagree with the Michigan school. In particular, they deny the theoretical utility of party identification. Their analysis shows extraordinary fluidity in the importance of current party identification, which accounts for 9 percent of the variation in 1974, 20 percent in 1979, and 3 percent in 1983. They also demonstrate declines in the proportion of the British electorate with psychological attachments to the parties, as well as a reduction in the proportion of voters with strong party identifications. They highlight the weakness of the concept and describe party identification as a "statistical artifact." Indeed, they insist that there really is no difference between the two variables: The relationship between party identification and vote choice is, they tell us, essentially tautological. Most Britons do not think of themselves as party supporters. As a result, analysis of vote choice should make little use of the concept of party identification in their opinion.

Notice some of the consequences of their research. If class, no matter how it is measured, has no impact on vote choice, then we may question the theoretical approaches that produced the hypotheses linking class position and voting, namely, the Marxist and Weberian approaches. Indeed, in the first part of this chapter, you saw how these two approaches appeared to contradict each other, and in the second part, you observed the difficulties in applying the approaches to the formation of political groups. Ultimately, Rose and McAllister's analysis gives you additional reason to doubt the utility of approaches that emphasize the importance of social structure on politics.

But even if you accept the finding that class does not determine political behavior in Britain, you need not accept the model of lifetime learning as an explanation of vote choice. Remember the rule of parsimony. A theory that contains eighteen explanatory variables is complicated—it is not at all simple and beautiful—and it calls out for more precise analyses. Note, too, that Rose and McAllister do not explain voting decisions in the full British electorate; they apply their model only to the portion of the electorate that voted for either the Labour or Conservative parties. If all voters are included, they are able to account only for a smaller portion of the variance: 59 percent in 1974, 67 percent in 1983, and 56 percent in 1983. By their standards of analysis, this is still rather successful. But note what it really means in this case: When you have information on the eighteen variables that go into the model, you will be able to predict successfully how a person will vote in about six of ten cases. That is not a great success rate relative to the complexity of the model. Furthermore, there are no tests of this model in any other democracy. Thus, before accepting Rose and McAllister's analysis as an alternative model of voting behavior, you should consider applying it to other cases. Although we have strong reason to believe that vote choice is not a function of class, we do not yet have an accepted theory of electoral behavior.

Political scientists who analyze voting behavior share a set of methods and questions, a list of explanatory variables, and standards for the evaluation of explanations. They disagree over the centrality of the concept of party identification and the relative importance of the assumptions of rational choice theory as applied to voting. Current research revolves around the statistical analysis of survey data, where the ability to account for variation in the choice of party or candidate (as measured by the R^2 statistic and regression coefficients) defines explanation. Here, theoretical debates deal with shared data and use the same methods of analysis.

THE ANALYSIS OF DEMONSTRATIONS AND POLITICAL VIOLENCE

Why do people demonstrate and riot? What sends them into the streets to pursue their political goals? And what accounts for variations in the level of collective violence? These questions are central to studies of demonstrations and political violence. They also indicate that the various research schools and theories disagree about whether to focus on the individual or the structural levels of analysis. They differ, as well, on the particular structural or individual variables that are tied together in the explanatory nets. And because there are no easy ways to measure and obtain data on demonstrations and violence, scholars frequently disagree on what they see and, therefore, on what to explain. As you saw in the analysis of turnout, political scientists who study demonstrations and riots ask related but distinct questions, offer competing theories, and propose alternative answers, despite the fact that they frequently use the same methods and statistical techniques.

Some scholars maintain that riots and rebellions are rare political phenomena, that relatively few poor or oppressed persons rebel, and that hardly anyone who suffers from discrimination takes violent action against the system. Barrington Moore, Jr., summarizes hundreds of years of political history in noting that

> the overwhelming majority of those whose "objective" situation would qualify them as being somehow the victims of injustice took no active part in the events of the period. As far as it is possible to tell now, they just sat tight, tried to make do in their lives, and waited for the outcome. Although in the twentieth century, the degree of popular participation has undoubtedly increased, I strongly suspect that doing nothing remains the real form of mass action in the main historical crises since the sixteenth century (1978, 156–157).

By themselves, Moore observes, poverty and oppression do not lead to collective violence. Indeed, he maintains that people will demonstrate, strike, and riot together only when they share a marked sense of injustice. This shared perception derives from the presence of a shared moral code and strong social ties among the members of the group and from a change—in work rules, salary, rights, or some other kind of standing expectation—that violates their shared code. When they act, they seek to redress the grievance. Furthermore, he says, there is no easy translation of local and particular issues into national and class politics. Examining detailed analyses of German coal- and steelworkers, as well as the demonstrations and violence that abounded in Germany in the aftermath of World War I, Moore searches for the conditions that account for the outbursts of such relatively rare political phenomena.

But Charles Tilly offers a very different analysis of the past four centuries of French history:

In our own century the involvement of national, politically active associations in the pursuit of shared interests—already visible in the nineteenth century—has become overwhelming. Amid the incessant activity of organized workers and organized capitalists, besides the increasing tendency of people to organize their demands in national strike waves and social movements, we notice the widening activity of students, intellectuals, government employees, independent farmers, shopkeepers, and service workers (1986, 388).

Tilly locates changes in "the repertoire of contentious political action." Festivals, charivaris, and grain and field seizures have given way to strikes, public meetings, rallies, and sit-ins. He also details how large portions of the French populace have engaged in such forms of demonstration. Drawing on an amended version of Marx's theory, Tilly maintains that the repertoires changed in response to massive alterations in the strength of the national state and capitalism in France. "In response to the shifts of power and capital, ordinary people invented and adopted new forms of action, creating the electoral campaign, the public meeting, the social movement" (Tilly 1986, 396). He analyzes demonstrations and collective violence as rational and frequent responses by groups of persons to fundamental changes in their lives wrought by capitalism and the French state.

G. Bingham Powell analyzes political violence (1982) with hypotheses from the same theoretical net that produced his study of turnout (1986). He states that characteristics of the social and political structures, especially those of the party system, powerfully and directly influence the level of political violence. Here, too, Powell tests his explanatory model with data on a large set of democracies—in the third world as well as North America and Western Europe—that is drawn from two periods of time. He distinguishes two dimensions of political violence. Riots are operationalized by examining data codified in source books of political statistics but without testing for the reliability and validity of the measures. He uses this information to assess numbers of deaths occurring during clandestine political acts, demonstrations, and riots. Powell offers a path analysis, which is a form of multiple regression, to demonstrate the proximate and immediate causes of political violence.

Powell asks which variables best account for variations in the level of riots and notes that three have direct impact: population size and two characteristics of the party system—the extent of voting for extremist parties and the number of parties in the legislature. Together, he says, they explain two-thirds of the cross-national variation in the level of rioting. But other characteristics of the polity and society also affect these variables (Powell 1982, 126). Furthermore, he shows that the same basic model accounts, as well, for variations in the cross-national level of peaceful protest (1982, 130). For Powell, the characteristics of the party system are powerful explainers of variations in the level of turnout, in peaceful protest, and in riots, but they do not help to explain differences in the level of political deaths (1982, 156). Indeed, Powell's analysis leads to the conclusion that these deaths result primarily from "organized attacks by political groups" (1982, 157). Therefore, they are not another manifestation of the general concept of political participation. Powell also associates the likelihood of revolution in democracy to the activities of party leaders (1982, 169). In other words, he maintains that characteristics of the party system are central to the explanation of variations in turnout, peaceful protest, political violence, and the demise of democracies. More generally, his analysis rests on the explanatory power of social and political structures.

Philippe C. Schmitter (1981) proposes a related but contradictory analysis of political protest and violence. He, too, analyzes democracies, concentrating on the 1960s and early 1970s, but restricts the focus to Western Europe and North America. Like Powell, Schmitter emphasizes the explanatory power of political structures, but he demonstrates that the organization of interest groups is of greater importance than the characteristics of the political parties.

Schmitter condenses his argument into a complex hypothesis: *"Polities in which interests are processed through formal associations that cover the widest variety of potential interests with national networks of representation, that have the highest proportion of those potentially affected as members, and whose pattern of interaction with the state is monopolistic, specialized, hierarchical, and mutually collusive should be more orderly, stable, and effective"* (1981, 292–293, emphasis in original). Before we turn to Schmitter's elaboration, note how many concepts must be defined and measured. The empirical evidence for this analysis will, therefore, rest heavily on the reliability and validity of the operational definitions.

Schmitter describes the "structure of interest intermediation." First, he asks about the proportion of the interests in a society (workers' demands, health, housing, religion, language, and any and all others) that are represented in formally organized interest groups. Second, he examines the proportion of persons involved in each of these interests who are members of formal organizations. Third, he explores the organizational characteristics of the interest groups, particularly the degree of centralization of each, and the extent to which one organization monopolizes each interest. Finally, he studies the relationship between the organized interests and the government, particularly the extent of direct and formal involvement of such interests in making and enforcing government policy. Schmitter narrows this daunting empirical task to questions about workers and unions. He assumes that the more a society is characterized by centralized unions and the fewer national unions exist, the higher the level of "societal corporatism" is. The presence of densely organized interest groups and high societal corporatism, argues Schmitter, makes for more orderly, stable, and effective democracies.

Although he presents three defining characteristics of democracies, I will focus only on "unruliness," which may be a synonym for political violence. Schmitter provides an abstract definition—"citizen initiated efforts to influence public choices in violent, illegal, or unprecedented ways" (1981, 302). He also provides three indicators—"the level of collective protest," "internal war," and "strike volume." His definition, operationalization, and sources indicate that Schmitter's "collective protest" is the same as Powell's "riots" and that Schmitter's "internal war" equals Powell's "deaths." (Powell, as you know, does not study the level of strikes in a society.) Examining the years 1958–1972, Schmitter places the democracies of North America and Western Europe into a rank-order that closely resembles that of Powell (1981, 23). He finds that the United States and France share the highest level of unruliness; Norway, the Netherlands, Sweden, and Switzerland have the lowest levels. Obviously, democracies vary in their levels of political violence.

Schmitter's analysis of unruliness diverges sharply from Powell's explanation of riots and deaths. Here, the structure of interest groups carries the explanatory weight. First, he examines the bivariate relationship and sees a strong negative correlation between each of the explanatory variables—density of association membership and level of societal corporatism—and citizen unruliness. Indeed, he identifies a negative correlation (.73) between societal corporatism and the dependent variable. Then, he shows that adding a variable that assesses the strength of voting for the Social Democratic parties—one measure of the party system—does not increase the correlation at all. Similarly, a variable labeled "predictability of voting patterns" (which closely resembles Powell's "party-group linkage") raises the correlation only slightly (Schmitter 1981, 317). In his analysis, the level of societal corporatism is the primary explanation of the level of citizen unruliness.

The contrasts among these analyses of demonstrations and political violence are striking.

1. Moore and Tilly examine diverse historical studies to generalize about the level of political demonstrations and violence in a

particular case and, in turn, to generalize about all European capitalist democracies.
2. Moore sees relatively low levels and Tilly sees relatively high levels of collective violence.
3. Moore accounts for outbursts of these phenomena by examining the sense of justice held by sets of persons and the extent to which these persons form a group. Tilly insists on the centrality of capitalist and state development and assumes that persons who are affected the same way by these changes will respond together to alleviate their conditions.
4. Powell and Schmitter examine similar dependent variables but offer very different explanations of the variations.
5. Powell does not examine the structure of the interest groups; instead, his argument rests heavily on the importance of political parties.
6. Schmitter demonstrates the relative importance of the characteristics of interest groups as compared to political parties.
7. Powell claims he can account for variations in the level of cabinet changes, something that Schmitter admits he cannot do. Indeed, it would seem that Powell's analysis demonstrates much greater theoretical import.
8. A close look at Schmitter's measures indicates that he ignores the effects of population size, a variable that Powell found to be very important in the analysis of political protest and violence. (Perhaps, however, Schmitter is right to overlook the effects of population size. Why should the mere number of persons in a society affect citizen unruliness? It would be difficult to propose a general hypothesis to account for this pattern.)
9. Furthermore, Schmitter's analysis of "government unstableness," another characteristic of a democracy, seems to confirm Powell's finding that there is an inverse relationship between the number of political parties and the level of political protest and violence.

The differences among these analyses highlight the need to assess them carefully. They also speak to the difficulties of this task. Remember that Moore focuses on Germany, and Tilly examines France. It is possible that the discrepancies are no more than the differences between the histories of two countries. Similarly, Powell and Schmitter do not examine the exact same set of democracies in precisely the same time period. Remember, too, that Schmitter's measure of citizen unruliness includes strikes. Are these differences in the dependent variables enough to account for the diverse results?

Perhaps you prefer to reject all these analyses on the grounds that none directly addresses the persons who engage in political violence. Structural variables may establish the conditions for riots, but they do not offer motives or calculations that send people into the streets. Neither Powell nor Schmitter defines explanation in terms of the psychological dispositions and goals of those who riot. And Tilly and Moore impute motives to members of groups without directly assessing their goals. If you insist that explanations require motives, then you will want to examine analyses of political violence that focus on individual actors.

Rational actor theorists and those who study the link between political attitudes and behavior offer their own analyses of political violence. The former speculate on the conditions that lead individuals to forego the tendency to free ride and instead join demonstrations, riots, and rebellions. The latter draw on psychological theories to examine how the perception of grievances triggers political violence and revolutions. The studies they produce offer direct alternatives to Moore's, Tilly's, Powell's, and Schmitter's structural analyses of political violence.

In an article entitled "An Evaluation of 'Does Economic Inequality Breed Political Conflict?' Studies" (1989), Mark Irving Lichbach has organized much of the literature on political violence. I will borrow from his summary of the differences between the hypotheses in political psychology, which Lichbach labels the "deprived actor school" and the "rational actor model."

As you know, political scientists who employ the theories of psychology emphasize the explanatory power of perceptions and evaluations. They believe that individuals assess their circumstances against a standard of fairness, which may be relative to friends and neighbors or to more general expectations.

> In sum, Deprived Actors care about relative income and wages. When economic inequality increases and in consequence, relative deprivation increases, some such actors become angry or frustrated enough to rebel. [These] theories of dissent argue that economic inequality will *generally* lead the poorer, impulse-driven actors to rebel, but only if some intermediate psychological processes (e.g., expectation formation and anger) are present to transform grievances about relative poverty into behavioral dissent (Lichbach 1989, 459).

According to Lichbach, persons who believe that they are not getting their proper share are particularly likely to riot, rebel, and revolt.

Lichbach presents Ted Robert Gurr's research (1968; 1970) on a large sample of countries in the 1960s as a classic illustration of this approach.

Gurr emphasizes the explanatory power of relative deprivation, defined as "actors' perceptions of discrepancy between their value expectations . . . and their value capabilities" (1968, 1104). However, his data do not permit a direct measurement of this variable. Instead, he combines many objective social, economic, and political characteristics into an operationalization of the critical psychological variable. Gurr's model explains more than one-third of the variance of civil strife: "The fundamental proposition that strife varies directly in magnitude with the intensity of relative deprivation is strongly supported; the three deprivation variables alone provide an R of .60 (R^2=.36), and when a fourth state-of-mind variable, legitimacy, is added the R^2 increases to .43" (1968, 1123). In this and related research, psychological perceptions, beliefs, and evaluations are believed to trigger political violence.

Rational actor modelers approach the problem from a very different angle. These theorists have no problem with Moore's claim that relatively few persons ever engage in collective protest and violence. As Lichbach states, "The key question here is: How do rational actors react to the returns from their economic activities compared to their dissident activities? [These] theories have suggested that actors use a simple cost-benefit calculus. Participants will spend an extra unit of their time on dissident activities only if the private reward is greater than the private reward from economic activities" (1989, 460). Given the free-rider issue and the particular problem here of high sanctions against this kind of political behavior, enforced by the police and the army, it is not surprising that civil strife is as infrequent as it is.

But just as we know that people vote and that interest groups, unions, and political parties form, we know that political dissidence occurs. The newspapers are filled with seemingly endless examples of demonstrations, riots, and rebellions. Even if the media exaggerate the sensational, violent politics is not nearly as infrequent as rational action theorists imply. How, then, do they explain its emergence?

Lichbach suggests that the answer lies in the presence of absolute, not relative, poverty and leaders of opposition groups with enough economic resources to attract followers (1989, 461). Persons enticed to action by the prospect of money, jobs, housing, or other personal benefits and persons coerced to join by threats of punishment will riot and join political groups. Staying within the boundaries of the rational actor model, Lichbach insists that violent political behavior, like other forms of political behavior, occurs when it is in the direct personal interest of the actor.

Edward N. Muller and Karl-Dieter Opp (1986) offer an alternative answer. First, they reason that individuals understand that the free-rider problem inhibits rebellious action and that people know that what they do is especially critical for this form of political behavior. In other words, they consciously act in order to overcome the normal limits of collective action. Second, Muller and Opp assume that individuals value psychic and social rewards, not only particularistic benefits. Thus, they move outside the strict definition of personal incentives. Muller and Opp amend rational choice theory by suggesting that individuals sometimes assume a "collectivist conception of rationality" (1986, 484). As we saw in the analysis of turnout and collective action, some rational action theorists are willing to relax their assumptions about individual motives.

If you believe that explanations of politics require variables that examine the motives of the actors, you should appreciate these studies. Such analyses, drawn from political psychology and rational choice theory, insist that the explanation of political violence is more than the specification of conditions that correlate with the dependent variable.

Each has its own problems. It is difficult, for example, to obtain direct measures of political attitudes and values, especially those of persons who have engaged in political violence. You must consider whether the use of indirect measures based on objective factors in the economy and polity serve as adequate surrogates. Gurr, himself, has his doubts (1968, 1123). Wolfinger and Rosenstone were able to solve this problem in regard to voting turnout by including data from a survey of voters, in addition to census data. Clearly, studies that demand that explanations examine motives must provide information on these attitudes. Similarly, keep in mind the tendency among rational choice theorists to relax the basic assumptions of their approach when confronted with the need to explain collective action, in general, and political violence, in particular. Muller and Opp seem to be repeating the procedure used by Downs, Riker, and Ordeshook in the analysis of turnout and the effort of Moe and Hechter in the explanation of collective action. This would seem to be a problem. After all, a primary justification for rational choice theory is that it makes use of deductive logic, and proponents of this school maintain that it is especially able to propose sets of related hypotheses. Remember, however, that to benefit from the power of deductive logic, it is necessary to stay within the limits of the original assumptions. You must consider whether Muller, Opp, Downs, Riker, Ordeshook, Moe, and Hechter, in deciding to relax the assumption that individuals act to maximize their own personal interest, actually weaken the analytic strength of the approach itself.

CONCLUSION

Hardly any questions in political science have one agreed-upon answer. Think of the issue of revolution in capitalist democracies: Marx ties this phenomenon to the formation of classes and class conflict; Weber emphasizes the rise of charismatic movements; and Powell focuses on the actions of party leaders. Or consider the problem of demonstrations and political violence in democracies: Moore stresses the shared sense of injustice among members of a group as a necessary condition for this kind of political action; Tilly specifies rational responses by groups of persons to the effects of capitalism and state-building; Powell uses population size and the characteristics of the party system as the primary explainers; Schmitter concentrates on the role of societal corporatism; theories drawn from political psychology use perceptions of relative deprivation as explanatory variables; and rational action models tie their explanations to overcoming the problem of collective action. Does political violence necessarily precede revolution in democracies? Weber, Moore, Tilly, Powell, Schmitter, Gurr, and the rational action modelers imply affirmative answers. Marx does not—or at least some readings of Marx do not. Each problem in political science seems to have a multitude of solutions.

Even the best-organized of the research schools that abound in political science exhibit slips in their internal rigor. This is certainly true for the two approaches that exhibit the highest levels of theoretical power and scope—Marxist and rational action theory. Marxists share a conceptual language and a stance that always directs them to examine the place of class in capitalist politics. But many critical Marxist hypotheses are now treated as empirical questions; they are no longer presented as true simply because they are derived from Marx's assumptions. Rational choice theorists insist that their approach best demonstrates the power of deductive logic in political science, and their theoretical net covers an exceptionally wide group of topics. Based on a limited set of assumptions about individuals, they derive analyses of cabinet coalitions, the formation of unions and political parties, voting behavior, the outbreak of political violence, and a host of other political phenomena. But rational action theorists relax these very assumptions in order to explain turnout, political violence, and collective action. Does this point to an inherent weakness in the approach, or is it little more than the standard need to adjust abstract theories to particular conditions?

Other studies display even less internal rigor. Powell's study utilizes a list of variables said to represent the social and economic environment and the party system. But what more general hypotheses justify the hypothesis in which population size is an explanatory variable? Rose and McAllister present eighteen variables to represent a model of lifetime learning, but they do not justify the order in which they use these variables. Similarly, students of political culture and attitudes offer a host of possibly important indicators of attitudes, perceptions, and beliefs, but, using theories with relatively weak nets, they do not always justify the particular variables and indicators they have examined.

We must now investigate the criteria by which you will accept or reject a claim to knowledge. Do Wolfinger and Rosenstone, Powell, Jackman, or Piven and Cloward provide the best analysis of turnout? Should you make your decision by examining each study by itself or relative to the others? How much importance do you attribute to the general approach from which these studies derive? If you maintain that political science must include data on motives, then you might be drawn to Wolfinger and Rosenstone's or Powell's analyses. If you emphasize the importance of theoretical scope, Jackman and Piven and Cloward beckon. Powell is the only one to answer Weber's call to provide data on the structural and individual levels of analysis: How important do you consider that to be? And how do you evaluate the empirical analyses offered by each study? Do you choose to apply the standards of explanation implied by thick description or established by the statistical analyses of variations in the dependent variable? You must also remember the criteria of validity and reliability in the assessment of definitions and operationalization, which we discussed in the first chapter. In the pages ahead, we will examine more fully the criteria that you may apply as you assess claims to knowledge in political science.

CHAPTER 5

How We Know When We Know: Testing Claims to Knowledge in Political Science

Political science is nothing if not diverse. In the second chapter, I presented four contrasting explanations of turnout in national elections. Following that, I reviewed five research schools in political science, each containing many studies. In Chapter 4, I displayed two contrasting theories of revolution in capitalist societies, six analyses of the formation of political groups, clashing research structures in the analysis of vote choice, and six different explanations of political violence. These illustrations depict a discipline that is not known for order and coherence.

Political scientists seem to know both too much and too little about their subject: too much because no one can be expected to keep track of so many alternative analyses; too little because there appears to be no pecking order among the studies. If you were to investigate political violence, for example, how would you begin the analysis? What would justify testing any of the hypotheses offered in the last chapter? It may be a waste of time to test all the hypotheses, and it is certainly not appropriate to allow your intuition to determine which you select.

What accounts for the cacophony in political science? First, political scientists have always borrowed concepts, hypotheses, theories, and methods from the other social sciences. The obvious links among the worlds of politics, economic and social relations, and the motives of individuals naturally induce political scientists to borrow from economics, sociology, anthropology, psychology, and the law. Second, many claims to knowledge in political science are not presented in ways that compel us to either accept or reject them. There are no unequivocal empirical tests whose results demand acceptance. Rigorous mathematical logics—with which one could simply decide what is a proper derivation of a theory and what is not—are rarely applied. As a result, it is sometimes as easy to accept as to reject a given proposition. Third, research at the frontiers of knowledge typically sounds cacophonous. And keep in mind that we have been reviewing how political scientists work. As a result, we have examined areas in which there can be no agreement yet. As you will see in the next chapter, dissensus and conflict characterize *all* research at the frontiers of knowledge, and this is true in all disciplines—in the physical sciences and the other social sciences as well as in political science. Fourth, to the extent that political scientists work on contemporary events, their work is bound to be affected by the absence of relevant data. They are less likely, therefore, to be able to propose especially compelling hypotheses. As a result, political science abounds in conflicting hypotheses, theories, and approaches to analysis.

Certainly, there *are* standards for claims to knowledge in political science, but the criteria offered will not force you to accept a particular conclusion. Indeed, because this is so, you must think especially carefully about the principles you use in your evaluation. You must develop rules that impel or constrain you to accept or reject a particular claim to knowledge. I emphasize impel, in the sense of moving you in the direction of an outcome. I emphasize constrain because a decision to accept one proposition usually entails a decision to reject an alternative one. We seek "credentialed knowledge" (Meehl 1986, 317) or knowledge defined by "objectively warranted assertability" (Brown 1987, 222)—claims to know the world that are so strong as to make it difficult not to accept them. You should realize, however, that the absence of unequivocal tests in political science means the decision to accept one research school over another must rest on more than rational criteria alone. Especially because this is so, you need to maximize the role of impersonal criteria in your assessment of claims to knowledge.

You must also consider how charitable you will be in your evaluations. Should you accept a claim until you have reason to reject it, or should you reject it until you have reason to accept it? The first position leads to utter confusion at all times. But if you were to always say "prove it," you would be rejecting some smart ideas that do not yet have adequate support. How long will you accept a claim that seems plausible but has little backing? And how long should it take you to challenge the utility of particular measures? Should you be more, less, or equally as generous to other persons as you are to yourself? In the pursuit of credentialed knowledge, there is reason to minimize our charitable feelings, and "the simple reason is that we well understand how easy it is to have a theory that turns out to be totally incorrect" (Newton-Smith 1981, 163).

As you proceed through this chapter, keep in mind that the rules help you address several related issues. They provide criteria to help you decide whether a claim to knowledge warrants testing or may simply be ignored and whether to accept the claim as knowledge. When you do political science, use the rules and techniques to strengthen your claims and thereby move others to accept them.

REQUISITES FOR EMPIRICAL PROPOSITIONS IN POLITICAL SCIENCE

The general characteristics of empirical knowledge, which I presented in the first chapter, imply specific rules that you should apply to all claims to knowledge about politics. When these expectations are violated, you need go no further. It is perfectly appropriate to refuse to use a concept because it is imprecise and to reject a hypothesis as nothing more than an assertion—a statement without logical or empirical support. Conversely, the more you can defend the precision of a concept or the theoretical significance and explanatory power of a hypothesis, the more reason you have to accept it.

1. First and foremost, you should expect political science to analyze the political world as it exists, not an imaginary universe. Propositions about politics must be demonstrated with empirical evidence—a criterion that political science shares with all empirical sciences. Philosopher of science Abraham Kaplan makes this general point:

> If science is to tell us anything about the world, it must somewhere contain empirical elements. . . . For it is by experience alone that information about the world is received. . . .
> It is in the empirical component that science is differentiated from fantasy. An inner coherence, even strict self-consistency, may mark a delusional system as well as a scientific one. Paraphrasing Archimedes we may each declare, "Give me a premise to stand on and I will deduce a world!" But it will be a fantasy world except in so far as the premise gives it a measure of reality (1974, 34–35).

All efforts to analyze politics seek to know how the existing political world operates. If they do not, if they are not at least potentially related to the political world, you may ignore them.

2. No matter how important observations of the empirical world are, there is neither description nor analysis without carefully demarcated concepts, variables, and hypotheses. Propositions require concepts.

You should never think that the facts speak for themselves. This is true in at least two senses. First, there are no unaided observations of politics. Without concepts, there are no data. And without thinking, we cannot perceive—much less describe or explain—the world "out there." All efforts to describe stem from conceptual and theoretical contexts. Two stories told by philosopher of science Karl Popper emphasize this point:

> But in fact the belief that we can start with pure observations alone, without anything in the nature of a theory, is absurd; as may be illustrated by the story of the man who dedicated his life to natural science, wrote down everything that he could observe, and bequeathed his priceless collection to the Royal Society to be used as inductive evidence. This story should show us that beetles may be profitably collected, observations may not.
>
> Twenty-five years ago I tried to bring home the same point to a group of physics students in Vienna by beginning a lecture with the following instructions: "Take a pencil and paper; carefully observe, and write down what you have observed!" They asked, of course, *what* I wanted them to observe. Clearly, the instruction, "Observe!" is absurd (1965, 46).

Without some idea, therefore, of what is important, we cannot cut into the seamless web that exists outside ourselves. Second, we know what to observe from the problem being analyzed, and the tentative answers—the hypotheses—propose to solve the problem. Theories structure all observations. Political science, like any discipline of knowledge, cannot proceed by observations alone.

3. Claims to empirical knowledge must be testable. In the words of Popper, "Irrefutability is not a virtue in a theory (as people often think) but a vice" (1965, 36). If you cannot test the claim, it is not an empirical proposition, and you need not consider it. "Our theories can touch the world only at those points at which they risk falsification through non-congruence with facts" (Gellner 1985, 59). Harold Brown links the standard of objectivity to the need to provide empirical tests. We should "return to nature again and again, and afford nature the opportunity of surprising us" (Brown 1987, 201). Remember to distinguish between taking a test and passing or failing a test, between shooting the ball at the basket and making or missing the shot. Success in the classroom demands taking and passing tests. Students who refuse to take them, who deny the need to submit themselves to the judgment of others, cannot convince others that they know anything. The same point holds for scholars who claim to know the world of politics. We must be assured that there is no good reason to reject their claims to knowledge.

Popper takes a very strong stand on this issue. In the aptly titled *Conjectures and Refutations: The Growth of Scientific Knowledge,* he argues that we know the world only by a process that revolves about the negation of hypotheses:

> Yet it is not the marvelous unfolding of the system which makes a theory rational or empirical but the fact that we can examine it critically; that is to say, subject it to attempted refutations, including observational tests, and the fact that, in certain cases, a theory may be able to withstand those criticisms and those tests—among them tests under which its predecessors broke down, and sometimes even further and more severe tests. It is in the rational choice of the new theory that the rationality of science lies, rather than in the deductive development of the theory (Popper 1965, 221).

Only with testable propositions can the decision be made to accept or reject any claim to knowledge.

4. Empirical evidence should be as precise as required by the theory being examined. Because you must make your abstractions visible, you need to provide indicators of the concepts and variables in your hypotheses. Moreover, you must make sure that the measures do not violate the requirements of reliability and validity. Where appropriate, this means that you will need to go into the field, rather than rely on the thin descriptions of surveys and published sources. Usually, the demand for precise empirical evidence means that you should attach numerical values to variables and relationships; where we need numbers and do not supply them, we are saying nothing. Paul Meehl's words bear underlining:

> It is necessary to think clearly about words and to realize that many of the words—I would say most words—both in ordinary language and in scholarly discourse that purport to explain anything are quantity words intrinsically. Not always, but almost always. . . . When a social scientist speaks of something—anything, a tribal custom or suicide tendencies or unconscious memories . . . he typically uses words like "always," "frequently," "typically," "rarely," "never," "oddly," "weakly," "under special conditions," "mostly." Every single one of these words is a claim of the degree to which some force or entity exists or influences; every single one indicates a probability with which something happens or the magnitude of a disposition (propensity). It is foolish for social scientists to get away from this simple fact about the descriptive language of their disciplines (1986, 320).

Note again that this does not imply that only information obtained from surveys or books of statistics should be used because it comes in the form of numbers. Rather, where required (and, as Meehl indicates, the obligation applies to most analyses), you should substantiate the quantity and degree words in your descriptions.

The importance of empirical tests in political science should not surprise you; we have been reviewing them throughout this book. Each of the studies in Chapters 2, 3, and 4, for example, contains empirical propositions. There are very few studies in political science that use only the language of mathematical reasoning or deductive logic to build an argument. And some rely heavily on verbal arguments, but they always make indirect or implicit empirical propositions. Ultimately, warrants to accept or reject knowledge in political science rest on the claim that they present empirical knowledge.

Not only should this not surprise you, it should also please you. Those of us who study politics are naturally attracted to the political world, and our desire to analyze it comes from this appeal as much, if not more, than from our passion for solving intellectual puzzles. Sometimes our yen to know the details, to get behind the scenes and learn what's really going on stands in the way of systematic knowledge. When we follow this call, forgetting the need to produce warrants for our knowledge claims, we really don't know whether we know anything. But when we assess empirical propositions about politics, we join our passion to know about politics with our need to know that we know.

In sum, claims to knowledge in political science must be tied to theories of politics. They must be testable, appropriately detailed, and linked to a conceptual foundation. Where they are not, they do not qualify as empirical propositions. We may ignore them; we have no warrant to accept them.

GOALS FOR EMPIRICAL PROPOSITIONS ABOUT POLITICS: STRIVE TO MAKE STRONG CLAIMS TO KNOWLEDGE

All empirical propositions are not alike even when they are testable and derived from theories of politics. They vary in theoretical significance, precision, power, and in the amount of evidence that supports them. But strong hypotheses attract other people's intellectual attention. By making powerful claims, they overcome our initial skepticism and justify the effort to test them. The stronger the proposition is, the more reason that we have to accept and provide further tests of its claims to knowledge about politics. The more tests passed and the more demanding the tests are, the more likely we are to accept the proposition.

1. Strong propositions are tied to many others in tightly knit theories. Recall the image of the web of ideas woven into a net or tapestry. A statement is strong when it is logically linked to other statements. And presenting reasons to support or reject the particular hypothesis influences the standing of those to which it is logically tied. Propositions drawn from Marx's theory and rational action theory rank higher on this dimension than those derived from the study of political attitudes and behavior and from Weber's analysis. We have good reason to examine strong hypotheses because the results of such examinations also test our ability to accept or deny many other propositions.

2. Strong hypotheses propose a powerful relationship between the explanatory and dependent variables. One way to propose a strong hypothesis is to specify a high regression coefficient or an especially high correlation. Do not suppose, however, that strong hypotheses always require numeric assessments of power. Marx's proposition that class conflict is a necessary and sufficient condition for revolution and Weber's hypothesis that revolutions in advanced industrial societies can only be led by charismatic movements certainly qualify as strong hypotheses. Such hypotheses propose that the explanatory variable has a marked effect on that which is being explained.

3. Strong hypotheses make precise claims about the way the explanatory and dependent variables covary. They specify the shape of the curve that describes the relationship, the numerical strength of the correlation, or the precise frequency with which the two sets of phenomena may be found together. Here, framing and testing hypotheses in ways that allow for precise assessments of the strength of the relationship is critical. These strong hypotheses demonstrate the principle that claims to knowledge need to be supported by numbers.

4. Strong claims to knowledge may display another characteristic: They may imply not only precise and powerful relationships among the variables but insist that the association observed is not spurious. Wolfinger and Rosenstone maintain that variations in the level of education and not some other factor, like registration laws or the number of political parties, best account for differences in the level of turnout. They use multivariate analyses to rule out the alternative explanations and tests for statistical significance to show that the proposition is not a result of random associations. A strong proposition like this asserts, therefore, that there is a real relationship between the designated explanatory variable or variables and that which is being explained.

5. Some strong statements make causal claims. As noted in the first chapter, causal explanations are a type of explanation that imply the strongest form of knowledge: the claim that we can point to a particular phenomenon that brings about some other. But what is a causal

relationship? Thomas D. Cook and Donald T. Campbell, in *Quasi-Experimentation: Design and Analysis Issues for Field Settings,* build on the three criteria for inferring cause that John Stuart Mill proposed more than a century ago: "(1) covariation between the presumed cause and effect; (2) the temporal precedence of the cause; and (3) the need to use the 'control' concept implicit in his Method of Concomitant Variation to rule out alternative interpretations for a possible cause and effect connection" (1979, 31). In other words, a cause and effect relationship is present when the two variables are always observed together, when the causal variable precedes the outcome, and when it can be shown that no other variable brings about the specific result. (This definition was used in the first chapter of this book.) Cook and Campbell add another characteristic of a causal explanation: "The causal laws of greatest practical significance and closest correspondence to common sense definitions of cause are those laws involving manipulable causes. These are causes we can do something about, and they can be likened to recipes for action" (1979, 31). In other words, causes are variables that can be manipulated and that always occur with, precede, and can be shown to have a direct impact on the outcome variable.

We can now restate one of the debates we observed in the analysis of turnout. Piven and Cloward insist on the explanatory importance of registration laws, but Wolfinger and Rosenstone offer education and other abstract skills as the critical variables in the explanation of turnout. Piven and Cloward also maintain that their variable has greater causal impact; it is much easier to change the rules for voting than it is to raise the general level of education in the United States. Because they offer causal or manipulable variables, their analysis has clear recommendations for policymakers. And because their analysis can explain turnout and provide the causal mechanism to raise the level of turnout, they insist that theirs is the stronger analysis of this phenomenon in the United States. They imply that one measure of the strength of a proposition is its ability to become policy and effect change.

To summarize this section, a proposition is strong when we are pushed to accept it. We are impelled to accept it when the force of reason and evidence is so great that we must overcome our initial skepticism. In the next section, I will review criteria by which we can decide whether there is strong reason to accept a proposition.

METHODS TO ACCEPT OR REJECT EMPIRICAL PROPOSITIONS

To accept a hypothesis, we must show that it has passed attempts designed to falsify it. As more and tougher tests are passed, the reasons not to reject and, therefore, to accept the proposition about politics become more powerful and compelling.

The Place of Experiments in Political Science

In some empirical sciences, it is possible to manipulate one factor—the designated independent or causal variable—and directly observe its effect on the proposed outcome. The results of these experiments compel the observer to accept or reject the proposition. Cook and Campbell maintain that because causal variables are manipulable, experimental controls are necessary to evaluate causal claims:

> The experiment is modest, seeking only to elucidate whether a particular cause or a restricted set of causes has an effect. . . . In a sense, our analysis of causation leads us to a conception of cause that avoids an essentialist explanation and settles for probing probabilistic causal connections. However, our analysis of causation leads us to prefer experimentation—one of the least modest methodological tools for field research—because a major requirement for experimentation (manipulability) mirrors the type of cause in which we are most interested (1979, 32).

These social scientists argue that by applying the tools of experimental analysis, we can test for the presence of causal relations in social science in general and, by implication, in political science in particular.

In disciplines like political science, in which research is done in the field and not in the laboratory, there are techniques that permit studies to resemble experiments. Cook and Campbell emphasize the use of large data sets and the importance of the technique by which the analyst randomly chooses the cases that will receive the treatment or causal variable. When Shanto Iyengar and Donald Kinder (1987) sought to determine the effects of watching the news on television on the ways individuals perceive the importance of public issues, they applied these guidelines. Similarly, to determine whether canvassing voters increases turnout, a test to randomly assign this treatment across a large number of election districts could be devised. Thus, in research involving a large number of cases where the analyst has the ability to manipulate the presence of an explanatory variable, political scientists may design studies that are close equivalents of experiments.

Nevertheless, there are very few of these kinds of studies in political science. In none of the work that we reviewed in the previous chapters did we observe the manipulation of an independent variable as a treatment and the observation of the dependent variable as an effect. Generally speaking, it is not easy to apply the criteria of randomization to much of what we study in political science, and it is often difficult to cite a large number of cases. For example, we cannot randomly assign a class-conscious working class and an apathetic working class to the existing cases of capitalist democracies. Nor can we randomly assign different levels of extremist party voting across these democracies. In the same way, we cannot observe what the effect on turnout would be if no one in the electorate had a university education. At best, there are too few such cases to allow us to claim that we have overcome the possible presence of any contaminating variables. As a result, the presentation of evidence in political science studies does not usually resemble a lab report, and the conclusions drawn from our analyses, even those aided by randomization and large samples, are not as compelling as the results of experiments.

In Place of Experiments, Strive to Eliminate Nuisance Factors

In the relative absence of experimental controls, randomization, and studies with very large samples, Cook and Campbell offer advice on how to structure research in order to eliminate alternative explanations. First, they instruct us to remove the possibility of confounding factors or simple mistakes. They offer tests for "mundane nuisance factors which suggest that an observed relationship may not be causal or may involve different constructs [i.e., concepts] than those in which the investigator may be interested. Like Popper, we stress the need for *many* tests to determine whether a causal proposition has or has not withstood falsification; such determination cannot be made on one or two failures to achieve predicted results" (Cook and Campbell 1979, 31, emphasis in original). Note that they stress the importance of multiple and repeated tests for the presence of each and all of the nuisance factors. As you show that your analysis has fewer and fewer errors, you provide an increasing number of reasons to accept the claim. Ultimately, generosity and skepticism will give way to reason.

In their discussion, which covers almost sixty densely printed pages, Cook and Campbell present four categories of tests for the presence of the nuisance factors: statistical conclusion validity, internal validity, construct validity of putative causes, and external validity (1979, 37–94). Their claims are outlined and their criteria are illustrated below.

1. *Tests for statistical conclusion validity eliminate the possibility that the wrong conclusions are being derived from information gathered in the form of statistics.*

Statistical claims are very sensitive to the size of the group being studied. The smaller the number (the n) in the population being observed, the more likely it is that the result is a fluke—the statistical equivalent of a lucky bounce—and the less reliable the findings are.

You must eliminate the possibility that the posited relationship is due to chance. Wolfinger and Rosenstone emphasize that their sample of the electorate was exceptionally large, thereby providing strong reason to accept their claims. They, Powell, and Jackman all use multivariate analyses and other statistical tests to assess the power of the explanatory variables on turnout, and a host of other scholars apply these techniques, as discussed in Chapters 4 and 5. Moreover, strong regression coefficients between education and turnout and age and turnout support Wolfinger and Rosenstone's argument. Powell and Jackman use these same measures to support alternative theories of turnout. Thus, these studies present tests for the validity of statistical conclusions in order to enhance their arguments. Put another way, they use statistical tests to ascertain the extent to which it is proper to draw the powerful conclusions that are implied when we use statistics.

2. *Tests for internal validity demonstrate the accuracy of the proposition in the particular setting. They ask questions about the source of the data, seeking to deny the alternative claim that the results obtained in the case at hand are an artifact of other explanatory factors.*

For example, as Cook and Campbell note, " 'History' is a threat when an observed effect might be due to an event which takes place between the pretest and the posttest, when this event is not the treatment of research interest" (1979, 51). If a massive storm dumped snow all over the United States during the first week of November 1972, one might ask whether the ability to get out of the house and to the polls was the real determinant of turnout in that election. When we test for "history," we seek to eliminate the possibility that some factor particular to the time or place (be it as obvious as a snowstorm or something less visible) actually brought about the effect. Obviously, "history" would not be a problem if there were nothing peculiar about events preceding the 1972 election that would deny the analytical power of the explanations offered by the authors we examined in the second chapter.

We must also ask if we have reason to question the reliability of the data. Perhaps there is something strange about the sample, apart from its size, that might hinder the analysis and detract from the accuracy of any conclusion. Are there problems with the questions asked in the survey or in the interview schedule followed by the political scientist engaged in fieldwork? One common mistake is asking one question that really has two parts. Such concerns point to the issue of *instrument reliability,* a nuisance factor that examines the techniques we use to provide descriptions. Or is it possible that some of the respondents are especially likely to offer distorted answers to given questions? This brings up the problem of *phenomenon reliability;* we must look for the presence of possible distortions in the accuracy of statements as related to the particular persons being studied. *Observer reliability* calls attention to errors that may be introduced by those doing the reporting. Furthermore, do not suppose that errors exist only in surveys. For example, aggregate data obtained from government agencies may present problems. Bookkeeping errors, the hesitance to report bad news, and inadequate resources all provide their own distortions. Similar problems appear in field studies, as well—via informants with their own axes to grind or anthropologists who are not sufficiently sensitive to what they are observing. The better you are able to address these problems, the more reason you have to accept the data.

Several of these mistakes are apparent in data on turnout. First, surveys overreport voting, asserting that more than three-fourths of eligible voters in the United States go to the polls although official data put the proportion at one-half. In addition, survey researchers may be particularly likely to interview persons who vote. If so, the extent to which this flaw affects the conclusions drawn from these surveys must be assessed. Do some respondents claim to have voted even though they, in fact, stayed away from the polls? Is there a pattern to this distortion, and how does it matter? Such questions are vital. For example, there is reason to believe that persons with relatively high levels of education are especially likely to claim to have voted when they actually did not. If so, we might conclude that Wolfinger and Rosenstone's fundamental argument is based on an illusion, and the appropriate hypothesis may be that the higher the level of education a person has attained, the more likely it is that he or she will *claim* to have voted. A hypothesis is, therefore, defended by denying the possibility that some other factor actually affected the outcome. And if you are unable to deny alternative explanations, others will be less inclined to accept your hypothesis.

Other data on turnout have different problems. I can say that surveys overreport voting because there is a baseline against which to compare them—a standard that comes from information reported by secretaries of state for each of the fifty states. But these data may also contain distortions, some of which come from simple mistakes. May we, for example, dismiss them on the grounds that overcounts are likely to be balanced by undercounts and that both are likely to be randomly distributed across the country? Piven and Cloward report a more significant flaw. "The source of bias is that local registration lists are clogged with names of millions of 'deadwood' registrants who have died or moved but who have not been purged from the local rolls"

(1988, 264-265). They use this as evidence to support their proposition that registration is the key to voting. If we knew the actual number of people registered to vote, they maintain, we would observe that nearly everyone who is registered does vote. Bias in the data distorts the analysis.

To assess the reliability of a set of indicators, the contention that the information contained in the operationalization is dependable must be supported. And as we eliminate nuisance factors, we increase the reliability of the descriptions.

Selecting a particular case for study because it has special characteristics may, in fact, distort the subsequent analysis, and you must strive to eliminate this possibility. Had Wolfinger and Rosenstone used a sample composed only of illiterate U.S. citizens, they would have found no relationship between education and turnout. With no variation in the explanatory variable, they would have been forced to deny their basic hypothesis.

One form of this problem is labeled "statistical regression." The general point is that in any large body of information, there is a tendency for phenomena to hover around the mean. If you choose to analyze a case because it is extraordinary, do not exaggerate the significance of a pattern that looks very much like a return to the normal state. Donald T. Campbell and H. Laurence Ross (1968) present what is now the classic illustration of this phenomenon in their study of the Connecticut crackdown on speeding in the mid-1950s. Following a year of exceptionally high traffic fatalities, the new governor inaugurated a policy of vigilantly enforcing speeding laws and severely punishing offenders. An immediate decline in traffic accidents and deaths followed this policy change. Should we say that the new policy worked, that it was the cause of the specified effect? Campbell and Ross demonstrate that we cannot rule out the possibility that the change was simply a return to the established average level of accidents and deaths.

"Selectivity bias" is another form of this problem. Let me cite Stanley Lieberson on this potential flaw:

> The absence of random assignment causes enormous difficulties if there is reason to believe that the subjects thereby placed in each condition differ in other ways that themselves have bearing on the outcome. . . .
> Suppose one wishes to determine the influence of military service on civilian earnings years later. The initial tendency will be to compare the incomes of those experiencing military service with those who did not. However, there would be every reason to believe that military service is not a random event, whether this be in a period where there is a draft or not. Rather, the subjects are sorted in some manner such that draftees,

volunteers, and those never serving will differ from one another on dimensions that in turn have a bearing on one's life chances later on (1985, 15).

Given the skewed distribution of the probability of serving in the military, we must rule out the possibility that what affects that probability also determines the ability to earn money after completing a military stint.

3. *Tests for construct validity of putative causes* seek to make sure that the variables are precisely linked to general concepts. Here, ensure that the concept's measures are used consistently and are appropriate for the abstract definition. Where they are not, we have reason to deny the explanatory hypothesis that uses the concept.

One form of this exercise assesses whether confounding results derive from contradictory operationalizations. For example, if religiosity is said to be a direct negative function of level of education, we must be certain that the same measures of each variable are used each time we test the hypothesis. If we measure religiosity by frequency of church attendance, with those who attend at least once per month defined as "religious," then we must be sure to defend and maintain that same operational definition. When we assess Marx's and Weber's analyses of revolution, we must determine whether they both would have measured the concept of revolution in the same way. When analyses use different indicators of the same concept, they speak past each other.

We should also check to be sure that the same indicators are not used to point to different concepts. Note, for example, that Wolfinger and Rosenstone use level of formal education to measure level of abstract skills, but Piven and Cloward and a host of other social scientists use years of formal education to measure class position in the United States. In one study, the indicator measures a psychological trait; in the others, it taps a social position. As a result, each approach may use data on education to prove different and contradictory points.

We must also assess construct validity, the relationship between the abstract concept and its operational definition. Although you should remember that no set of indicators is the same as the concept being defined, operationalizations vary in how successfully they capture the abstract meaning of the concept.

I will use the measures of education that we discussed in Chapter 2 to illustrate a test for construct validity. Wolfinger and Rosenstone do not directly justify their decision to use age and formal schooling to measure the concept of the ability to handle abstract skills. They present very few measures of personal attitudes and use objective characteristics as surrogates for the missing data. This gap is a critical weakness in their analysis because they use the general hypothesis to cover the specific relationship between age and education and turnout. They can show a positive direct relationship in the United States between age and turnout and education and turnout, but they cannot show a direct positive relationship between the ability to handle abstract issues and turnout. Similarly, they do not show that turnout may be used as a synonym for political participation. Thus, they have not sustained the general hypothesis that ties together those psychological attributes and political participation. Similarly, there is a critical problem in Piven and Cloward's operationalization of the working class. The theoretical power of their analysis derives from Marxist theory, in which the working class concept plays a critical role. But there is a gap between Piven and Cloward's illustrations—blacks and poor whites in the South and steelworkers, miners, and immigrants in big cities of the North—and Marx's concept. They are hard pressed to show how their analysis of variations in the rate of turnout by different social categories can be clearly linked to Marx's proletariat. And without that, the theoretical power of their analysis crumbles. We can see, then, that as we rule out problems of construct validity, we enhance the theoretical power of our analysis and our ability to maintain that the particular relationship is an example of a general hypothesis.

4. *Tests for external validity seek to determine the extent to which it is appropriate to propose that the pattern observed in a particular case is an instance of a widespread generalization.* Here, we strive to maximize the ability to generalize to particular target groups and to generalize across types of persons, settings, and times. If we want to make statements about general propositions, we must make sure that there is no reason to think that the case or cases studied preclude the ability to generalize beyond them. Let's say that you accept Wolfinger and Rosenstone's claim that education and turnout covary in the United States in the 1972 presidential election. Tests for external validity can help you decide whether the proposition may be extended to other presidential elections, to other elections in the United States, to other national elections, to all elections, or to other forms of political participation.

The issue of U.S. exceptionalism is an example of what Cook and Campbell call "the interaction of selection and treatment" (1979, 73). If, as is sometimes argued, the United States is fundamentally different from all other democracies, you should not generalize results obtained there to the general category of all democracies; an unrepresentative sample produces unrepresentative effects. Powell, for instance, presents evidence that the relationship between education and turnout does not hold true in the democracies of Western Europe. This claim does not deny the proposition that education covaries with and perhaps even causes turnout in the United States. But it suggests that the uniqueness of the particular case denies the general proposition that education and turnout *always* covary in democracies.

How, then, can we generalize from Wolfinger and Rosenstone's findings for the 1972 presidential election to other presidential contests? One justification is the implicit claim that there was nothing so different about that election that would preclude generalizing a finding from that contest to neighboring elections. Indeed, the authors take this position to imply that the particular relationship between abstract skills, as measured by level of education and age, and turnout do, indeed, apply to all U.S. elections. They would defend their right to generalize to other elections in the United States, but they do not insist on the right or need to offer a proposition that applies to all democracies.

Anthropologists are particularly cautious about generalizing from their studies to a wider universe. Because they emphasize the unique qualities of each community, they deny that any one case may represent all other cases. We may not reason, maintains Geertz, that "Jonesville is America (writ small) or that America is Jonesville (writ large)." Nor may we treat each case as if it were a testing ground for a general theory (1973, 21–22). At best, we can treat each community as representative of a small number of like communities. In this view, there is almost always a problem of selection-treatment interaction because each community is likely to be unrepresentative of almost all other communities.

By eliminating Cook and Campbell's nuisance factors, we increase the number of reasons to accept a specific empirical proposition. Conversely, we cannot deny the plausibility of rival explanations if:

- we have failed to test the statistical conclusion validity and ruled out the possibility that wrong conclusions have been drawn from our statistical data;
- it is possible that "history," "statistical regression," "selectivity," or other factors may limit the internal validity of our claim;
- we have poor justification for the construct validity of our claim; or
- the problem of selection-treatment interaction has limited the claim's external validity.

In Place of Experiments, Strive to Eliminate Rival Hypotheses

We can make a claim to knowledge when we show that other hypotheses do not stand up to the empirical tests that ours has passed.

And the more alternatives denied, the more reason there is to accept our hypothesis. On the other hand, when we cannot eliminate rival hypotheses, we must be skeptical about the one we offer.

Why do we stress the negation of alternative explanations? Popper insists that it is possible to know only when a hypothesis is negated and that confirmation is always provisional. After all, you can never be sure that subsequent tests will not negate a theory. He maintains that it *is* possible, however, to show precisely that one theory bests another by pointing to the tests passed by one and failed by the other. Science progresses, therefore, by rejecting some claims to knowledge and provisionally accepting alternative hypotheses. Cook and Campbell summarize Popper's position: "This leads to an emphasis upon a rivalry of theories in an environment of experimental and observational facts" (1979, 23). Popper offers a method of assessing competing theories, not single propositions.

Many of the studies that we examined in the previous chapters exemplify this method of testing empirical propositions. In *The Protestant Ethic and the Spirit of Capitalism* (1958), Weber denies Marx's exclusive focus on the economic determinants of capitalism's rise. And in the essay "Socialism," he explicitly refutes the empirical accuracy of several of Marx's critical propositions regarding revolution in capitalist societies. Wolfinger and Rosenstone demonstrate that socioeconomic status does not account for variations in the level of turnout in the 1972 U.S. presidential election. Powell details the inability of education to explain turnout as part of his argument for a theory that stresses the importance of political structures. Walker designs his analysis of the formation of interest groups in the United States as an explicit test of Olson's theory of collective action. By finding relatively few persons who either joined in order to obtain private benefits or were coerced to become members, Walker strengthens his own explanation, which rests on structural variables—spread of education and mass communication, growing levels of social protest, and a major increase in government and private funding for political organizations. In Schmitter's analysis of political violence, he did not control for population size, a variable that Powell showed to have a major impact in his analysis. There is, however, one common thread in these analyses: They all test rival hypotheses in order to provide reasons to accept or reject claims to knowledge.

In Place of Experiments, Strive to Devise Tough Tests

Some efforts to evaluate empirical propositions are more demanding than others. When we apply "tough" tests, we do more than attempt to assess the importance of nuisance factors as alternative explanations. We use a method that allows us to draw powerful conclusions.

A tough test examines a proposition where you have strong reason to suppose that it will fail. Proponents of the Michigan model of vote choice gave their theory a tough test when they used it to analyze electoral behavior in Great Britain and France, knowing that many scholars had denied that party identification would explain vote choice outside the United States. When findings revealed that party identification consistently has the highest regression coefficient and explains the greatest portion of the variance in vote choice in Britain and France, the strength of their theory was greatly enhanced. The Michigan model bested two particularly demanding tests, providing stronger reason to accept it.

Testing the null hypothesis usually is not a tough test. Here, an explanatory relationship is claimed to be present when its absence—the proposition that there is no relationship between the variables (the null hypothesis)—is denied. Any correlation that can be shown to be statistically significant (that is, not due to random factors) is taken to support the hypothesis. But simply positing and then examining the null hypothesis does not provide a genuinely tough test. Paul Meehl is sharply critical of this form of research:

> "Everything is correlated with everything," and .25 is not a bad average value. Randomly chosen [variates] do not tend to correlate zero. Of course in real life, the experimenter is usually correlating variates that belong, at least commonsensically [sic], to some restricted domain. We don't usually do studies correlating social dominance with spool-packing ability or eye color. So a more realistic guesstimate of the crud factor, the expected correlation between a randomly chosen pair of variates belonging to a substantive domain, would be higher than that, maybe as high as .30 (1986, 327).

Finding a relatively low correlation between the explanatory and dependent variables, Meehl maintains, tells us very little about the world that we did not already know. Would anyone have suggested that there was *no* relationship between two closely tied phenomena like occupation and vote, attitudes toward the candidates and vote, or party identification and vote? Consequently, the null hypothesis is seen as an easy test because we have strong reason to know before the test that the null hypothesis will be false. As a result, very little is learned from this test. The findings are significant only when it is suggested that no relationship exists between the variables; it is a tough test only when you examine a hypothesis derived from a theory that denies the possibility of any relationship at all among such variables. Even a small correlation negates this hypothesis and raises questions about the theory from which it is derived.

By giving our ideas demanding tests, we stack the deck against ourselves, and we are able, therefore, to derive powerful support if test evidence backs up our propositions. The importance of tough tests derives from several rules offered by Karl Popper: "It is easy to obtain confirmations, or verifications, for nearly every theory—if we look for confirmations. Confirmations should count only if they are the result of *risky predictions*. . . . Confirming evidence should not count *except when it is the result of a genuine test of the theory;* and this means that it can be presented as a serious but unsuccessful attempt to falsify the theory" (1965, 36, emphases in original). When you locate evidence to support your proposition, do not look for the places where the theory is most likely to hold and proclaim success. Confirmation comes only after we apply and pass tough tests that are designed to negate, and even then it is only provisional. Once again, we are told to be suspicious rather than generous when we evaluate our propositions.

Note the converse of this claim: When your hypothesis fails an easy test, you should recognize that it is probably in deep trouble. Consider the research on the relationship between social class and vote choice. It would seem that Great Britain is an especially likely case in which to find evidence that class position determines vote choice. Yet, I cited studies in the previous chapter that find no more than a very weak association between the two variables. If the relationship between class and vote does not hold in Great Britain, it is unlikely that it would hold anywhere else. As a result, there would seem to be good reason to deny both the general and the particular propositions of this research. Failing an easy test gives us strong reason to reject a claim to knowledge.

The general principle is simple: Empirical propositions must be evaluated. The more tests applied and the tougher the tests, the more we are pushed to accept their conclusions. But the application of the principle is not so easy. Consider Wolfinger and Rosenstone's analysis of voter turnout in the presidential election of 1972. How much significance do you attribute to the large sample and to the rigorous statistical tests applied to the data? What do you do with the claim that better-educated citizens are most likely to overreport their voting? How significant is it that there is little evidence that education and turnout covary outside the United States? What about the problem of construct validity? How much does it matter that there is no clear link between the ability to handle abstract problems and a person's age and formal schooling? Severe weaknesses in this study pull me in the direction of rejecting both Wolfinger and Rosenstone's analysis of turnout in the presidential election of 1972 and their general analysis of turnout and political participation. However, that does not imply that I accept Piven and Cloward's alternative analysis for I am particularly concerned about the problems of construct validity in their analysis, as well. Studies that rely on the power of Marxist theory must be very careful in how they define and measure the working class.

Do not be dismayed by questions like those posed above. Although they insist that you choose, you may not feel ready to evaluate scholarship. If so, you should remember that skepticism seems to be the appropriate initial position in the evaluation of any claims to knowledge. Indeed, I have assumed this posture in some of my own assessments of the studies of turnout because I have not performed my own tests of the propositions. Do not accept a proposition until you have good reason not to reject it. And even then, accept it only provisionally.

However, you must eventually move beyond this essentially negative stance. To assist you further, I will demonstrate why I have decided to no longer use party identification in the analysis of vote choice and highlight some of the weaknesses of case studies in politics. As we proceed through this exercise, you should decide whether, when, and why you are willing to defend or jettison a given claim.

EVALUATING WHAT WE KNOW ABOUT THE RELATIONSHIP BETWEEN PARTY IDENTIFICATION AND VOTE CHOICE

Do you accept or reject the proposition that party identification explains vote choice? To address the question, you must bear in mind several points. First, students of voting share the view that something may be said to explain vote choice when it has a high regression coefficient and contributes a very large portion to the observed variance in electoral choice. Second, the studies focus on voting in presidential or parliamentary elections. And third, they use survey data as evidence to test their hypotheses. The evaluation of this proposition thus benefits from a shared set of evidence and method.

There are many reasons to accept the proposition that party identification explains vote choice. Consider the evidence when the proposition is applied to voting patterns in the United States. As I indicated in Chapter 4, numerous tests run on more election surveys than anyone would want to count over the past thirty years consistently show a strong relationship between party identification and vote choice in both presidential and congressional elections. Scholars have eliminated potential problems of statistical conclusion validity and internal validity by employing large and well-conceived samples of the voting population.

For these same reasons, we can eliminate the possible interference of "historical" events. Because very large portions of the electorate claim to have a party attachment, there is no reason to worry that the survey instrument itself distorts the analysis. Indeed, even those political scientists who emphasize the importance of issues and candidate evaluations on electoral decisions in the United States do not deny the overriding significance of party identification. All in all, I can think of few reasons to doubt the internal validity and the statistical conclusion validity of the proposition when it is applied to the United States.

Furthermore, by demonstrating the strength of the proposition in surveys taken in Great Britain and France, the Michigan model has passed many tough tests, including demonstrations of external validity. In one such exercise, Mark Lichbach and I (1977) compared the relative explanatory power of party identification and two indicators of social class—occupation and subjective identity—on voting behavior, using data from a British panel survey taken between 1963 and 1970. By placing the class variables before the question tapping party loyalty in our regression analysis, we purposefully arranged it to favor class and thereby provide a very demanding test for party identification. Despite this, we found that party identification in 1963 far outperformed the class variables on reported voting during the subsequent seven years. Indeed, occupation and class identification had barely any predictive power at all.

At that point, I was a believer. Building on the proposition that party identification explains vote choice, Lichbach and I expanded the theoretical net by deriving hypotheses to analyze aggregate change in electorates, as well. Ronald Rogowski (1981) replicated our analysis, including additional measures of social class. Much to his amazement, the class variables had no impact on vote choice, and party identification remained the best predictor of subsequent voting behavior. Think now about Rose and McAllister's (1986) analysis, which I presented in the previous chapter. Despite the fact that they label party identification as a statistical artifact, they include it in their model of electoral choice in Britain. And Converse and Pierce (1986) demonstrate that party identification exists in France much as it does in the United States and Britain. Given these findings, one might well maintain that the proposition has demonstrated external validity. The proposition that party identification explains vote choice has passed numerous and tough tests, and there would seem to be strong reason to accept it.

Nonetheless, I have reached the conclusion that the proposed association between party identification and vote choice is illusory (Feldman and Zuckerman 1982; Zuckerman 1989). I make this claim neither because I have a hypothesis to put in its place nor because I reject the theory that produces the proposition. Rather, the proposition itself, as well as a number of logically related hypotheses, have failed tests of construct validity, giving me good reason to doubt its internal and external validity.

Consider Cook and Campbell's criterion of construct validity of putative causes when applied to party identification and vote. The concept is measured by the response to this survey question: "Generally speaking, do you think of yourself as a Xite, Yite . . . ?" (where X and Y indicate the major political parties). A following question probes the strength of the party identification: "How strongly do you feel [about your party]?" But this operationalization can imply several different meanings. It may mean a psychological attachment, as the underlying theory claims; a short-term commitment; a relative preference at a particular point in time; a psychological attachment to one party together with a dislike of alternative parties, as well as an identification while liking or not caring about the other parties; a usual vote choice; or a host of other meanings. Each of these alternatives has a different psychological meaning and behavioral implication. Because operationalization reduces a complex notion of political loyalty to responses to two ambiguous questions, we cannot tell what it really means.

Suppose that, rather than tapping a psychological attachment to the party, the operationalization actually answers the question "How do you intend to vote?" To the extent that this occurs, the measure contaminates the dependent variable with the explanatory variable, and the relationship then becomes a tautology. Hence, we should not put much stock in the high regression coefficients found between party identification and vote choice. The two questions may be little more than different ways of asking a person how he or she intends to vote. If many of the persons surveyed interpret the questions in that way, then all they are reporting is what they usually do, which does not address their psychological attachments or loyalties. Whether the question taps psychological attachments or whether it is interpreted to mean how a voter will vote, there would be reason to deny the construct validity of the accepted operational definition for the concept of party identification.

There are still other problems for this proposition. One of the key hypotheses attached to the proposition is that party loyalty strengthens with age. Consider the results of recent studies of panel data in Britain and the United States, cases with relatively persistent political parties that should therefore provide easy tests for this proposition (Nie, Verba, and Petrocik 1976; Crewe, Sarlvick, and Alt 1977; Katz, Niemi, and Newman 1980; Niemi, Katz, and Newman 1980; Feldman and Zuckerman 1982; Beck 1984; Alt 1984). These data exhibit changes in party identification among those who are otherwise not expected to lose their attachment. As a result, they deny the claim that party identification strengthens over time. Rogowski (1981) also provides evidence that persons who report party identification at one election are not especially likely to vote persistently for that party. Furthermore, Rose and McAllister (1986, 105) detail increases in the proportion of the British electorate who know their parents' party identification and decreases in the proportion who vote according to what they learned at home. They also show much more flux in the presence and explanatory power of party identification than the concept's theoretical foundations permit. Converse and Pierce's own data on France show considerable variation in the proportion of people who identify with one of the political parties: 60 percent in 1967, 49 percent in 1968, and 45 percent in 1969 (1986, 75). They indicate, as well, that 65 percent of the French electorate who reported a party attachment in 1967 retained that loyalty one year later, compared to 88 percent of the British electorate in 1964–1966 and 90 percent of the U.S. voters between 1958 and 1960. In addition, more French voters in 1967 and 1968 voted for the same party than kept the same party identification (1986, 87–88). Furthermore, although Converse and Pierce show that persons with party identification are more likely than those with no partisan loyalty to vote for their party after having supported another in the previous election, their data indicate that among French voters who cast ballots in both 1967 and 1968, persons with a party identification were no more likely than those without this attachment to vote for the same party in the two elections (1986, 95). Indeed, the relative similarity in the stability of vote choice among those with and without party identification appears in the British and U.S. data, as well. There is good reason to maintain that party identification does not hold voters to stable electoral behavior.

The problems continue. The French surveys underline the importance of variations in number of political parties in explaining differences in vote choice in adjacent elections. This pattern runs counter to the psychological foundations of the concept of party identification. In Converse and Pierce's own words, "Identification is identification; it does not take cognizance of neighborly relations" (1986, 91). The theory cannot explain why the entry of new political parties affects the stability of vote choice between adjacent elections.

As a result, I have concluded that party identification, as currently measured, is too imprecise to classify voters in theoretically meaningful ways. Relatively few of those persons who answer affirmatively to the survey question have a psychological attachment to a political party that guides their political behavior. And by merging these voters with others for whom the affirmative answer on the party identification question has no clear psychological meaning and little or no behavioral implication, the concept's operationalization confuses, rather than strengthens, the analysis. For all these reasons, I would conclude that party identification does not explain electoral behavior.

Where do you stand on this issue? Do you feel you have sufficient reason to accept the claim that party identification explains vote choice in democracies? Should we limit the proposition only to the United States? (Note that the full implication of my position would deny even this decision.) Although I am convinced that it is best to analyze electoral choice without using the party identification concept, you may not be. As I noted at the start of this chapter, empirical tests in political science do not usually compel us to accept a particular conclusion; indeed, even the proponents of the Michigan model now stand bowed, if not bent. Nonetheless, almost all research on voting in the United States places party identification at the heart of the analysis. My decision to drop the concept clearly runs against the accepted wisdom.

EVALUATING THE UTILITY OF DETAILED CASE STUDIES

The Case Studies of Class Politics Must Be Tied to Precise Hypotheses

The central importance of theoretical scope, conceptual precision, and empirical accuracy is reiterated in the evaluation of some of the detailed case studies that we have examined in this volume. The importance of case studies rests on the extent to which they are closely tied to theories. When studies lose track of the general covering hypotheses (as happens in the work of Shefter, Kocka, and Nolan that we reviewed in Chapter 4), their analyses do not advance the study of class politics.

The essays of Shefter, Kocka, and Nolan on class politics in the United States and Germany exemplify how theory and case studies may pull in different directions. The thicker the description and the more the analysis narrates events, the easier it is to break the tie between data, variable, concept, and theory. As the authors detail differences in modes of dispositions and collective action by workers in different countries, they lose sight of the general arguments about the formation of working-class movements. Indeed, as you will see, in the absence of guiding hypotheses—not just frameworks and statements in the form of "sometimes the relationship holds and sometimes it does not"—we may not be able to describe it.

Shefter maintains that the disjunction of workplace and political activity was not an inevitable characteristic of the U.S. working class. What then accounts for the success of "pure and simple" trade unionism? "Efforts to pursue a strategy of mobilization in the economic arena encountered serious difficulties. Businessmen fought back furiously: they organized employers' associations, drove unions to strike, and then called upon the government to defend their right to hire strike-breakers" (Shefter 1986, 254). Employers usually obtained the support of government troops to scatter mobilized workers. Efforts to sustain a militant electoral movement ran up against the power of race-baiting in the South and the political machines in the northern industrial cities. "The experience of the post–Civil War decades clearly indicated the great difficulties trade unions confronted to sustain themselves in the face of periodic business depressions, bitter employer resistance, and hostile public authorities" (Shefter 1986, 254–255). Craft unionism survived because union leaders viewed that strategy as the only viable alternative in the face of the overwhelming power of their opponents.

Kocka and Nolan provide overlapping explanations for the success of the Socialists and the failure of the liberal parties and unions among the Protestant workers. Kocka posits, "The public was alarmed by the successes of the socialist parties at the polls and the wave of strikes; state repression increased. In 1875, the two parties united. . . . The increasing tensions between capital and labor, dramatized by the waves of strikes and other disputes, had to strain a liberal-radical alliance comprising workers and businessmen" (1986, 346). Nolan summarizes her explanation of the sea change in the political and economic organization of the German workers: "The era of the Great Depression saw a fundamental transformation of worker politics in the economic arena and in society at large. In the wake of economic crisis, repressive state policies, and the restructuring of the labor force, the embryonic Social Democratic organization of the 1870s became a mass movement by the 1890s" (1986, 348). State repression, economic crises, and resistance by the middle class and the liberal parties, Kocka and Nolan agree, explain the Socialists' ability to control collective action by Protestant workers.

Placing Shefter's, Kocka's, and Nolan's hypotheses next to each other introduces fundamental questions about each and all the analyses. The three authors agree on the variables that account for the structure of working-class politics. They depict economic crises, state repression, and employers' resistance to militant unions and political parties in both countries. Shefter argues that the presence of these variables explains the development of a labor reform movement, in which workplace and electoral activity remained sharply separated and the workers' movement did not attack capitalism and liberal democracy. Kocka and Nolan, however, associate the same explanatory variables with a centralized structure of national unions and political organizations controlled by the Socialist party. The analyses rebut each other.

If Shefter is right, then Kocka and Nolan are wrong. If Kocka and Nolan are right, then Shefter is wrong. How can this be? How can a study that presents so much empirical detail about one particular case imply that an analysis of another case is false? How can such case studies negate each other?

An analysis of the web between hypothesis and theory denies the power of each of the studies. Recall that a particular hypothesis needs a general hypothesis to demonstrate that it is not simply a coincidence and to justify the expected relationship among the explanatory and dependent variables. Shefter's explanation of "pure and simple" trade unionism in the United States is covered, therefore, by this general hypothesis: The higher the level of economic crises, state repression, and employers' resistance is, the less politically radical the labor movement will be. At the same time, Nolan's and Kocka's explanations of the radical nature of the labor movement in Germany are justified by this more general hypothesis: The higher the level of economic crises, state repression, and employers' resistance is, the more politically radical the labor movement will be. But two important theoretical consequences here deny the power of each analysis. (1) The two general hypotheses contradict each other; if one is right, the other must be wrong. (2) Each general hypothesis denies the other particular hypothesis. Given the existence of the general hypothesis covering Shefter's analysis, there is no theoretical justification for the particular hypothesis suggested by Nolan and Kocka. Conversely, given Nolan's and Kocka's covering hypothesis, there is no justification for Shefter's explanation. As a result, theoretical problems plague each and all the studies.

Furthermore, the empirical evidence provided in these essays denies each of the hypotheses in the same manner. Suppose that Shefter, Nolan, and Kocka have painted accurate pictures of the economic crises, state repression, and employers' resistance in the United States and Germany. If so, then the U.S. evidence denies Nolan's and Kocka's general hypotheses and consequently their particular explanations; conversely, the German evidence denies Shefter's general hypothesis and consequently his particular explanation. It follows once again that both of these hypotheses must be wrong.

The explanatory analysis of each case must rest on a more general hypothesis linking the presence of economic crisis, state repression, and resistance by the middle classes with a particular form of political action by workers (Newton-Smith 1981, 223–224; Brown 1987, 141).

There is no theory that specifies that these same conditions lead to a "pure and simple" trade union in one case and a united revolutionary movement in another. The authors have explained neither the differences between what happened in Germany and the United States nor the particular patterns of each case. They have pursued the demands of thick description at the expense of theoretical rigor. And because neither hypothesis stands on a secure theoretical base, there is no reason to accept either one.

Case studies need to be tied to precise theories of politics. Zolberg suggests that political scientists "treat each historical situation as a case of working-class formation—that is, as something akin to one of several states of a dependent variable that can be accounted for by reference to variation among a set of factors considered, for this purpose, as theoretically grounded independent variables" (1986, 401). No case is exceptional; each is a particular instance of a more general phenomenon, amenable to analysis by hypotheses.

My criticisms raise questions about efforts to analyze politics that emphasize the particulars of individual cases. They imply that it is very difficult to move from detailed description to theory. I consider such efforts to be the fundamental weaknesses in Shefter's, Kocka's, and Nolan's analyses. I have leveled the same criticisms at Wolfinger and Rosenstone's analysis and would apply similar objections to Geertz's call for thick description. Above all, I would underline the need to frame research questions and hypotheses in the context of more general theories.

THE LIMITS OF EMPIRICAL TESTS OF PROPOSITIONS

By now, you should be struck by the difficulties of evaluation. To know whether to accept a proposition, we must test it. With more demanding tests and a greater number of them, we can be more certain about the conclusions that we draw from them. At the same time, there are no unequivocal tests in political science. Reasonable persons, those who seek to apply rational criteria to their decision to accept or reject a claim to knowledge, will disagree. You should no longer be surprised by the cacophony of theories and research schools that characterizes political science. Several other points are pertinent here.

1. There is no precise number of tests that must be passed in order to certify a proposition. Indeed, if we follow Popper, then we may never claim that the proposition is confirmed, only that it is not negated. We can apply no simple accounting rules to empirical tests of propositions.

2. There is a tendency to exaggerate the level of empirical support for a hypothesis. Meehl reports that factors internal to scholarly communities in the social sciences magnify the number of positive results and ignore many negative findings. Too many scholars count the negation of a null hypothesis as an accomplishment. Too many editors refuse to publish articles that report that hypotheses have been falsified. As a result, Meehl maintains that a 4 to 1 ratio in support of a hypothesis is probably no better than 1 to 1 (that is, there are an equal number of failures and successes) or even, in the pessimistic view, "9 to 1 against the theory" (1986, 328). Even if he overstates this point, there is good reason to suppose that political scientists and others in the social sciences overlook the need to reject hypotheses.

3. Equally as important, empirical tests frequently produce contradictory results. The question of ambiguous results is compounded not only because one test may fail to produce a compelling conclusion but because the results of some tests may confirm the propositions, others may negate them, and still others may produce conflicting conclusions.

Consider one portion of the controversy that surrounds the analysis of political violence, some of which we explored in the previous chapter. Lichbach reviews dozens of studies using statistical data and applying careful assessments of statistical conclusion validity (among them Powell's work, discussed in Chapter 4), but he finds no unequivocal answer to the question of whether variation in economic inequality is associated with variation in the level of political violence. As a result, he denies that the solution to the puzzle will come from more empirical tests. Equivocal tests can only produce equivocal results: "Producing one more empirical variation of the . . . argument in an effort to clarify the confusion created by previous variations has been a source and not remedy of the confusion" (Lichbach 1989, 447). He adds that no matter how hard these analysts have tried to overcome problems of statistical conclusion and internal validity, they have not succeeded:

> These replications have revealed that the [economic inequality-political conflict] nexus is very sensitive to all the aspects of research design mentioned earlier: measurement, the inclusion of cases, time frames, and the specification of control variables.
>
> In consequence, [these] studies have been ad hoc because they were unsuccessful: robust . . . laws have not been discovered. Researchers have been unable to locate empirical generalizations applicable across studies because the replications and the regression experiments produced inconsistency, not consistency (Lichbach 1989, 448).

There may or may not be a positive relationship between economic inequality and political violence. After two decades of empirical tests, maintains Lichbach, we still cannot confirm the proposition.

4. Therefore, adding another test, no matter how demanding, will never completely certify or decertify a proposition. Empirical tests by themselves do not allow us to certify knowledge in political science.

In sum, we do not have rules that allow us to decide when to accept or reject a proposition. We are drawn to exaggerate the level of empirical support for our hypotheses. And when we apply several tests, we frequently obtain contradictory results. Political scientists have yet to devise designs for their research that produce unequivocal test results.

THE ROLE OF THEORY IN THE EVALUATION OF EMPIRICAL PROPOSITIONS

Here, too, there is a paradox, one we can label "the paradox of theory and test results": The greater the role of theory is in our analysis, the more we can learn from empirical tests; the greater the role of theory is in our analysis, the more we are drawn to deny evidence that negates our hypothesis. We naturally have strong reasons and motives to defend our claims to knowledge in the face of apparent negations.

Returning to the image of theory as a net of hypotheses, we can see that the more strands that can be tied to a hypothesis, the more reason we have to test it. When we negate or support a hypothesis, we affect the theory from which it comes. Consequently, a single test can have significant implications. When the proposition cannot be tied to other theoretical strands in a network of ideas, we have reason not to use it. Thus, for example, because of the conceptual weakness of the concept of party identification and the negation of many propositions that use this concept, I have decided not to use it anymore. But when we derive precise hypotheses from the general principles of a theory, we know how to organize an empirical test that will have significant theoretical results. The converse of this claim is also important: The more that the tests are designed to evaluate theories, the more we can learn from them.

One problem with some of the empirical tests that we have observed is that they are not designed to reject or confirm hypotheses embedded in theoretical networks. Lichbach makes this criticism of work on political violence: "One must conclude that to most statistical modelers, 'theory' is nothing more than a set of weakly linked empirical generalizations, or behavioral or regression equations, justified by an informal and ad hoc discussion of the expected signs of the variables" (1989,

449). As a result, it is not easy to draw a general conclusion from such tests. If a proposition is more clearly derived from a theory, the payoff that can result from a test is greater. This criterion brings us back to the need for strong claims to knowledge. When we make them, it is easier to decide when we are wrong and when we are right.

Lichbach contends that empirical studies allow us to evaluate claims to knowledge only when they are tied to precisely defined hypotheses derived from theories. To resolve the controversy surrounding the proposition linking economic inequality and political violence, he maintains that the research should be organized as a test of two competing theories—the deprived actor model (drawn from political psychology) and the rational actor model.

> Simple collective action theory implies that any distributional measure that one cares to construct . . . will be uncorrelated with dissent. More importantly, Olson's arguments imply that if an [economic inequality–political conflict] relationship is located in a particular sample of data, then it must be spurious. On the other hand, simple [deprived actor] theory predicts that an [economic inequality–political conflict] relationship will exist. More importantly, [deprived actor] theories offer no reason why an [economic inequality–political conflict] should become spurious once collective action factors are controlled for. Hence, the test: determine if strong bivariate relationships between economic inequality and political conflict are spurious once factors relating to the collective action problem are controlled for. If [the] relationships are spurious, then [rational actor] theories are correct. If [the] relationships are strong and direct, then [deprived actor] theories are correct. Such a test would go a long way toward settling both the specific . . . puzzle and the general [deprived actor] versus [rational actor] issue in conflict studies (Lichbach 1989, 464).

When the propositions being examined are derived from theories, we can use empirical tests to evaluate knowledge claims. We can even use tests of the null hypothesis to make powerful statements. Negating or supporting these hypotheses tells about the theories from which they come. In turn, we sustain our theories by devising and passing tough tests.

This position is closely tied to Popper's philosophy of science. He notes that knowledge progresses when we derive testable hypotheses from theories. When we negate these hypotheses, we know what we do not know, and these results constrain us to look in another direction. When we support these hypotheses, we have reason to continue to view the world through the lens of the theory. This position also echoes Popper's principle that we should organize research so as to evaluate alternative theories. Lichbach's solution does not call for the examination of hypotheses drawn from one theory alone but from alternative and competing theories. He tells us that the logic of the test is that only one can be right. By applying the test, we will be able to decide between rational choice theory and deprived actor theory. Other tests like this one will allow us to pick among the alternative hypotheses that compete to explain turnout, revolution, the formation of political movements, and other phenomena studied by political scientists.

Alas, the other proposition in the paradox must be confronted: Theorists of politics (and, as I will note in the next chapter, theorists of everything else) are not usually willing to accept the results of tests that falsify their hypotheses. I am not as sanguine as Lichbach that rational actor theorists or proponents of political psychology will easily accept the results of a test if the findings run counter to their hypotheses. Remember how hard the proponents of the Michigan model have fought to retain the validity of party identification in electoral analysis. Theorists have strong intellectual reasons and other motives for remaining loyal to their hypotheses.

It is instructive to see how rational choice theorists respond to challenges. Conceding that the precise application of their model was not able to account for an individual's decision to vote, Downs, Riker, and Ordeshook relax the assumption that individuals do not intrinsically value social goods. This changes a fundamental premise of their deductive theory, calling into question whether they have altered the definition of self-interest so much that they violate the theory's principle. Moe (1980; 1981) and Hechter (1988) did the same thing in the analysis of political groups and collective action, and Muller and Opp (1986) relaxed key assumptions when they applied rational choice theory to political violence. Now consider Riker's response (1982) to Meehl's attack (1977), the substance of which I presented in Chapter 4. In an article on theory development in political science, Riker uses propositions about sophisticated voters and vote calculi, derived from rational choice theory, in order to cover Maurice Duverger's law (1967) that states that plurality voting systems are always associated with two-party systems: "Meehl (1977) has . . . insisted that the 'wasted vote' argument is at best meaningless and at worst a fraud. Voters' motivations are rational, he argued, only in terms of their sense of moral obligation. . . . Granting some persuasiveness to Meehl's argument, the theoretical underpinning of Duverger's law is surely weak if behavior in accord with the psychological factor of individual voters' calculation of expected utility is itself irrational" (1982, 764). In an understatement, Riker concedes that Meehl's argument demands a new theoretical justification for Duverger's law. At the same time, he denies the general thrust of the criticism. Instead, he shifts from the claim that all voters seek to maximize their expected utility to the proposition that politicians do: "The direction one must go, I believe, is to turn attention away from the expected utility calculus of the individual voter and to the expected utility calculus of the politician and other more substantial participants in the system" (1982, 764). Riker deflects the attack on rational choice theory, claiming that the core assumptions may still be applied to some citizens, namely, politicians. In so doing, he does not acknowledge the consequences that derive from denying the claim that most voters are maximizers of their expected utility; after all, politicians compose fewer than 5 percent of a population. He also does not concede that Meehl's criticism is a blow to rational action theory as such. These theorists insist on retaining the centrality of rational choice even as they tinker with its application and meaning.

Political scientists who use Marx's theory are equally determined to sustain their core assumptions in the face of attack. Much evidence refutes the proposition that class explains vote choice in capitalist democracies; many analysts—including Rose and McAllister (1986), Rogowski (1981), and Lichbach and myself (1977)—have tested and negated the claim with British data. But in an effort to save the proposition, proponents of Marxist theory have devised a score of different measures of social class, despite the fact that none has anything but a weak association with electoral choice. In the face of these criticisms, some Marxist scholars keep calling for other measures, some deny the reliability of survey samples, some insist that electoral behavior is not central to politics in capitalist democracies, and some make all three claims. They seem to disregard the rather obvious point that no proletariat-led revolutions have yet occurred in capitalist societies. Furthermore, Marxist theory is silent about the racial, ethnic, and religious violence that has marked capitalist societies. On that score, it is particularly noteworthy that Marxists have offered no analyses of the Holocaust of European Jewry that occurred during World War II (Goldscheider and Zuckerman 1984). Finally, recall the efforts to use Marx's theory that are illustrated by the essays in Katznelson and Zolberg's book (1986). The authors propose that sometimes those who share the same relationship to the means of production live near each other and develop persistent social ties, sometimes they define themselves the same way, and sometimes they engage in collective political action. Each analysis seeks to specify the particular conditions for one or more of these dimensions of class formation. As they reject the deductive and determinist elements of the theory, they offer weaker conditional claims. Still, they insist that analyses of politics in capitalist democracies must use the concept of social class.

It is also interesting to see how Marxists analyze the formation of new social and political movements. Claus Offe distinguishes between what he calls the "old" and "new" paradigms. He argues that the former, which center on class conflict, are being supplanted by groups involved in the new issues of "preservation of the environment, human rights, peace, and unalienated forms of work. Thus the new paradigm would correspond to greater individuation, namely, to a type of social structure in which the collectivities of the old paradigm have become both less distinctive and less durable as points of reference" (Offe 1987, 73). He accounts for this development with changes in the structure of family relations and professional and job relations, which lead to greater "migration" via various occupations, places of employment, and living arrangements. He says that these new social movements are characterized by persons of the same class background seeking not class specific goals but the general good (Offe 1987, 73). Offe never views these new social movements as challenges to propositions derived from Marx. Instead, he couches his analysis in the language of class politics. Thus, even as they drop the premises and power of Marx's deductive theory, Marxists retain the basic intellectual position that democracies must be analyzed through the prism of class politics.

Proponents of all theories—not only political scientists who use the Michigan model of electoral choice or rational choice and Marxist theorists—are loath to jettison them. Popper's description of progress in science through the refutation of claims to knowledge is too simple. Newton-Smith's general point is instructive: "The presence of an anomaly does not, just like that, show the theory to be false. . . . All we know is that something went wrong, but we cannot conclude without further ado that our theory is at fault. The fact that we recognize the need to ignore anomalies where some extraneous factors have intervened makes theories particularly resistant to easy falsification. . . . To reject a theory just because it has generated an anomaly will deprive us of any theories whatsoever" (1981, 71–72). As you will see in the next chapter, all scientists attempt to "wriggle" their hypotheses off the hook of defeat. They must. First, they have to guard against the premature dismissal of their good idea; even if a theory produces a hypothesis that fails a test it should pass, that still may not be reason enough to dismiss the theory as such. Second, there are relatively few unequivocal test results. Problems of measures and concerns about the reliability of data always produce cloudy test results. Again, you should keep in mind that this applies to political science and to other sciences, as well. Third, it is unreasonable to suppose that scientists will easily abandon a theory to which they have devoted much of their time and energy. In the presence of a theory that has been successful in the past, equivocal test results, and the psychological need to defend prior work, scientists are easily moved to defend their claims to knowledge.

The role of theory in the evaluation of empirical propositions can be stated as a series of somewhat contradictory claims:

1. We need theories in order to determine what hypotheses to test and how to test them.
2. The more closely propositions are tied to a theory, the greater the consequences that may be derived from these tests.
3. The more we adhere to a theory, the more likely we are to reject negations and accept confirmations of its hypotheses.
4. Sometimes, it is appropriate to defend the theory against attack; at other times, it is appropriate to concede defeat.
5. There is no criterion that allows you to know when to defend and when to concede defeat.

Therefore, no matter how carefully the hypotheses are derived from theories, there are no unequivocal test results. It follows from the paradox of evaluation and the paradox of theory and test results that reasonable persons—those who apply rational criteria to their decision to accept or reject a claim to knowledge—will disagree in their evaluations.

CONCLUSIONS AND IMPLICATIONS

Political scientists find it difficult to reject their knowledge claims; the abundance of alternative studies on the same topic prove nothing if not that. This is not a psychological trait exclusive to those of us who study politics, nor is it a criticism of this practice. In fact, it stems from the ambiguities inherent in doing political science. There are always problems in moving from abstract concepts to empirical measures: No measures are perfect, and data sets have flaws. And because there are no experiments by which we can determine the absolute veracity of a claim, alternative analyses of politics abound.

The networks of theory in political science are not so tightly woven that a negation of a hypothesis denies the entire structure. Proponents of Marxist theory and rational choice analysis, the best examples of deductive theories in political science, do not feel compelled to reject their theories in the face of disappointing empirical tests. Students of political attitudes and behavior, political anthropologists, and those who continue to follow the methodological and theoretical strictures of Max Weber are equally reluctant to abandon their core assumptions. In the absence of an internal logic that dictates how to respond to tests and in the presence of evidence that sustains their approaches, political scientists quite logically defend their basic principles.

The cacophony of research schools, theories, and hypotheses that continue to characterize this field does not mean that political science goes in circles. There are numerous examples of the accumulation of knowledge. For example, the research in political attitudes and behavior, noted in Chapter 3, moves beyond party identification to include additional variables that precisely specify the relationship between attitudes and political behavior.

Lichbach offers this advice on where to go next in the analysis of political violence: "Researchers should take the bottom-line, stylized fact that results from this literature to be the following: economic inequality may either have a positive, negative, or no impact on dissent. . . . Researchers need, in other words, a 'conditionalization' of the [economic inequality–political conflict] nexus, to discover the necessary and sufficient conditions under which economic inequality produces positive, negative, or no effects on conflict" (1989, 465). He also suggests that rational choice theory will produce the hypothesis that will solve the problem (1989, 465). He joins many political scientists who propose to develop and apply the hypotheses of rational action theory.

Those who propose emendations to Marx's theory and the analysis of vote choice agree on new directions in the analysis of electoral behavior. Researchers must now begin, they say, with the understanding that no social cleavage is easily transformed into a basis of widespread and persistent political divisions. Future research must specify the probability that persons who share the same objective position in a society will identify with each other. Then, it must examine the independent probability that they will vote, demonstrate, or riot together (Zuckerman 1989). By phrasing the questions of research in new ways, we will learn more and more about the world.

In these and other cases, demanding tests of different types have been applied to hypotheses. Their results, even if they are not unequivocal, limit our ability to accept some propositions and impel us to accept others. They point us in the direction of new hypotheses and new research efforts. Above all, we can and must test knowledge claims. We must apply rational criteria to such claims, knowing the difficulties and limitations involved in doing that, because they are the only criteria we have.

In the face of this diversity of research schools, theories, and hypotheses, how do you and other students of political science choose which approach to use, not only which proposition to accept or reject?

Followers of Popper's philosophy of science would suggest that you work with the theory that displays the greatest number of well-supported strands in their analytic tapestry. But as you will see in the next chapter, Popper's guidelines are not so easily followed. Newton-Smith reminds us that no science contains definitive tests. "The guiding principles in science can point in different directions, and even if they all point in the same direction it may turn out to be the wrong direction" (1981, 226). In reality, there are no easy guidelines to help you select one theory over another.

How then do you choose? The answer is, you don't. More precisely, you are likely to bring more than rational criteria alone to this decision. In fact, the question is unfair because it assumes that one selects a research school only after winnowing out alternatives, much as we choose which hypotheses to accept and which to reject. Indeed, because rational criteria are even more difficult to apply to the evaluation of research schools than to propositions, we are even less likely to make this selection using the rules offered in this chapter. We accept one school of analysis rather than others less because we have carefully chosen among them and more because our teachers have taught us to use it, because of our private hunches, and because of our personal successes in using it. Thus, nonrational criteria enter the process. Decisions to accept or reject research schools, theories, and hypotheses are always based on nonrational as well as rational criteria. In the next chapter, I will show that scholars apply both types of criteria in all fields of knowledge, not only political science.

CHAPTER 6

What We Mean When We Call Political Science a Science: Ambiguity and Certainty in the Pursuit of Knowledge

Political science *is* a science. Don't be confused by the variety of research schools, the diversity of hypotheses, the dearth of experiments, and the inability to draw binding conclusions from analysis. Don't be put off by the absence of universally accepted general laws of politics. Certainly, you have no reason to assert that a science of politics is impossible. Following Weber and Geertz, you might contend that the social sciences need to include methods not found in the physical sciences, but that is not a reason to deny the label "science" to the study of politics.

The criteria of science are rather straightforward. To do science, we must assume that the world outside our minds is real and that we may know it. How we know it is critical. In science, claims to knowledge are based on the public criteria of evidence and reason. Meehl accentuates "reproducibility, degree of quantification, and conceptual neatness" (1986, 316), and Gellner lists "accurate observation, testing, mathematicisation, shared conceptual currency, the abstention from transcedence or circularity, and perhaps others" (1985, 119–120). To the extent that political scientists present claims to knowledge about politics that fit these criteria, they do science.

To relate political science to other disciplines, you must develop a properly nuanced view of science as it is actually pursued. Following the pathbreaking study of Thomas Kuhn, *The Structure of Scientific Revolutions* (1962), we have come to recognize the conceptual, social, and political factors that condition all of the sciences. Nonrational factors also enter into the process by which knowledge is claimed and tested. Who controls power in a laboratory or in an academic journal, for example, always affects the certification of claims to knowledge. However, these factors join with but do not replace reason and evidence. Furthermore, disciplines vary in the extent to which they are characterized by widely accepted claims to knowledge and in the extent to which they possess universal laws. Both conceptual confusion and conceptual neatness appear in all fields. A plethora of hypotheses and theories, a relative absence of unequivocal experiments and other demonstrations of empirical claims, and a dearth of formal logics characterize many, if not all, fields; such traits are neither unique to political science in particular nor to the social sciences in general. As a result, all disciplines are necessarily limited in the claims that they make.

ALL SCIENCES SEEK ORDER IN "THE MULTIPLICITY OF IMMEDIATE SENSE EXPERIENCES"

The effort to make sense of the world "out there" is pivotal to all fields of knowledge that bear the title "science." Each attempt to describe and explain an event or pattern of events addresses the question of the relationship between our minds and the apparent confusion in the world outside ourselves.

Recall the passage that guides Max Weber's philosophy of social science, which I cited in Chapter 3. Life "confronts us," notes Weber, as "an infinite multiplicity of successively and coexistently emerging and disappearing events both 'within' and 'outside' ourselves" (cited in Eldridge 1980, 11). Although he directs this view to social phenomena, there is no reason to accept his limitation. Indeed, the same language appears in the work of Albert Einstein. He defines the "experiences given to us" or the "multiplicity [or variety] of immediate (sense) experiences."

> [It is] an infinite plane on which the separate and diverse sense experiences or observations that clamor for our attention are laid out, like so many separate points. It does indeed represent the "totality of empirical fact" . . . or "totality of sense experiences." In themselves the points on this plane are bewildering, a universe of elements, a veritable "labyrinth of sense impressions," of which, moreover, we never can be completely sure that they are not "the result of an illusion or an hallucination" (Holton 1986, 31–32).

Consider the rush of news events, the kaleidoscope of sense impressions, and the mixed chorus of sounds that surround us. Scientists must confront the question of how we can know the complicated world in which we live.

Nature Exists, Scientists Seek to Know It

Scientists accept the reality of that world and strive to devise ways to understand it. They disagree over methods and whether there are limits on our ability to analyze, but they accept the claim that nature exists. It is not possible to do science while maintaining that every effort to know the world is an artificial and, therefore, fundamentally doomed attempt to assert an intellectual order over a chaotic universe.

We stretch and push our minds to discover the order that exists in the world outside our minds. Einstein defines science as the effort to build intellectual edifices that correspond to the order in the universe. I will continue with Holton's presentation of Einstein's views: "In fact the ultimate aim of science can be defined in this manner: 'Science is the attempt to make the chaotic diversity of our sense-experience correspond to a logically uniform [unified] system of thought.' The chaotic diversity of 'facts' is mastered by erecting a structure of thought on it that points to relations and order" (1986, 32). In this view, we strive to create a set of logically bound propositions that mirror the regularities of the universe itself. Analysis is the effort to create a model of the world in order to predict and explain particular elements of it.

Think back to the contrast between Marx and Weber that we explored in the third and fourth chapters. Marx's theory implies a position that is even more optimistic than that of Einstein. Not only does he see order in the universe that we strive to uncover, but he insists that he has discovered the logic of social, economic, and political development. His theory, Marx maintains, is exactly in line with reality. Furthermore, it demonstrates that our lives will change for the better as we proceed to socialism and communism. In essence, Marx claims to know the world exactly and to know that it will end wonderfully; you cannot be more optimistic than that. But Weber is much less confident about science's ability to uncover the order in nature. He offers ideal-types, claiming that each concrete case will more or less resemble the order erected by our minds. Weber offers "shafts of light," which he sometimes develops into precise hypotheses and policy recommendations. Fundamentally, though, all the approaches to political science that we have examined accept the reality of the political world. Einstein, Marx, Weber, and other social and physical scientists agree that we may, indeed, know the world around us.

As noted earlier, it is impossible to do science without assuming that the natural world exists and that it is amenable to our efforts to analyze it. The reports of scientists, even those who are self-conscious about the limits of scientific knowledge, reiterate this point. Take, for example, the views of biologist Stephen Jay Gould: "If I didn't believe that in working with these snails I was really finding out something about nature, I couldn't keep going. I'd like to be honest enough to admit that everything that I'm doing is filtered through my psychological presuppositions, my cultural vices. . . . *The truth value of a statement has to do with the nature of the world, and there I do take the notion that you can test and you can refute*" (1988, 147, emphasis added).

Notice the imagery, passion, and purpose in the comments of Mitchell Feigenbaum, a mathematician and leader of the newly developing field of chaos theory: "I truly want to know how to describe the clouds. . . . Somehow the wondrous promise of the earth is that there are things beautiful in it, things wondrous and alluring, and by virtue of your trade you want to understand them" (cited in Gleick 1987, 187). Feigenbaum seeks not just another interpretation but the accurate description of that portion of the world that interests him.

Paul Meehl summarizes the scientist's response to the question of the reality of the outside world: "As to realism, I have never met any scientist who, when doing science, held to a phenomenalist or idealist view; and I cannot force myself to take a nonrealist view seriously even when I work at it. So I begin with the presupposition that the external world is really there, there is a difference between the world and my view of it, and the business of science is to get my view in harmony with what the world really is to the extent that is possible" (1986, 322).

Any effort to do science assumes that the world out there is something other than an extension of the analyst's thoughts. This does not mean that our minds do not structure how we perceive. When we do science—political science or any other variety—we create abstractions, knowing that our concepts, hypotheses, and theories are our inventions and knowing that there is a world out there against which they are to be tested, no matter how difficult and equivocal the results of the tests may be.

THERE IS NO KNOWLEDGE WITHOUT EMOTIONS: THE ROLE OF PASSION IN SCIENCE

Do not suppose that scientists approach the effort to know the world in a cold, dispassionate frame of mind. Numerous reports demonstrate that no research occurs without emotion; passion drives the effort to uncover the order in the world. Sometimes, our passions lead us astray.

At other times, they direct us to powerful insights. Not only are you entitled to your political preferences, your personal goals, and your fascination with the world of politics, without them you may not be able to pursue the task of knowing the world. Without passion, there is no knowledge.

A prime illustration is a study of scientists involved in the early stages of the exploration of space. Ian Mitroff analyzed forty-two of the top scientists in the Apollo moon project in order "to study the nature and function of the commitment of scientists to their pet hypotheses in the face of possibly disconfirming evidence" (1974, 581). They were an elite group: Two held a Nobel Prize, six were members of the National Academy of Science, all but four had doctorates, thirteen were major editors of leading scientific journals in the field, and nearly all were employed at prestigious universities or research laboratories (1974, 584).

In the interviews, the scientists openly displayed deep and strong emotions and a powerful competitive drive. Mitroff cites the following typical description: "X is so committed to the idea that the moon is Q that you could literally take the moon apart piece by piece, ship it back to Earth, reassemble it in X's backyard and shove the whole thing . . . and X would still continue to believe that the moon is Q. X's belief in Q is unshakeable. He refuses to listen to reason or to evidence. I no longer regard him as a scientist. He's so hopped up on the idea of Q that I think that he's unbalanced" (1974, 586). These views really did not place X outside the boundaries of science; after all, he was part of the research group, and Mitroff presents the report of his opponent. In fact, those scientists most strongly attached to their own ideas were judged to be the most creative and the most outstanding in the group (Mitroff 1974, 586). Furthermore, all the scientists agreed that emotional commitment is essential to science. Numerous examples of this claim fill Mitroff's article:

> **Scientist A.** Commitment, even extreme commitment, such as bias, has a role to play in science and it can serve science well. . . . We must be emotionally committed to the things we do energetically. No one is able to do anything with liberal energy if there is no emotion connected with it.
>
> **Scientist B.** Most of the scientists I know have theories and are looking for data to support them; they're not sorting impersonally through the data looking for a theory to fit the data. You've got to make a clear distinction between not being objective and cheating. A good scientist will not be above changing his theory if he gets a preponderance of evidence that doesn't support it, but basically he's looking to defend it.

156 ■ POLITICAL SCIENCE AS A SCIENCE

> Without [emotional] commitment one wouldn't have the energy, the drive to press forward, sometimes against extremely difficult odds. . . .
> **Scientist D**. One thing that spurs a scientist on is competition, warding off attacks against what you've published. . . .
> **Scientist G.** Science is an intensely personal enterprise. Every scientific idea needs a personal representative who will defend and nourish that idea so that it won't suffer a premature death (Mitroff 1974, 588–589).

Notice how far these statements take us from the mythical scientist, coldly sifting through the evidence or applying a mathematical formula. Doing science takes deep personal commitment. We drive ourselves and need passions and emotions to do the work.

Do not suppose that Mitroff's group of astronomers, physicists, and engineers involved in the Apollo mission is unique. Emotional commitments to ideas, competition, and passion shine through every report that I have read of how scientists work. The following selections are taken from Lewis Wolpert and Alison Richards's volume entitled, *A Passion for Science* (1988), which gathers together the reports of scientists about their careers.

> I was so excited by these quite new ideas that I was almost stopping people in the street to tell them. Perhaps it is, above all, the thrill of the ideas which binds scientists together, it is the passion which drives them and enables them to survive (Lewis Wolpert quoted in Wolpert and Richards 1988, 9).

> The intellectual gratification is much less than the expected reward that I'll have when I see my buddies the next time, and tell them "Look here man, I found this!" This is what I like best about science. I'm always thinking about the papers you see. Even before I have found something, I'm already thinking of the opening phrase of the paper in which I will describe this discovery (molecular biologist Gunther Stent quoted in Wolpert and Richards 1988, 115).

> It's playing a game either against one's colleagues or somebody who's written a book you think might be silly or, perhaps, wiser than oneself; but particularly it's a game against nature, against the way things are. And you try to win—there's a certain competitive streak here, I think—against reality itself (neuropsychologist Richard Gregory quoted in Wolpert and Richardson 1988, 195).

Feel the joy in the expression of the physicist Leo Kadanoff: "It's an experience like no other experience I can describe, the best thing that can happen to a scientist, realizing that something that's happened in his or her mind exactly corresponds to something that happens in nature" (cited in Gleick 1987, 189). Excitement, pleasure, the strength of an advocate, pride, anger, the drive that comes from conflict, the effort to defeat nature, and other similar emotions motivate scientists.

Notice, too, the importance of daring in Holton's description of how Einstein proposed to develop theories about "the multiplicity of immediate [sense] experiences." "Rising out of an area just above a portion of the chaos of observables E, there is an arrow-tipped arch reaching to the very top of the whole scheme. It symbolizes what under various circumstances could be a bold leap, a 'widely speculative' attempt, a 'groping constructive attempt,' or a desperate proposal, made when one has despaired of finding other roads. There, high above the infinite plane of E, is suspended a well-delimited entity labeled 'A, system of axioms' " (1986, 32-33).

Only someone bold enough to apply his or her mind to the "chaos of observables" can devise a coherent system of propositions that matches the order inherent in the universe. This involves acrobatics, not only rules and procedures. Holton cites other adjectives that Einstein used for this effort—"inspiration," "guess," "hunch" (1986, 33). "But the leap to the top of the schema symbolizes precisely the precious moment of great energy, the response to the motivation of 'wonder' and the 'passion of comprehension' . . . which can come from the encounter with the chaotic E" (1986, 33).

No scientist has developed a more comprehensive and systematic theory of the world outside himself than Einstein. In his own words, this effort required passion and feats of intellectual daring as much as it did the application of reason and evidence.

Emotion drives science. In order to do science, you must dare to know the world; dreams of glory, competition, the drive to conquer, and other powerful emotions urge the scientist to take the challenge.

THERE IS NO KNOWLEDGE WITHOUT REASON AND EVIDENCE

To do science, rules of logic and evidence that are outside your control must limit your passion. Scientists obviously must test their claims to know the world, and though they may work in private, they must present their knowledge in public. They know that their hunches, dreams, and competitive needs do not provide compelling reasons for others to accept their claims to know the world. But reason and evidence do.

As you saw in the last chapter, the willingness to test and accept the falsification of one's hypothesis defines science. Numerous philosophers of science and scientists themselves exclude from their field any school of analysis whose proponents act as if their propositions could never be falsified. "Again, the crucial idea is that to hold a claim in an objective manner, I must be prepared to subject it to the widest possible range of observational tests" (Brown 1987, 203). David Hull, a biologist who uses the tools of philosophy and sociology as well as his own observations and understanding of his specialty, makes this point:

> Nearly all the views that we tend to dismiss as not being "scientific" because they are not "falsifiable" are actually quite falsifiable. The problem is that their proponents are not interested. . . . If a theory handles a wide range of phenomena and only a few anomalies crop up, a scientist can afford to set these counterinstances by the side for the moment. Perhaps the data are in error or possibly a slight modification can account for them. However, if through time enough phenomena turn out to be sufficiently recalcitrant, he or she might well be led to abandon the theory altogether (1988, 81).

Holton presents Einstein's frame of mind, which joins reason and evidence with passion at the frontiers of science: "Below this upper layer of a few grand laws lies a layer of experimental facts—not the latest news from the laboratory, but hard-won, well-established, aged-in-the-bottle results. . . . But between these two solid levels is the uncertain and shifting region of concepts, theories, and recent findings. They deserve to be looked at skeptically; they are man-made, limited, fallible, and if necessary, disposable" (1986, 13). Einstein does not argue that you should let your passions and hunches run wild. No matter how strongly you are committed to your hypotheses, you must approach these ideas with a willingness to abandon them.

However much scientists may seek to advance their own ideas, they remain constrained by the rules of logic and evidence, standards that lie beyond their control. Gould is particularly sensitive to the importance of selfish motives in science, and, therefore, he insists on the need to check oneself: "Science is done by human beings who are after status, wealth, and power, like everybody else. That's why I advocate self scrutiny. I say, if you don't scrutinize yourself carefully, and you really think that you are just objectively depicting the world, then you're self-deluding. The capacity for self-delusion is amazing" (1988, 147). Hull would argue with those who maintain that power and career interests, not empirical tests, determine claims to knowledge in evolutionary biology: "Regardless of the impression that one might get from reading the recent literature in the sociology of knowledge, scientists really do make extensive observations and run exhaustive and exhausting experiments. All this effort is not mythical behavior designed to camouflage the causal factors that are actually operative in their arriving at their conclusions" (1988, 342).

Sciences and Scientists Vary in the Extent to Which They Use Theoretical and Empirical Tests

In James Gleick's account of the development of chaos theory, he emphasizes the basic difference between the theorists' and empiricists' approaches to research in the physical sciences. "Theorists conduct experiments with their brains. Experimenters have to use their hands, too. Theorists are thinkers, experimenters are craftsmen. The theorist needs no accomplice. The experimenter has to muster graduate students, cajole machinists, flatter lab assistants" (1987, 125). Both organize their work to develop and test efforts and thereby know the world. And both seek compelling reasons to accept or reject hypotheses.

Einstein was a theorist, not an experimentalist, preferring the precision of mathematical proofs to the vagaries of empirical tests. "The criterion is simply this: 'The theory must not contradict empirical fact'" (Einstein, cited in Holton 1986, 40–41). This position rests on the principle that cognition precedes observation. "We must be able to tell how nature functions, know the natural laws at least in practical terms, before we can claim to have observed" (Einstein, cited in Holton 1986, 41). Einstein did not, therefore, place much store in the role of experiments in physics or in the work of experimental physicists:

> Einstein's attitude was perhaps best expressed in a remark reported to me by one of his colleagues in Berlin: "Einstein once told me in the lab: 'You make experiments and I make theories. Do you know the difference? A theory is something nobody believes except the person who made it, while an experiment is something everybody believes except the person who made it'" (Holton 1986, 13).

As a result, Einstein would ignore empirical findings that ran counter to his theory: "Even though the 'experimental facts' seem clearly to favor the theory of his opponents, Einstein found the limited scope and ad hoc character of their theories more significant and objectionable than the apparent disagreement between his own theory and the new results of experimental measurements" (Holton 1986, 71). In Einstein's view, test results, even predictions of heretofore unknown events, cannot determine the truth value of a theory. Although his fame spread when he was acclaimed for having predicted an eclipse as a derivation of his general theory of relativity, he himself was much less impressed by his feat:

Einstein . . . though pleased by the eclipse results, gave them little weight as evidence for his theory. According to his student, Ilse Rosenthal-Schneider, after showing her a cable he received from Arthur Eddington about the measurements, Einstein remarked "But I knew that the theory is correct." When she asked what he would have done if the prediction had not been confirmed, he said "Then I would have been sorry for the dear Lord—the theory *is* correct." Later, he wrote: "I do not by any means find the chief significance of the general theory of relativity in the fact that it has predicted a few minute observable facts, but rather in the simplicity of its foundation and in its logical consistency (Brush 1989, 1125, emphasis in original).

Einstein offers theoretical scope and logical rigor (especially as expressed in mathematical form) more than—perhaps even rather than—the results of empirical tests as compelling reasons to accept his theory.

Nobel Prize winner Sheldon Glashow reiterates Einstein's position about the centrality of theoretical criteria for claims to knowledge: "Our hypotheses may be wrong and our speculations idle, but the uniqueness and simplicity of our scheme are reasons enough to be taken seriously" (cited in Holton 1986, 172). For him, the ability to solve existing problems in distinctive ways and the clarity with which the hypotheses relate to each other guard against "illusion and hallucination." This position also allows the scientist to ignore results of empirical tests that run counter to the expectations of his or her theory. Above all, theoretical physicists insist on the primacy of reason over evidence in the efforts to analyze the world.

The way in which theorists view the relationship between theory and evidence is significant. They assert that when the set of hypotheses conforms to the rules of logic and mathematics and does not run counter to what we know about the world, we have reason to proceed as if it were true. They maintain that a theory develops by the internal unfolding of its own logic. The vagaries of any and all empirical tests, they reason, imply that we should not put great store in the ability of experiments to assess the explanatory power of our theories.

Rational choice theorists emphasize the importance of deductive logic in their analysis. Riker's theory of political coalitions, for instance, illustrates one of many applications of the mathematical theory of games to political analysis. These political scientists also present empirical evidence to illustrate but not test or substantiate their analyses. Doubting the reliability and validity of empirical evidence, rational choice theorists use the power of mathematical logics to test their claims to knowledge.

Others, in physics and other sciences, insist that the effort to know the world must confront its object directly. Keep in mind Abraham

Kaplan's admonition: Seek to know this world, not one that is solely the creation of our minds. Geertz makes a similar point: "Coherence cannot be the major test of validity for a cultural description. Cultural systems must have a minimal degree of coherence, else we could not call them systems; and, by observation they normally have a good degree more. But there is nothing so coherent as a paranoid's delusion or a swindler's story" (1973, 17–18). The real world that we seek to analyze is too complex for simple formulations that are not grounded in empirical tests. Psychologists and biologists are especially known for the use of carefully designed observations. Anthony Epstein, who discovered the first virus known to cause cancer in humans—the Epstein-Barr virus—spent years grappling with puzzling results in the laboratory. He posited his discovery only after exhausting all available alternative hypotheses. An experimenter, not a theoretician, Epstein describes how he works: "I think just sort of messing about is the answer. You've got to keep messing about at the bench. You see how to change this just a little bit . . . and you want to tinker with something. . . . I'm not sure it's right in astrophysics or big science, but it's very important in certain kinds of biological work. It means registering inside yourself minute changes, tiny things which may have a big influence" (1988, 164–166). In Hull's description of the critical role of laboratory experiments for biologists, he notes that psychologists and biologists use empirical evidence to guide claims to knowledge more frequently than they use mathematical proofs.

As you know, most research in political science accepts the centrality of empirical evidence. Political scientists examine survey data, organize demanding empirical tests of their hypotheses, and conduct fieldwork in order to directly observe the world of politics. Many of them, no matter what their research school, use the same statistical methods to evaluate their hypotheses.

Scientists Seek to Check but Not Inhibit Their Work

There is always tension between the scientist's claim to know the world—the passion that drives research—and the need to test the claim. Each scholar seeks a balance among these contradictory demands. He or she must wriggle off the hook of negative tests and perhaps concede failure. Successful scientists view both practices as obligations.

Because we can never be absolutely certain about our claims to knowledge, we must guard against the premature rejection of smart ideas. Indeed, the more committed we are to the view that we have uncovered the order of the universe, the more right we have to suspend disbelief, assume that our hypotheses are accurate, and proceed to derive further implications from them (Lakatos 1974; Van Fraasen 1980 and 1986). Holton discusses Einstein's views that balance the pull toward skepticism and emotional distance with the drive to say, "I know." "Hence in this early and usually private stage of theorizing the researcher has to grant himself a freedom, the right of 'suspension of disbelief,' a moratorium of premature attempts at falsification. . . . Though the very idea is contrary to the naive picture of the scientist, it is an essential part of the scientific imagination" (1986, 38). Consider how theoretical physicist Michael Berry uses mathematics in his work:

> As the physicist Richard Feynman said, "A great many more things are known than can be proved." And while a physicist wants to be right, he doesn't want rigour to turn into rigour mortis. And if you're trying to create some rather elaborate edifice, and calling on lots of branches of mathematics, you just can't afford to be perfectly rigorous with every step. It's as though, for example, a printer would, in printing a book, have to insist that every letter was absolutely perfectly formed, that there wasn't a shadow of a smudge anywhere. You'd never get beyond the first line if you did that (1988, 46).

Hull, too, balances the need to wriggle off the hook of negative test results and the need to accept defeat. "As Darwin himself remarked, he was a master wriggler. Any scientist who is incapable of wriggling a bit will never succeed in science, but there are limits to wriggling. If it becomes too pervasive, the scientist ceases to be a 'scientist' " (1988, 280–281). Successful scientists necessarily defend their ideas against efforts to deny them. The need to test and the need to wriggle underline the contradictory demands of reason, evidence, commitment, and passion in seeking order in the world outside ourselves.

IN SCIENCE, NONRATIONAL FACTORS INFLUENCE BUT DO NOT DETERMINE CLAIMS TO KNOWLEDGE

As we move away from the myth that equates science and absolute truth, we can better understand that nonrational and even irrational factors influence the decision to accept or reject a claim to knowledge. Certainly, scientists make mistakes. But more importantly, the psychological requirements of the process of doing research and the limitations of their minds lead them to produce less than ideal studies. Passion, the drive to uncover nature's secrets, and conflict with intellectual opponents provide the psychological commitment to work long hours and solve research puzzles. Political interests, the demands of careers, and social pressures affect research, as well. Thus, nonrational and irrational factors play exceedingly important roles in science.

Conceptual Schema and Cognitive Limitations Influence but Do Not Determine Knowledge Claims

All perceptions of the world require concepts, and all concepts are embedded in wider frameworks of understandings. As a result, all research reflects these intellectual structures, which Kuhn (1962) labeled paradigms. Groups of scholars at work on a topic reach consensus on the questions to be asked, the proposed answers to be tested, the standards for evidence, and the techniques of gathering data. Containing both conceptual and theoretical elements, the paradigms offer the puzzles that guide future research. Normal science adds to the precision of the paradigm, filling in the blanks in the accepted understanding of the world while ruling out competing questions, hypotheses, and methods. Paradigms shield the analyst from alternative points of view.

There is no basis for the naive view that truth is simply out there, calling attention to itself. Rather, the analyst must perceive, analyze, and judge. From this claim, David Faust derives two critical points: "Scientists, along with other individuals, evidence cognitive limitations that lead to frequent judgment error and that set surprisingly harsh restrictions on the capacity to manage complex information and make decisions." Because we cannot eliminate the role of the scientist, we must understand how the mind is limited in its ability to know the world (Faust 1984, 3; see also Brown 1987, 157–167). At the same time, he says, science is not the creation of the analyst, having no relationship to the natural world: "To admit this does not necessitate the retreat into fictionalism that some have chosen—the view that scientific knowledge reflects nothing but the inner workings and imaginations of minds, and that the external world contributes nothing to what is known" (Faust 1984, 4). Faust's book specifies these limitations and offers mechanisms to maximize the role of rational factors in decisions about claims to knowledge.

Intellectual paradigms and the cognitive limitations of scientists highlight the nonrational elements that are always present in research. The paradigms inhibit the scientist's range of vision. The need to judge, the tendency to overvalue the first piece of evidence, and other cognitive characteristics that scientists share with other humans necessarily distort their ability to observe and analyze the world. Such principles lead students of political attitudes and behavior to structure their analyses around the individual's perceptions. Attitudes contain affective, intellectual, and intentional components. And what applies to political attitudes holds for attitudes toward scientific subjects, as well. Affect always accompanies intellectual judgment; both nonrational and rational factors influence all analyses.

Because Science Is a Social Phenomenon, Power, Interests, and Status Affect but Do Not Determine Claims to Knowledge

Kuhn's study of scientific revolutions (1962) drew initial attention to the role of social and political factors in the creation and defense of claims to knowledge. The philosopher Paul Feyerabend (1975) and some sociologists of science suggest a fundamental revision of how we understand science by arguing that these factors impede and even doom all efforts to know the world. Most students of science accept the limited point that politics and social pressures affect claims to knowledge but not the sweeping position that only these factors determine what stands as science.

The revisionists maintain that nonrational factors, not the impersonal standards of reason and evidence, determine what knowledge is. Sociologists of science have entered laboratories in biology, chemistry, and physics and returned to report the central role played by power and social pressures in the development and certification of truth claims. Donald T. Campbell has summarized the conclusions that may be drawn from such studies (1986, 112–113), along the following lines:

1. Nonrational factors distort analyses, inducing some scholars to accept "false" ideas, but they also influence scientists to accept ideas as "true."
2. There are no empirical or logical tests with absolutely clear results. "The Quine-Duhem observation on the equivocality of 'factual' (experimental, observational) falsifications or confirmations of theoretical predictions is an unavoidable predicament in all scientific belief change and allows for extrascientific beliefs and preferences to influence the inevitably discretionary judgments involved. No certain proof, logical or observational, is ever available or socially compelling" (Campbell 1986, 113). In *no* science, social or otherwise, is it possible to devise experiments or mathematical proofs that compel the acceptance or rejection of claims to knowledge.
3. If we accept the second point and the principle that no theory is ever more than temporarily true, the truth value of a claim cannot be the reason that it was accepted as true. Truth does

not guide research toward itself. Rather, it is ephemeral, always subject to nonrational judgments.
4. Political power within scientific professions frequently affects the acceptance of ideas as true. Because some professors control access to jobs in laboratories, appointments to university faculties and research institutes, allocation of research funds, and editorial decisions on publications, many find it difficult to oppose their analyses and conclusions. As a result, power determines judgments.
5. "Scientists do not live up to the so-called norms of science, for example, of neutrality, objectivity, and the sharing of all information" (Campbell 1986, 113).
6. In the laboratory, "social persuasion and selection" affect the outcome of research results. The views of one's colleagues, not only the power of the head of the research group, help determine whether hypotheses are confirmed or rejected.

Campbell reports that the revisionist sociologists of science believe the distinctions between science and nonscience are artificial and temporary, and nonrational factors draw scientists to reject or accept claims to knowledge. He concludes that the work of the revisionists leads them to claim that "history and current practice in both astronomy and astrology should be studied with equal trust and respect" (1986, 114). In this view, then, the decision as to what constitutes scientific knowledge reflects social and political pressures; it does not derive from analyses based on impersonal and rational evaluations.

This view takes us back to the question of the nature of reality. Campbell summarizes two recent studies of life in the laboratory, seeking to determine whether the results of research decide questions of knowledge. He notes that the authors of both argue:

> The production of scientific belief assertions of truth claims is shown by participant observation and ethnographic research to be a process in which order is imposed upon a chaotic welter of inconsistent and inconclusive observations through quasi-conspiratorial social negotiations. Thus when life in the scientific laboratory is examined in detail, the factual proof that might be expected never appears. Ambiguity, equivocality, and discretionary judgment pervade. A point at which Nature intrudes and says yes or no to theory is never encountered. This research experience increases doubts about the reputed objectivity of science (Campbell 1986, 118).

This perspective fosters the belief that scientists impose an artificial order on an essentially chaotic reality. The kind of order they propose reflects the needs of their careers and the social pressures of the laboratory, rather than any notion of objective truth.

Note the radical extension of the revisionists' argument: Knowledge is what a community of people, especially those in powerful positions (in regard to professorships, journals, grants), define it to be. There are no absolute standards, no objective facts, no definitive rules of logic. Personal, careerist, and social interests, as well as—and perhaps even more than—intellectual factors, dominate decisions about what science and knowledge are.

I do not accept the revisionists' view of science. In my opinion, doing science combines nonrational, irrational, and rational elements, but there is no reason to maintain that all analyses are equally and only based on subjective, political, careerist, and other such factors. Conceptual biases and intellectual weaknesses do not make all claims to know the world equally false. Faust admonishes us not to retreat into the view of science as fiction. As Newton-Smith responded to Kuhn: "Even if there is no rationally grounded algorithm to guide our decisions [about theories] there may none the less be rational considerations which it is relevant to appeal to in justifying our decisions" (1981, 116). Our passions vary in the extent to which they drive us to push on with powerful and weak ideas. And the fact that the decisions of scientists—like those of other human beings—are affected by the demands of those with power, the perceived needs of self-interest and careers, and other social effects does not mean that rational criteria have no place in the establishment of truth claims. Hull makes this point in a particularly telling fashion: "Scientists form social groups. They cooperate with each other, compete, build on each other's work, sometimes give credit where it is due. Studying the world in which we live is a social process, but from this platitude it does *not* follow that our knowledge of the world is socially determined. It might be, but it need not be" (1988, 15, emphasis in original). We must not exaggerate the importance of conceptual blinders, power, interests, and status in science. Indeed, although the relative importance of these factors necessarily varies, rarely do the nonrational factors completely displace reason and evidence.

Furthermore, there is a fundamental difficulty with the radical extension of the revisionists' account of science, such as the argument that Feyerabend (1975) offers. On what grounds should you accept their claims? If you find them convincing because they are in accord with your experience or because of the power of their logic or the wealth of their empirical detail, then reason and evidence underpin your decision. But this negates their very argument. If the power and status of the revisionists convince you, then they are in the awkward position of making reasoned claims to knowledge but having them accepted only because of social persuasion and arm-twisting—and they are not likely to be satisfied with this outcome. Furthermore, to the extent that they hold no social, economic, or political power over you (which is likely to be true for most readers of this book), they can convince you only on rational grounds. Hence, your acceptance must be based on rational grounds. So, whether we accept or reject the claims of the revisionists, we must use reason and evidence to assess their claims to knowledge. All analyses, *including* those of the revisionists, must be amenable to rational tests (Putnam 1981; Newton-Smith 1981; Brown 1987).

As a result, there is good reason to reject the revisionist sociology of science. Even though Campbell applauds their research, he rejects the radical implications of their position. He provides several instances in which scientists changed their minds and accepted new ideas in the face of social, political, and intellectual pressures to maintain the orthodox position. Noting that the revisionists accept the claim that "the natural world has [at least] a small . . . role in the construction of scientific knowledge," Campbell devises ways to maximize that role, using the findings of these sociologists to enhance the "fallible, corrigible, presumptive, and contingent" nature of these claims to knowledge. Indeed, he defines science by these very criteria (Campbell 1986, 115).

In all sciences, the accumulation of knowledge involves both a deep emotional commitment to a way of seeing the world and tests of that vision. It requires the ability to know when the vision has failed, while realizing that there need be no definitive tests that will ever absolutely certify propositions. Regardless of the importance of nonrational factors in the assessment of hypotheses and theories, they are always tempered and limited by rational criteria. To do science, we must make our vision of the world comprehensible to others. Ultimately, science revolves around knowledge that is accepted or rejected on grounds of reason and evidence, as well as nonrational and irrational criteria.

AMBIGUITY AND CERTAINTY IN SCIENCE

By now, you should recognize the need to discard two critical myths about science: Science is truth, and science is power. Both statements are false because they are exaggerations. The search to uncover and posit the order in nature is always limited by the methods and theories used and by the social and psychological processes inherent in the activities of the scientist. No study is perfect, but that does not mean that all studies are equally and fatally flawed. The process of research involves disagreement as well as agreement, conflict as well as cooperation. Using reason and evidence as best we can to evaluate claims to knowledge, we sometimes produce powerful analyses. Rarely, however, are they so powerful that they compel others to accept them.

In All Sciences, Research at the Frontiers of Knowledge Is Characterized by Alternative Approaches, Contrasting Methods, and Sharp Disagreements

Sciences vary in the extent to which they exhibit consensus over what constitutes knowledge. It is important not to exaggerate the extent to which paradigms structure research within an entire field. In reality, competing schools of analysis divide all disciplines, and dissension always characterizes work at the frontiers of knowledge. Furthermore, no two scientists ever agree on everything. Inevitably, dissension, as well as consensus, is a constant feature of all fields, not only political science.

Stephen Cole offers strong evidence for refuting the proposition that there is a hierarchy of sciences that sharply distinguishes between the physical and social sciences. Using the same standards of science that I presented at the start of this chapter, he examines whether there are clear and systematic differences with regard to the development of theory, quantification, cognitive consensus, predictability, rate of obsolescence, and rate of growth. According to Cole, disciplines at the top of such a hierarchy—physics and associated fields, in most people's minds—would be characterized by highly developed theories, high levels of codification of knowledge, "ideas expressed in mathematical language," much agreement on research findings and methods to test hypotheses, and other characteristics that indicate the absence of diversity and the presence of consensus on what constitutes knowledge (1983, 113). He notes that most persons who accept the existence of a hierarchy of sciences place the social sciences far from the top, expecting them to be characterized by the absence of most or all of these traits. To test for differences in current research, he studies scientific journals and the process by which proposals for grants are evaluated at the National Science Foundation (NSF). He also examines citations in text books for variations in the presence of codified knowledge. Cole's work is one of the few systematic efforts to assess the hierarchy of the sciences.

At the research frontier, Cole's study finds scientists of all kinds using diverse methods and hypotheses, with little consensus on what stands for accepted claims to knowledge. In the journals of psychology, sociology, geology, and chemistry, he locates no significant differences in the level of intellectual agreement, measured as the tendency to cite "a relatively small number of papers and authors" (Cole 1983, 121). He expands this test by studying the process of peer review for research grants at the NSF, looking at decisions in ten fields: algebra, anthropology, biochemistry, chemical dynamics, ecology, economics, fluid mechanics, geophysics, meteorology, and solid-state physics. His examination reveals that all fields are characterized by a relatively high measure of disagreement and that the two social sciences, economics and anthropology, had the lowest level of disagreement on proposals (1983, 123). Additional tests of the levels of consensus further corroborate the claim that all sciences display much disagreement over methods, findings, and the prospects of research proposals. Similarly, Cole identifies no significant differences across the journals of the disciplines in the tendency to cite recent, rather than older, studies; research in the physical sciences is no more characterized by an "immediacy effect" than is work in sociology and economics (1983, 126–127). Developing the general significance of his findings, Cole maintains that "science at the research frontier is a great deal less rational and predictable than our imagery suggests" (1983, 131). Furthermore, he points to a growing body of evidence that indicates that scientists have a very poor record of predicting which ideas at the research frontier will be successful and which will fail (1983, 132). Disagreements about the methods, hypotheses, theories, and results of current research and the likelihood of future success apply to *all* the sciences, and diversity and dissension are constant features of current research.

The same descriptions fill reports on the state of cosmology, a subfield of physics. In an article written for the "Science Times" section of the *New York Times,* entitled "If Theory Is Right, Most of the Universe Is Missing," William J. Broad writes:

> According to astrophysicists, calculations show that the sum of all the known dust, planets, comets, asteroids, stars, pulsars and quasars now accounts for about 1 percent of the matter that theory says ought to make up the universe—that is, unless there is a flaw in current understanding of the laws of nature. . . .
> The depth of the mystery is illustrated by the odd suspects now being put forward to account for the invisible mass: Giant slush balls, swarms of black holes, cosmic rocks, and exotic new types of hypothetical subatomic particles with names like photinos and winos (1984, C1, C5).

In his book *Science à la Mode,* cosmologist Tony Rothman provides another characterization of the research frontier of his field: "We have presented the reader with a number of cosmological models: isotropic, closed, open, anisotropic inhomogenous, halls or mirrors, Variable-G, with constants, without constants, Big Bang, and Steady-State, Inflation, and Quantum. Each has its attractive features and each has its failings; undoubtedly the reader has a headache. In the end we must simply say that we don't know. But before the end, we should remind the reader that the Garden of Cosmological Delights is very large" (1989, 28). Confusion and disarray—in the form of competing hypotheses, theories, and schools of analysis—are constant and conspicuous features of research frontiers. But they provide their fields with a sumptuous array of intellectual fare.

Cole's research also uncovers differences among the sciences regarding the extent to which they possess a shared core of knowledge. Because text books codify what scholars claim to know about a field, Cole compares texts in physics, chemistry, and sociology. He measures the extent of codification by examining the age and number of references that are cited. The older the references are and the smaller their number is, Cole reasons, the higher the level of intellectual agreement in the science would be. His results show that the studies cited in physics and chemistry are far older and fewer than those in sociology. The sociology texts contained an average of 800 references, three-fourths of which were published after 1959, and the physics texts averaged 74 references, only 3 percent of which appeared for the first time after 1959 (Cole 1983, 134). Interestingly, texts in political science resemble those in sociology. As an exercise for this chapter, I examined two recent textbooks on U.S. politics (Janda, Berry, and Goldman 1989, and Keefe et al. 1989). One contained 339 references, 75 percent of which were published after 1969. In the other, there were 419 references, 83 percent appearing for the first time in 1970 or after. Such tests indicate that physics and chemistry have a stable core of knowledge and that political science and sociology do not. Thus, sciences appear to differ only with regard to the presence of a research core.

Disagreement at the research frontier reappears in David Hull's work, reaffirming that each discipline is a cacophonous orchestra. Indeed, the sound of music comes only from the work of small clusters, "cliques" of scholars. As a result, Hull cautions against the use of phrases like the "scientific community" or "physicists." "No such groups exist. They are worse than useless fictions; they are highly misleading" (Hull 1988, 22). Working on shared problems with shared methods, he says, cliques form research clusters that divide the broader discipline.

At the same time, Hull insists that we not exaggerate the cohesion of the cliques:

Although members of scientific research groups frequently go to great lengths to hide their disagreements both from each other and from outsiders, they still exist. The preceding observations apply even to the smallest, most highly integrated research groups (or cliques). Such diversity only increases when the groups in question are larger and more amorphous. In short, cooperation in science does not require total agreement, nor does agreement necessarily imply extensive cooperation. Pick any two members of a research group and they will agree with each other on all but a few of the issues relevant to their research. However, it does not follow from this sort of pair-wise agreement that there is one set (or even cluster) of propositions about which all members of the group agree (1988, 113).

Examining patterns of rejection and acceptance in the journal *Systematic Zoology* for evidence of conflict and cohesion, Hull uncovers very little proof that members of each clique are particularly kind to each other and especially harsh on others (1988, 335). Not only is dissension apparent at the level of entire disciplines but it abounds within research clusters as well.

As a result, you should not suppose that any one scientist sits down at the desk to create a "seamless web" or "net" of theory. It may be possible to construct a set of tightly related propositions that join a body of research, but rarely does the work of any one scholar involve the full net itself. Indeed, Hull suggests that we have used the wrong imagery, and he proposes that "patchwork nets" should replace "seamless webs" and "nets."

> Although there are areas of systematicity in any scientist's conceptual system, few scientists succeed in forming a totally seamless worldview. Areas are partially dependent, partially independent. When one expands this picture to include other scientists, conceptual development in science becomes even patchier. . . . No two scientists are ever in total agreement with each other even in their areas of most concentrated investigation. . . .
> If one is interested in science as a process, conceptual systems cannot be viewed as seamless wholes. . . . A more appropriate picture is scientists casting their patchwork nets, one after the other, retrieving them, reworking them piecemeal on the basis of the most recent fit, and then casting them again. . . .
> According to the logical empiricist analysis of science, scientific theories are totally explicit, perfectly precise inferential systems. . . . But scientific theories as they function in science are much cruder. . . . Frequently it is very difficult to decide which observation statements follow from a particular theory without worrying about deriving a particular observation

from one theory and its contradictory from another (Hull 1988, 493–494).

Hull describes the consensus over methods, hypotheses, and results that exists (though never all the time and for all purposes) within small clusters of scholars. Another researcher, James Gleick, depicts physicists, biologists, mathematicians, meteorologists, and others cutting divisions into their traditional disciplines as they formed a research cluster to examine chaos: "Those who recognized chaos in the early days agonized over how to shape their thoughts and findings into publishable form. Work fell between disciplines—for example, too abstract for physicists yet too experimental for mathematicians" (1987, 37–38).

The descriptions above should remind you of the differences among political scientists who study turnout, the conflict among those who analyze demonstrations and political violence, and the divisions among the other political scientists whose research you have observed in the previous chapters. In this and all scientific disciplines, conflict and dissension at the frontiers of knowledge are organized by the consensus that prevails among members of the same research cluster.

Where There Are Passion, Power, and Disagreement, We Find Conflict

Unconventional analyses, explanations, and theories usually encounter opposition. Indeed, given the strength of intellectual paradigms, the psychological difficulty of assimilating information that is markedly different, and the exhortation that scientists be skeptical about new claims to knowledge, it would be unreasonable to expect any other response to a radically new analysis. Each effort to advance an unorthodox perspective encounters opposition, and when scientists persist in this effort, conflict ensues.

The history of science is populated with scholars whose work was ignored for long periods of time but who persevered against powerful odds and finally succeeded. Another selection from the *New York Times,* entitled "A Psychiatrist Who Wouldn't Take No for an Answer" illustrates this point:

> For years, Aaron T. Beck had to struggle. In the 1970s he published his own journal to, as he puts it, "bootleg" reports of his studies that other psychiatric journals rejected. He wrote a textbook to get the word out about the discipline he called "cognitive therapy."
>
> "He really was a pariah," says Dr. Beck's colleague Ruth Greenberg. "Talk about people who stuck to an idea when other people had no use for it!" . . .

> The approach is so straightforward in shunning traditional complexities that Dr. Beck says it befuddled many psychiatrists. "Analysts view me as a behaviorist and behaviorists view me as an analyst" (Greenberg 1981, C1, C2).

Anthony Epstein describes the difficulties he faced in the pursuit of clues that led him to conclude that a virus causes cancer in humans: "It was a tremendous uphill battle from the very beginning. First of all conventional virologists in those days would not accept that something seen in the electron microscope was a virus" (1988, 163).

Holding to the accuracy of his view, Epstein persisted: "Well, I knew I was right, so I really didn't care." But in order to convince others, he needed reason and evidence. Epstein prefers experiments, so he sought but was refused permission to test his hypotheses in laboratories in Britain. "I remember that Yvonne Barr was very upset that in fact we had to send it abroad, to America . . . in order to pursue these further studies and get some independent confirmation of our . . . findings" (Epstein 1988, 164). Scientists with revolutionary claims always encounter powerful opposition.

Where research clusters form, they benefit from the research and political successes of their adherents. Once again, I will cite Gleick's work on chaos theory to illustrate a point:

> Every scientist who turned to chaos early had a story to tell of discouragement or open hostility. Graduate students were warned that their careers could be jeopardized if they wrote theses in an untested discipline. . . . A particle physicist . . . might begin playing with it on his own . . . but would feel that he could never tell his colleagues about it. Older professors felt they were suffering a kind of midlife crisis, gambling on a line of research that many colleagues were likely to misunderstand and resent. . . .
> To some the difficulty of communicating the new ideas and the ferocious resistance from traditional quarters showed how revolutionary the new science was. . . .
> As the chaos specialists spread, some departments frowned on these somewhat deviant scholars; others advertised for more. Some journals established unwritten rules against submissions on chaos; other journals came forth to handle chaos exclusively. . . . By the middle of the eighties a process of academic diffusion had brought chaos specialists into influential positions within university bureaucracies (1987, 37–38).

New questions and answers, especially those that challenge existing approaches, engender active opposition. Research success requires political success, and political success requires research success—the two go hand in hand.

Passion and controversy filled the media during the spring and summer of 1989 when two chemists claimed to have discovered "fusion in a flask" or "cold fusion." It is impossible to exaggerate the significance of their claims: Developing the engineering consequences of their discovery would solve all of our energy problems. At the same time, their successes would have destroyed theories long held dear by almost all physicists. As a result, their first reports received enormous media attention and rabid opposition from physicists. Indeed, the conflict spread to involve leaders of the national associations of both chemists and physicists. Consider this report from the battlefront:

> In mid-April, at a meeting of the American Chemical Society in Dallas, chemists cheered the work of their colleagues, Drs. B. Stanley Pons . . . and Martin Fleischmann. . . .
> After years of expensive failure by physicists, "it appears that chemists may have come to the rescue," the society's president, Dr. Clayton F. Callis, told an enthusiastic crowd.
> Last week, the other team struck back.
> At a meeting of the American Physical Society in Baltimore, physicists smugly reported that, try as they might, some of the best laboratories in the country have failed to replicate the cold fusion experiment. Physicists applauded when Dr. Steven E. Koonin said the phenomenon was a result of "the incompetence and delusion of Pons and Fleischmann" (Johnson 1989, E6).

A year later, the controversy no longer involved physicists in battle against chemists, and the media no longer kept score on whether the breakthrough had occurred. Pons, Fleischmann, and others interested in cold fusion were still at work trying to provide compelling evidence to support their claims.

The disciplines, fields, research schools, clusters, and cliques of science have different levels of conflict and, as these reports emphasize, conflicts do abound. But as Kuhn points out, most research falls within the category of normal science and does not challenge accepted schools of analysis. Such studies naturally are not greeted with hostility and do not generate conflict. And many, if not most, challenges to orthodox wisdom fail. Only the successful scientists get to tell their tales for only the successful combine adequate reason, evidence, and political support.

Where There Are Power, Dissension, and Conflict, We Find Ambiguous Conclusions

It should be evident by now that political science is not the only science in which claims to knowledge are more or less compelling. Nowhere are there simple rules that may be applied in order to certify knowledge. The existing rules allow us to assess claims to knowledge, but they do not provide definitive evaluations. But all scientists must accept and reject propositions. In the words of Scientist G, quoted in Mitroff's study of the Apollo researchers:

> In every real scientific problem I've ever seen, the evidence by itself never settled anything because two scientists of different outlook could both take the same evidence and reach entirely different conclusions. You eventually settle the differences, but not because of the evidence itself but because you develop a preference for one set of assumptions over the other. How you do this is not clear. . . .
>
> I've learned by now that you never completely prove or disprove anything; you just make it more or less probable with the best of what means you've got at the time (1974, 588–589).

Hull reiterates this position time and again, emphasizing one of the central theses of this chapter:

> Reason, argument, and evidence are supposed to decide controversies in science, but when scientists have to make choices, evidence is never totally determinate, nor arguments overwhelmingly convincing. More than one alternative is not just possible but also plausible. The appropriate conclusion to such realizations is not that anything goes. There has to be some middle ground between the one and only possible answer and total arbitrariness (1988, 288).
>
> In any instance of apparent falsification, too many alternative sources of error are not only possible but plausible. If one could be absolutely sure that a particular observation is veridical and that no modification elsewhere can save a particular hypothesis, then single-minded attention to falsification would be justified. However, in the real world, scientists must balance confirming instances against apparent disconfirmations and make their decisions accordingly (1988, 342–343).

These points apply not only to work in physics and biology but to political science in particular and the social sciences in general. We seek to know the world, while accepting that there are no simple techniques to ensure the brilliance of our analysis and no rules to certify the reliability and generalizability of our claims. But there are rules to guide analyses, allowing us to reach reasoned choices among alternatives. And over time, there are successes. "We have in [the scientific] community the tradition of argument and counter-argument . . . and the success of science gives us reason to rely on the element of judgment that is inevitably involved in resolving these disputes" (Newton-Smith 1981, 117). Science is a successful and necessarily limited effort to know the world.

**Where Science Takes Us and Where It Does Not:
The Limits of Knowledge at the University**

These studies produce a complex and realistic view of science. This scientific mode of reasoning has produced enormous intellectual and technological successes. Reason and evidence always matter, even if nonrational factors affect the effort to know the world. And science is more than the manipulation of knowledge in the defense and pursuit of power. A discipline that merits the claim of science produces knowledge, even if it does not produce absolute truth. All efforts to understand the world are aided and limited by the questions asked, the theories and hypotheses offered, and the methods used to test the claims to knowledge. In addition, all disciplines are characterized by alternative schools of analysis, by dissension, and by conflict. Every scientist faces the problem that reason and evidence rarely compel acceptance or rejection of a particular hypothesis. And all recognize that their analyses can provide only partial understandings of the world. In science, using reason and evidence to create public knowledge, we know that we may be wrong even as we strive to be right. We seek not to be a science but to do science.

In the process, we confront powerful frustrations. Recall Weber's discussion of science, which we examined in the second chapter. Using the image of the "disenchantment of the world," Weber remarks that when we assume that everything may be known, as we do in science, we place a weighty burden on our own shoulders. Because we expect to know more and more, whatever we know now is only temporarily true. Each success is only a step toward the next success, which, in turn, is a step toward the next, and so on, forever. Scientists never die "old and satiated with life," as the Bible describes Abraham. Rather, we must expect that our claims to know the world, as partial as they may be, will become outmoded. We devote ourselves to uncovering the order in the universe, knowing that we can have no more than limited successes. Indeed, given the descriptions presented in this chapter, we know that our efforts will meet disagreement, sometimes even strident opposition. But to do science, we must either ignore or overcome these frustrations.

Don't let these pressures and limitations block your studies. "Of course, the history of science is a history of flux. Of course, our current theories are doomed. Of course, in so far as truth (strictly speaking) is concerned all theories stand together. For they are all false. But admitting that the historical scene is a flux does not mean that nothing is preserved or that there is no progress" (Newton-Smith 1981, 260). We continue to seek to know the world because we *need* to know it and because that is what we do at the university. We also strive to learn in order to improve the world and to limit the harm that might happen in the future.

The tools of reason and evidence define our work and lives at the university. Only when we use them can we know the world in ways that produce public, as opposed to private, knowledge. These activities do not define our sum and substance as humans, but they guide our efforts to know the world beyond the university's walls.

At the same time, you should remember that we are not only creatures of the university, of science, and of reason and evidence. Weber fears that the rational calculations of science illustrate the spread of instrumental value rational orientations to action in every aspect of our lives. But Weber errs. There is no reason to maintain that emotions and commitments to absolute values are not important in the lives of most people or even in the lives of scientists. We have not become "clerks," and there is little basis to the claim that we are all rational maximizers of our personal interests at all times and in all circumstances. Max Weber to the contrary, you need not be reduced to a rational calculator, coldly sifting through the evidence, in order to do science. Indeed, to do science you must engage your passion as well as your reason.

POLITICAL SCIENCE AS A SCIENCE

Political scientists agree that there is a "real world" of politics and that we strive to analyze it. They display a shared language of research, which emphasizes conceptual neatness and the analysis of empirical evidence. When you do political science, you should specify hypotheses, properly define concepts and variables, and locate the hypotheses in logically coherent arguments or theories. Where appropriate, you should do fieldwork, and if you have reliable and valid data, you should display supporting numbers, graphs, tables, and equations. At the same time, you know that work in political science varies in the extent to which it possesses tightly knit logics and makes use of the full powers of statistical analyses.

Agreement over the language of analysis gives way to disagreement over approaches to analysis. Looked at as a whole, the study of turnout is characterized by four competing research schools: Wolfinger and Rosenstone's hypotheses, which draw on political attitudes; Powell's combination of structural and attitudinal variables; Jackman's emphasis on structural variables linked to assumptions about voters that are rooted in rational choice theory; and Piven and Cloward's structural analysis, which utilizes Marxist theory. Taken together, they do not provide a coherent answer to the question of how to explain variation in the level of turnout. There is, as well, disagreement over the analysis of electoral behavior. In the Michigan model, party identification is basic to the analysis, yet Rose and McAllister, I, and numerous other political scientists have offered many reasons to dismiss studies that use this variable. Rational choice theorists have offered new hypotheses for electoral behavior that contradict propositions taken from structural analyses, as well as models based on political attitudes. As Hull notes with regard to the term "physicists," it makes little sense to speak of "political scientists" as such, given the diversity of this field.

The cacophony of theoretical dissension gives way to the distinct choruses of separate research clusters. From the perspective of each approach, we are given explanations of turnout, electoral behavior, political violence, and a host of other subjects with varied amounts of theoretical power and empirical evidence to support them. No hypothesis is so weak that it denies the utility of its theoretical approach or causes members of the research cluster that offers it to abandon their theory. And no hypothesis is so strong as to compel its acceptance. Research occurs within clusters of scientists who share language, method, and argument and pay little regard to alternative schools of analysis.

Note as well that such research clusters usually examine different subject matters, further dividing political science. Wolfinger and Rosenstone reflect a long-standing orientation among students of political attitudes that emphasizes the uniqueness of U.S. politics; indeed, it even defines "American Politics" as a separate field. Following the logic of Marxist theory, Piven and Cloward locate the special characteristics of U.S. politics under a broader concept, implying the need for cross-national analyses. Both Powell's and Jackman's approaches, which use the explanatory power of structural variables, also emphasize the need for cross-national analysis. Students of voting behavior also disagree over the utility of carving along geographical lines. And for a long time, proponents of the Michigan model (and other studies emphasizing political attitudes) examined voting in the United States to the near exclusion of all other cases, while analyses employing the structural perspectives (especially the emphasis on social class) focused on voting in other democracies. Differences in subject matter, as well as methodology and theory, separate the research clusters of political science.

In political science, as in other disciplines, dissension is frequently accompanied by conflict. The clash between Wolfinger and Rosenstone and Piven and Cloward over how best to increase the level of turnout in the United States is typical. Different recommendations to political candidates would flow from Marxist theorists, rational choice proponents, and students of electoral behavior that use the Michigan model. And deep differences separate rational actor, Marxist, Weberian, and deprived actor models of political violence. In our field, interest in current events and the pull of political ideologies further exacerbate these conflicts. Inevitably, as political scientists compete for professional appointments, research grants, and influence over government officials, members of research clusters come into conflict with each.

Do not expect to find absolute truth in political science. As in all sciences, knowledge in this field is limited by the methods employed, the questions asked, and the hypotheses offered. This does not mean that political science is a hallucination; rather, it implies that you must be very careful about how you use the theories of political science to engineer changes in the world around you. Knowledge is relative to the theoretical approaches used.

DOING POLITICAL SCIENCE

Strive to know the political world: Engage your passions, check them with reason and evidence, and push ahead with the work. When you do that, you do political science.

In political science, you take leaps of intellectual daring, and you take them in public. Success does not come to the timid. The more sweeping your hypotheses are and the more tightly drawn the threads of your theories are, the stronger your claims will be and the more reason you will have to test them. Do not be intimidated by the thought that politics is "oh so complicated." This fear will tie you down and limit your daring.

Present your hypotheses and test them. As tougher tests are applied to your ideas, you will find added reasons to hold them and an increased ability to convince others.

Do not fix your sights on current events. Analyzing only the immediate and the familiar inhibits knowledge. It does not make for expertise. An important reason why so many people were surprised by the revolutions in Eastern Europe during 1989 was that political scientists had not been working on the broad problem of revolution in Communist systems. Too many students of these political systems busied themselves with day-to-day events, especially the nuances of politics among the leaders of the various Communist parties, and too few examined the conditions that lead to revolution in authoritarian regimes. Do not limit yourself to the analysis of the most recent election or war. For example, keep in mind that, as political scientists, we are interested in the determinants of turnout in the United States as part of the general analysis of political participation and that we care about the changes in Eastern Europe because it helps us to analyze the general question of revolution. Allow your mind to soar to questions of theoretical importance.

Strive to control the influence of your political preferences on your analysis. Do not give them up, but use the tools of analysis to keep you from being led by your dreams alone. In a field like political science, in which everyone has views about the subject matter and in which there are relatively few theories, insufficient data, and few compelling claims to knowledge, it is all too easy to allow your wishes to replace reason and evidence. The best way to keep your political preferences in check is to purposefully and consciously increase the role of theory and observation in your analysis.

Push yourself to follow the implications of your hypotheses. Tie your claims to other propositions, and increase the net and strength of your ideas. Follow through on a decision to use only a defined set of explanatory variables by exploring the logical implications and empirical outcomes of this choice. Hull is probably right when he cautions us not to expect seamless webs of proposition. Still, weaving patchwork nets takes the willingness to push your thread through coarse material.

Consider when it is time to discard critical assumptions. I have argued that rational choice theorists have been too quick to modify their assumptions and that Marxists and exponents of the Michigan school of electoral analysis have been too slow. Where do you stand on these questions?

The use of mathematical reasoning enhances your ability to elaborate your ideas. Indeed, Einstein, rational choice theorists, and many others imply that only the use of mathematical proofs permits the development of these implications. And it is clearly true that precision about evidence demands appropriate measures and quantification. If you intend to examine the world out there as it exists, you must make sure that your indicators are both reliable and valid. Where appropriate, you should do fieldwork. You also need to master the relevant statistical techniques that facilitate data analysis. These points are crucial.

Shift the level of analysis from the particular to the more general so that you enhance your ability to speak to questions of theory. I have argued that we cannot explain cases without reference to theories, but do not suppose that you must offer universal laws of politics. Strive, instead, to advance hypotheses that apply to types of political systems.

Tackle big questions. Look at the problem of the social sciences in the context of all the sciences. Why does so much research occur at the frontier? Why do so many citations refer to recent work and not to the classics that compose a core of knowledge? In the absence of well-developed theories and in the presence of pervasive interest in current problems, you should not be surprised that political science, like its related disciplines in the social sciences, stands apart from the other sciences. Contemplate, too, the issue of explanation in the social sciences. Weber reiterated a widely held principle when he insisted that the way to study politics, economics, and society derives from the unique characteristics of humans. This position demands that you focus on the purposeful action of humans, and it suggests that explanations in the social sciences should include motives as explanatory variables. Many of the analyses you examined accept this point. Indeed, most of you began this book with that assumption in mind, and many may still retain it. Is there reason to jettison this principle? I would urge you to study the means by which political scientists can develop techniques to address the unique properties of humans. Consider whether the search for motives has inhibited the ability of political scientists to offer powerful hypotheses, which explain by offering statistical patterns and theoretical principles but no motives. Above all, as you strive to analyze politics, strive, as well, to examine the basic questions of the discipline itself.

REFERENCES

Almond, Gabriel A., and Verba, Sidney. *The Civic Culture: Political Attitudes and Democracy in Five Nations.* Princeton: Princeton University Press, 1963.

Alt, James. "Dealignment and the Dynamics of Partisanship in Britain." In *Electoral Change in Advanced Industrial Democracies: Realignment or Dealignment,* edited by Russell J. Dalton, Scott C. Flanagan, and Paul Allen Beck. Princeton: Princeton University Press, 1984.

Asher, Herbert. "Voting Behavior Research in the 1980s: An Examination of Some Old and New Problem Areas." In *Political Science: The State of the Discipline,* edited by Ada Finifter. Washington, D.C.: American Political Science Association, 1983.

Beck, Paul Allen. "The Dealignment Era in America." In *Electoral Change in Advanced Industrial Democracies: Realignment or Dealignment,* edited by Russell J. Dalton, Scott C. Flanagan, and Paul Allen Beck. Princeton: Princeton University Press, 1984.

Bentley, Arthur. *The Process of Government.* Chicago: University of Chicago Press, 1909.

Berry, Michael. "The Electron at the End of the Universe." In *A Passion for Science,* edited by Lewis Wolpert and Alison Richards. Oxford: Oxford University Press, 1988.

Bottomore, T. B., and Rubel, Maximilien, eds. *Karl Marx: Selected Writings in Sociology and Social Philosophy.* New York: McGraw-Hill, 1964.

Broad, William J. "If Theory Is Right, Most of the Universe Is Missing." *New York Times,* September 11, 1984.

Brown, Harold I. *Observation and Objectivity.* New York: Oxford University Press, 1987.

Brush, Stephen G. "Prediction and Theory Evaluation: The Case of Light Bending." *Science* 246 (1989):1124–1129.

Butler, David and Stokes, Donald. *Political Change in Britain: The Evolution of Electoral Choice.* New York: St. Martin's Press, 1974.

Campbell, Angus, Converse, Philip E., Miller, Warren E., and Stokes, Donald E. *The American Voter.* New York: Wiley, 1960.

Campbell, Donald T. "Science's Social System of Validity-Enhancing Collective Belief Change and the Problems of the Social Sciences." In *Metatheory and Social Science: Pluralisms and Subjectivities,* edited by Donald W. Fiske and Richard A. Shweder. Chicago: University of Chicago Press, 1986.

Campbell, Donald T., and Ross, H. Laurence. "The Connecticut Crackdown on Speeding: Time Series Data in Quasi-Experimental Analysis." *Law and Society Review* 3 (1968):33–53.

Carmines, Edward G., and Stimson, James A. "The Two Faces of Issue Voting." *American Political Science Review* 74 (1980):78–91.

Cole, Stephen. "The Hierarchy of the Sciences?" *American Journal of Sociology* 89 (1983):111–139.

Converse, Philip E., and Markus, Gregory. " 'Plus Ça Change . . . ': The New CPS Election Study Panel." In *Controversies in Voting Behavior,* edited by Richard Niemi and Herbert F. Weisberg. 2d ed. Washington, D.C.: Congressional Quarterly Press, 1984.

Converse, Philip E., and Pierce, Roy. *Political Representation in France.* Cambridge, Mass.: Harvard University Press, 1986.

Cook, Thomas D., and Campbell, Donald T. *Quasi-Experimentation: Design and Analysis Issues for Field Settings.* Boston: Houghton Mifflin, 1979.

Crewe, Ivor, Sarlvick, Bo, and Alt, James. "Partisan Realignment in Britain." *British Journal of Political Science* 7 (1977):129–190.

Dalton, Russell J. *Citizen Politics in Western Democracies.* Chatham, N.J.: Chatham House, 1988.

Dalton, Russell J., Flanagan, Scott C., and Beck, Paul Allen. "Political Forces and Partisan Change." In *Electoral Change in Advanced Industrial Democracies: Realignment or Dealignment,* edited by Russell J. Dalton, Scott C. Flanagan, and Paul Allen Beck. Princeton: Princeton University Press, 1984.

Downs, Anthony. *An Economic Theory of Democracy.* New York: Harper and Row, 1957.

Duverger, Maurice. *Political Parties: Their Organization and Activity in the Modern State.* Translated by Barbara and Robert North. New York: Wiley, 1967.

Eisenstadt, S. N., ed. *Max Weber on Charisma and Institution Building.* Chicago: University of Chicago Press, 1968.

Eldridge, J.E.T., ed. *Max Weber: The Interpretation of Social Reality.* New York: Schocken, 1980.

Elster, John, ed. *Rational Choice.* Oxford: Basil Blackwell, 1986.

Epstein, Anthony. "Between the Lines." In *A Passion for Science,* edited by Lewis Wolpert and Alison Richards. Oxford: Oxford University Press, 1988.

Faust, David. *The Limits of Scientific Reasoning.* Minneapolis: University of Minnesota Press, 1984.

Fazio, Russell H. "How Do Attitudes Guide Behavior?" In *The Handbook of Motivation and Cognition,* edited by R. M. Sorrentino and E. T. Higgins. New York: Guilford Press, 1986.

Fazio, Russell H., and Williams, Carol J. "Attitude Accessibility As a Moderator of the Attitude-Perception and Attitude-Behavior Relations: An Investigation of the 1984 Presidential Election." *Journal of Personality and Social Psychology* 51 (1986):505–514.

Feldman, Stanley, and Zuckerman, Alan S. "Partisan Attitudes and the Vote: Moving Beyond Party Identification." *Comparative Political Studies* 15 (1982):197–222.

Ferejohn, John, and Fiorina, Morris. "The Paradox of Not Voting: A Decision Theoretic Analysis." *American Political Science Review* 69 (1974):525–536.

Feyerabend, Paul. *Against Method.* Atlantic Highlands, N.J.: Humanities Press, 1975.

Fiorina, Morris. *Retrospective Voting in American National Elections.* New Haven: Yale University Press, 1981.

Fiske, Donald W., and Shweder, Richard A., eds. *Metatheory and Social Science: Pluralisms and Subjectivities.* Chicago: University of Chicago Press, 1986.

Franklin, Mark, and Mughan, Anthony. "The Decline of Class Voting In Britain: Problems of Analysis and Interpretation." *American Political Science Review* 72 (1978):523–534.

Frolich, Norman, and Oppenheimer, Joe A. *Modern Political Economy.* Englewood Cliffs, N.J.: Prentice-Hall, 1978.

Geertz, Clifford. *The Interpretation of Cultures.* New York: Basic Books, 1973.

Gellner, Ernest. *Relativism and the Social Sciences.* Cambridge: Cambridge University Press, 1985.

Gerth, Hans, and Mills, C. Wright, eds. *From Max Weber: Essays in Sociology.* New York: Oxford University Press, 1958.

Gleick, James. *Chaos: Making a New Science.* New York: Viking, 1987.

Goldscheider, Calvin, and Zuckerman, Alan S. *The Transformation of the Jews.* Chicago: University of Chicago Press, 1984.

Gould, Stephen Jay. "Roots Writ Large." In *A Passion for Science,* edited by Lewis Wolpert and Alison Richards. Oxford: Oxford University Press, 1988.

Greenberg, Joel. "A Psychiatrist Who Wouldn't Take No for an Answer." *New York Times,* August 11, 1981.

Gurr, Ted Robert. "A Causal Model of Civil Strife: A Comparative Analysis Using New Indices." *American Political Science Review* 62 (1968):1004–1024.

―――. *Why Men Rebel.* Princeton: Princeton University Press, 1970.

Hechter, Michael. *The Principles of Group Solidarity.* Berkeley: University of California Press, 1988.

Hempel, Carl G. *Aspects of Scientific Explanation.* New York: The Free Press, 1965.

Hendel, Charles, ed. *David Hume's Political Essays.* New York: Liberal Arts Press, 1953.

Hobbes, Thomas. *Leviathan.* New York: Liberal Arts Press, 1958.

Holton, Gerald. *The Advancement of Science, and Its Burdens.* Cambridge: Cambridge University Press, 1986.

Hull, David L. *Science As a Process: An Evolutionary Account of the Social and Conceptual Development of Science.* Chicago: University of Chicago Press, 1988.

Inglehart, Ronald. *The Silent Revolution: Changing Values and Political Styles in Western Publics.* Princeton: Princeton University Press, 1977.

Iyengar, Shanto, and Kinder, Donald R. *News That Matters: Television and American Opinion.* Chicago: University of Chicago Press, 1987.

Jackman, Robert W. "Political Institutions and Voter Turnout in the Industrial Democracies." *American Political Science Review* 81 (1987):405–423.

Jackson, John E. "Issues, Party Choices, and Presidential Votes." *American Journal of Political Science* 19 (1975):161–185.

Janda, Kenneth, Berry, Jeffrey, and Goldman, Jerry. *The Challenge of Democracy: Government in America.* 2d ed. Boston: Houghton Mifflin, 1989.

Johnson, George. "On Fusion, the Chemists Have the Ball Now," *New York Times,* May 7, 1989.
Kaplan, Abraham. *The Conduct of Inquiry: Methodology for Behavioral Science.* New York: Chandler, 1974.
Katz, Richard S., Niemi, Richard D., and Newman, David. "Reconstructing Past Partisanship in Britain." *British Journal of Political Science* 10 (1980):505–515.
Katznelson, Ira. "Working-Class Formation: Constructing Cases and Comparisons." In *Working-Class Formation: Nineteenth Century Patterns in Western Europe and the United States,* edited by Ira Katznelson and Aristide R. Zolberg. Princeton: Princeton University Press, 1986.
Katznelson, Ira, and Zolberg, Aristide R., eds. *Working-Class Formation: Nineteenth Century Patterns in Western Europe and the United States.* Princeton: Princeton University Press, 1986.
Keefe, William J., Abraham, Henry J., Flanigan, William H., Jones, Charles O., Ogul, Morris S., and Spanier, John. *American Democracy: Institutions, Politics, and Policies.* 3d ed. New York: Harper and Row, 1989.
Kelley, Stanley, Jr., and Mirer, Thad W. "The Simple Act of Voting." *American Political Science Review* 68 (1974):572–591.
Key, V. O. *The Responsible Electorate.* Cambridge, Mass.: Harvard University Press, 1966.
Kimberling, William C. "Voting for President: Participation in America." *The Federal Election Commission Journal of Election Administration* 15 (1988):21–28.
Kinder, Donald R., and Kiewiet, D. Roderick. "Sociotropic Politics: The American Case." *British Journal of Political Science* 11 (1981):129–161.
Kocka, Jurgen. "Problems of Working-Class Formation in Germany: The Early Years, 1800–1875." In *Working-Class Formation: Nineteenth Century Patterns in Western Europe and the United States,* edited by Ira Katznelson and Aristide R. Zolberg. Princeton: Princeton University Press, 1986.
Kuhn, Thomas S. *The Structure of Scientific Revolutions.* Chicago: University of Chicago Press, 1962.
Laakso, Markku, and Taagapera, Rein. " 'Effective' Number of Parties: A Measure with Application to Western Europe." *Comparative Political Studies* 12 (1979):3–27.
Lakatos, Imre. "Falsification and the Methodology of Scientific Research Programs." In *Criticism and the Growth of Knowledge,* edited by Imre Lakatos and Alan Musgrave. Cambridge: Cambridge University Press, 1974.
Lasswell, Harold. *Power and Personality.* New York: Viking, 1962a.
———. *Psychopathology and Politics.* New York: Viking, 1962b.
Laver, Michael. *The Politics of Private Desires: The Guide to the Politics of Rational Choice.* New York: Penguin, 1981.
Lenin, V. I. *What Is to Be Done?* New York: International Publishers, 1943.
Lichbach, Mark Irving. "An Evaluation of 'Does Economic Inequality Breed Political Conflict?' Studies." *World Politics* 41 (1989):431–470.
Lieberson, Stanley. *Making It Count: The Improvement of Social Research and Theory.* Berkeley: University of California Press, 1985.

Marx, Karl. *Capital: A Critique of Political Economy.* New York: The Modern Library, 1906.
Marx, Karl, and Engels, Friedrich. *The German Ideology: Parts I and II.* New York: International Publishers, 1963.
McGaw, Dickinson, and Watson, George. *Political and Social Inquiry.* New York: Wiley, 1976.
Meehl, Paul. "The Selfish Voter Paradox and the Thrown-Away Vote Argument." *American Political Science Review* 71 (1977):11–30.
———. "What Social Scientists Don't Understand." In *Metatheory and Social Science: Pluralisms and Subjectivities,* edited by Donald W. Fiske and Richard A. Shweder. Chicago: University of Chicago Press, 1986.
Milbrath, Lester W., and Goel, M. L. *Political Participation.* 2d ed. Chicago: Rand, McNally, 1977.
Mitroff, Ian I. "Norms and Counter-Norms in a Select Group of the Apollo Moon Scientists: A Case Study of Ambivalence of Scientists." *American Sociological Review* 39 (1974):579–595.
Moe, Terry M. "A Calculus of Group Membership." *American Journal of Political Science* 24 (1980):593–633.
———. "Toward a Broader View of Interest Groups." *Journal of Politics* 43 (1981):531–543.
Mommsen, Wolfgang J. *The Age of Bureaucracy: Perspectives on the Political Sociology of Max Weber.* New York: Harper and Row, 1974.
Moore, Barrington, Jr. *Injustice: The Social Bases of Obedience and Revolt.* White Plains, N.Y.: M. E. Sharpe, 1978.
Muller, Edward N., and Opp, Karl-Dieter. "Rational Choice and Rebellious Collective Action." *American Political Science Review* 80 (1986):471–488.
Newton-Smith, W. H. *The Rationality of Science.* Boston: Routledge and Kegan Paul, 1981.
Nie, Norman, Verba, Sidney, and Petrocik, John. *The Changing American Voter.* Cambridge, Mass.: Harvard University Press, 1976.
Niemi, Richard D., Katz, Richard S., and Newman, David. "Reconstructing Past Partisanship: The Failure of the Party Identification Recall Questions." *American Journal of Political Science* 24 (1980):633–651.
Nolan, Mary. "Economic Crisis, State Policy, and Working-Class Formation in Germany, 1870–1900." In *Working-Class Formation: Nineteenth Century Patterns in Western Europe and the United States,* edited by Ira Katznelson and Aristide R. Zolberg. Princeton: Princeton University Press, 1986.
Offe, Claus. "Challenging the Boundaries of Institutional Politics: Social Movements Since the 1960s." In *Changing Boundaries of the Political: Essays on the Evolving Balance Between the State and the Society, Public and Private in Europe,* edited by Charles S. Maier. Cambridge: Cambridge University Press, 1987.
Olson, Mancur, Jr. *The Logic of Collective Action: Public Goods and the Theory of Groups.* New York: Schocken, 1968.
Ordeshook, Peter C. *Game Theory and Political Theory: An Introduction.* Cambridge: Cambridge University Press, 1986.

Page, Benjamin, and Jones, Calvin. "Reciprocal Effects of Policy Preferences, Party Loyalties, and the Vote." *American Political Science Review* 66 (1972):979–995.

Parsons, Talcott, ed. *Max Weber: The Theory of Social and Economic Organization.* New York: Free Press, 1964.

Pitt-Rivers, Julian A. *The People of the Sierra.* 2d ed. Chicago: University of Chicago Press, 1971.

Piven, Frances Fox, and Cloward, Richard A. *Why Americans Don't Vote.* New York: Pantheon, 1988.

Popper, Karl R. *Conjectures and Refutations: The Growth of Scientific Knowledge.* New York: Harper Torchbooks, 1965.

Powell, G. Bingham, Jr. *Contemporary Democracies: Participation, Stability, and Violence.* Cambridge, Mass.: Harvard University Press, 1982.

———. "American Voter Turnout in Comparative Perspective." *American Political Science Review* 80 (1986):17–43.

Pulzer, Peter G. J. *Political Representation and Elections: Parties and Voting in Great Britain.* New York: Praeger, 1967.

Putnam, Hilary. *Reason, Truth, and History.* Cambridge: Cambridge University Press, 1981.

Riker, William H. *The Theory of Political Coalitions.* New Haven: Yale University Press, 1962.

———. "The Two-party System and Duverger's Law: An Essay on the History of Political Science." *American Political Science Review* 76 (1982):753–766.

Riker, William H., and Ordeshook, Peter C. "The Calculus of Voting." *American Political Science Review* 62 (1968):25–42.

Rogowski, Ronald. "Social Class and Partisanship in European Electorates: A Reassessment." *World Politics* 33 (1981):639–649.

Rose, Richard, and McAllister, Ian. *Voters Begin to Choose: From Closed-Class to Open Elections in Britain.* Beverly Hills, Calif.: Sage, 1986.

Ross, Marc Howard. "Political Organization and Political Participation: Exit, Voice, and Loyalty in Pre-Industrial Societies." *Comparative Politics* 21 (1988a): 73–90.

———. "Studying Politics Cross-Culturally: Key Concepts and Issues." *Behavior Science Research* (1988b):105–129.

Rothman, Tony. *Science à la Mode: Physical Fashions and Fictions.* Princeton: Princeton University Press, 1989.

Runciman, W. G. *Weber: Selections in Translation.* Cambridge: Cambridge University Press, 1978.

Sarlvick, Bo, and Crewe, Ivor. *Decade of Dealignment: The Conservative Victory in 1979 and Electoral Trends in the 1970s.* Cambridge: Cambridge University Press, 1983.

Schmitter, Philippe C. "Interest Intermediation and Regime Governability in Contemporary Western Europe and North America." In *Organizing Interests in Western Europe,* edited by Suzanne Berger. Cambridge: Cambridge University Press, 1981.

Shefter, Martin. "Trade Unions and Political Machines: The Organization and Disorganization of the American Working Class in the Late Nineteenth Century." In *Working-Class Formation: Nineteenth Century Patterns in Western Europe and the United States,* edited by Ira Katznelson and Aristide R. Zolberg. Princeton: Princeton University Press, 1986.

Shively, W. Phillips. "The Development of Party Identification Among Adults: Exploration of a Functional Model." *American Political Science Review* 73 (1979):1039–1054.

Smelser, Neil J., ed. *Karl Marx on Society and Social Change.* Chicago: University of Chicago Press, 1973.

Stent, Gunther. "Telling Nature." In *A Passion for Science,* edited by Lewis Wolpert and Alison Richards. Oxford: Oxford University Press, 1988.

Tilly, Charles. *The Contentious French.* Cambridge, Mass.: Harvard University Press, 1986.

Tucker, Robert C., ed. *The Marx-Engels Reader.* 2d ed. New York: Norton, 1978.

Van der Eijk, C., and Niemoller, B. "The Netherlands." In *Electoral Change in Western Democracies: Patterns and Sources of Electoral Volatility,* edited by Ivor Crewe and David Denver. New York: St. Martin's Press, 1985.

Van Fraasen, Bas C. *The Scientific Image.* Oxford: The Clarendon Press, 1980.

———. "Empiricism in the Philosophy of Science." In *Images of Science: Essays on Realism and Empiricism with a Reply from Bas C. Van Fraasen,* edited by Paul M. Churchland and Clifford A. Hooker. Chicago: University of Chicago Press, 1986.

Verba, Sidney, and Nie, Norman H. *Participation in America.* New York: Harper and Row, 1972.

Verba, Sidney, Nie, Norman H., and Kim, Jae-on. *Participation and Political Equality: A Seven Nation Comparison.* Cambridge: Cambridge University Press, 1978.

Walker, Jack L. "The Origins and Maintenance of Interest Groups in America." *American Political Science Review* 81 (1983):390–405.

Weber, Max. *The Protestant Ethic and the Spirit of Capitalism.* New York: Scribner's, 1958.

Weisberg, Herbert F. "A Multidimensional Conceptualization of Party Identification." In *Controversies in Voting Behavior,* edited by Richard Niemi and Herbert F. Weisberg. 2d ed. Washington, D.C.: Congressional Quarterly Press, 1984.

Wolfinger, Raymond E., and Steven J. Rosenstone. *Who Votes?* New Haven: Yale University Press, 1980.

Wolpert, Lewis, and Richards, Alison. "A Passion for Science." In *A Passion for Science,* edited by Lewis Wolpert and Alison Richards. Oxford: Oxford University Press, 1988.

Zolberg, Aristide R. "How Many Exceptionalisms?" In *Working-Class Formation: Nineteenth Century Patterns in Western Europe and the United States,* edited by Ira Katznelson and Aristide R. Zolberg. Princeton: Princeton University Press, 1986.

Zuckerman, Alan S. "New Approaches to Political Cleavage: A Theoretical Introduction." *Comparative Political Studies* 15 (1982):131–144.

———. "The Bases of Political Cohesion: Applying and Reconstructing Crumbling Theories." *Comparative Politics* 21 (1989):473–496.

Zuckerman, Alan S., and Lichbach, Mark Irving. "Stability and Change in European Electorates." *World Politics* 29 (1977):523–552.

ABOUT THE BOOK
AND AUTHOR

In this concise but wide-ranging text, Alan Zuckerman introduces the reader to the various approaches to political explanation. He shows how researchers espousing different theoretical assumptions, levels of explanation, variables, and data come to offer conflicting accounts of the phenomena to be studied. He then introduces five paradigms of political explanation—those associated primarily with rational choice theory, political psychology, community analysis, Marx, and Weber.

Zuckerman brings out not only what these explanatory models say about politics but, more importantly, what they presuppose about the nature of political explanation. Good explanations in any field require variables that can be operationalized and hypotheses that can be tested intersubjectively, and Zuckerman shows how political scientists use these methods. But his discussions are also informed by contemporary philosophy of science, which leads to an appreciation of how even the most firmly established claims are in fact limited and tentative. This appreciation is especially important when explanations from different paradigms must be compared and evaluated.

Zuckerman conveys confidence in the value of good political analysis to his readers, helping them to develop a sophisticated understanding of the analytical options for thinking about politics. This is a splendid text for beginning students of political science as well as for those more advanced students who want to review and reflect on contemporary modes of thought in political analysis.

Alan S. Zuckerman is professor of political science and Judaic studies and director of the social science data center at Brown University. He has also served as Fulbright professor of political science at Tel-Aviv University and the University of Pisa and visiting research fellow at the University of Essex. Among his publications are *The Politics of Faction: Christian Democratic Rule in Italy* and *The Transformation of the Jews* as well as numerous articles on Jewish communities, the Holocaust of European Jewry, political cleavages, political parties, and electoral behavior.

INDEX

Almond, Gabriel and Sidney Verba, 55, 76
Alternative explanations, 13–14, 26, 62, 84–87, 124–131
"American exceptionalism," 40–41
"American Politics" as a research field, 178–179
American Voter, The (Campbell et al.), 54, 95
Anthropological approach, 58–60, 60–63, 113–114
Austria, 31
Authority structures, 77–78

Berry, Michael, 162
Brown, Harold, 4, 5, 6, 12–13, 116, 118, 158
Bureaucracy, 78, 86–87
Butler, David and Donald Stokes, 99

Campbell, Angus, Philip E. Converse, Warren E. Miller, and Donald E. Stokes, 95
Campbell, Donald T., 164–165, 167
Campbell Donald T. and H. Laurence Ross, 127
Canada, 30
Capital: A Critique of Political Economy (Marx), 64
Capitalism, 68–72, 105–106, 109
Carmines, Edward and James Stimson, 98
Changing American Voter, The (Nie, Verba, and Petrocik), 97–98
Chaos theory and ambiguity in science, 159, 172, 173
Charismatic leadership, 78, 86–87
Civic Culture, The (Almond and Verba), 55
Class, 87–89, 92–94
 and Marxist theory, 66–72, 73–74, 81
 and voting behavior, 34–38, 99
Class Struggles in France: 1848 to 1850, The (Marx), 64

Coalitions, 47–48
Cole, Stephen, 168–169, 170
Conceptual contexts, 2, 3, 8–10, 117–118
Conjectures and Refutations: The Growth of Scientific Knowledge (Popper), 119
Construct validity of putative causes, 37, 128–129, 136
Contribution to the Critique of Political Economy, A (Marx), 64, 65–66
Converse, Philip E. and Gregory Markus, 97, 98
Converse, Philip E. and Roy Pierce, 99–100, 101, 135, 137
Cook, Thomas D. and Donald T. Campbell, 122, 123, 124, 130
Cross-cultural generalizations, 58, 60–63
Current events and political science, 1, 14–15, 179–180

Diversity of political science, 13–14, 18, 177–179
Downs, Anthony, 50, 51, 112, 145

"Economic Crisis, State Policy, and Working-Class Formation in Germany, 1870-1900" (Nolan), 93
Economic issues, 21–24, 97
 and Marxist theory, 65–66
 and political violence, 144–145, 149
Economic Theory of Democracy, An (Downs), 97
Education and voter turnout, 19–20, 21–24
Eighteenth Brumaire of Louis Bonaparte, The (Marx), 64, 70
Einstein, Albert, 152, 153, 157, 158, 159, 162
Electoral behavior. *See* Voting behavior

Electoral Change in Advanced Industrial Democracies (Dalton, Flanagan, and Beck), 102
Epstein, Anthony, 161, 173
Ethnic violence and Marxist theory, 146
"Evaluation of 'Does Economic Inequality Breed Political Conflict?' Studies, An" (Lichbach), 110
Experimentation and political science, 123–124
Explanation, 81, 121
  in political science, 5, 6–7, 10–13, 181
  Weber on, 74, 75–78, 80
External validity, 129–130, 136

Faust, David, 163, 166
Fazio, Russell, 56–57
Feigenbaum, Mitchell, 154
Ferejohn, John and Morris Fiorina, 51
Feyerabend, Paul, 166–167
Finland, 31
Fiorina, Morris, 97
France, 99, 100
  political violence in, 105–106, 108, 109
  voting behavior in, 132, 135, 137

Geertz, Clifford, 59–63, 75, 81, 92, 130, 141
Gellner, Ernest, 4, 13, 79, 118, 151
German Ideology, The (Marx and Engels), 64, 66, 68–69, 70
Germany, 94, 138, 139–140, 141
  political violence in, 109
  Socialist party of, 85
  See also West Germany
Glashow, Sheldon, 160
Gleick, James, 159, 172, 173
Gould, Stephen Jay, 154, 158
Great Britain, 31, 55, 100, 137
  and the Michigan model, 99, 132, 135
  voting behavior in, 101, 102–104, 133, 146
Gurr, Ted Robert, 83, 110–111, 112, 113

Hechter, Michael, 91–92, 112, 145
Hierarchy of the sciences, 168–169, 170

Historical processes, 34–38, 37, 66–67
"Historical Specifics of the Class Struggle, The" (Marx), 70
Holton, Gerald, 153, 162
Holy Family, The (Marx and Engels), 65
Hull, David, 11, 158–159, 161, 162, 166, 175
  on explanation, 180
  on research clusters, 170–171
Hume, David, 48–49

Ideal-types, 77, 153
"If Theory Is Right, Most of the Universe Is Missing" (Broad), 169
Individual levels of analysis, 21, 39, 80, 81, 83, 105
Inglehart, Ronald, 101
Institutional context. *See* Structural level of analysis
Instrument reliability, 125
Interest groups, 90–92, 107–108, 109
Internal validity, 125–128, 130, 134–135, 136
Israel, 30
Italy, 31, 55
Iyengar, Shanto and Donald Kinder, 123

Jackman, Robert, 39, 40, 43–44, 83, 114, 125
  and the structural level of analysis, 63, 84, 178
Jackson, John, 97
Japan, 30

Kaplan, Abraham, 117, 160–161
Katznelson, Ira, 92–93
Kelley, Stanley, Jr. and Thad Mirer, 54, 97
Key, V. O., 97
Kinder, Donald and D. Roderick Kiewiet, 97
Kocka, Jurgen, 92–94, 138, 139, 140, 141
Kuhn, Thomas, 151, 163, 164, 174

Labor unions, 89–90, 93–94, 139
Laver, Michael, 45–46, 49, 51
Lichbach, Mark Irving, 110, 111, 142–145, 149

Logic of Collective Action, The (Olson), 88, 89

Marx, Karl, 72, 77, 78, 81, 84, 88, 153
  on class, 21, 93
  on revolution, 112–113, 131
  and the structural level of analysis, 80, 101
Marxist theory, 15, 44–45, 83–84, 113, 121
  and "American exceptionalism," 40–41
  and collective action, 87–88, 92–94
  and the nature of reality, 153
  and proposition evaluation, 146–147
Mathematical theory of games, 47–48
Meehl, Paul, 52, 119–120, 145, 146
  on the nature of reality, 154
  on testing knowledge claims, 132, 142, 151
Methodology of the Social Sciences, The (Weber), 72–73, 74
Mexico, 55
Michigan model, 54–55, 94, 95–97, 145, 178–179
  and continuing support of, 98–100
  reevaluations of, 103, 132, 135, 138
Mill, John Stuart, 122
"Minimax regret," 51
Mitroff, Ian, 155–156, 175
Moe, Terry, 91–92, 112, 145
Moore, Barrington, Jr., 7, 105, 108, 109, 110, 111, 113
Motivation, individual, 20, 21, 25, 40, 110
  and Weber on social science, 75–77, 80
Muller, Edward N. and Karl-Dieter Opp, 111–112, 145

National states and political violence, 105–106, 109
Netherlands, 31, 101–102, 108
Newton-Smith, W. H., 6, 8, 10, 116, 147, 150, 166
Nie, Norman, Sidney Verba, John Petrocik, 98
Nolan, Mary, 93–94, 138–141
Norway, 108

Observation, 117–118, 126, 180

Offe, Claus, 147
Olson, Mancur, Jr., 88, 89–90, 91, 144
Ordeshook, Peter, 51–52, 112, 145
Origins and Maintenance of Interest Groups in America (Walker), 90–91

Page, Benjamin and Calvin Jones, 97
Parties, political, 27, 54–55
  and political violence, 106–108, 109
Party identification, 11–12, 95–104, 134–138
Passion for Science, A (Wolpert and Richards), 156
Phenomenon reliability, 126
Piven, Frances Fox and Richard A. Cloward, 39, 40, 92, 114, 128–129, 179
  and Marxist theory, 44, 72, 83, 178
  on registration laws, 122, 126–127
Policy recommendations and political analysis, 27, 35, 38, 122
Political attitude analysis, 53–54, 83–84, 110–112, 113
  and Marxist theory, 65
  and the Michigan model, 98
  and proposition evaluation, 143–144
Political culture approach, 40, 54, 55
Political efficacy, 55, 59
Political ideologies and political science, 26–27, 179, 180
Political institutions. See Structural level of analysis
"Political Organization and Political Participation" (Ross), 60
Political psychology. See Political attitude analysis
Political Representation in France (Converse and Pierce), 99
Political socialization, 22–23, 52, 69, 96, 103
Politics of Private Desires, The (Laver), 45–46
Popper, Karl, 144, 147, 150
  on testing knowledge claims, 124, 131, 133, 141
  on theory, 11, 118, 119
Powell, G. Bingham Jr., 39, 40, 83, 106–107, 109, 110, 113
  and political efficacy, 55, 59

and the structural level of analysis, 63, 84, 178
on voting behavior, 54, 114, 125, 131
and Weberian analysis, 45, 76
Principles of Group Solidarity, The (Hechter), 91
"Problems of Working-Class Formation in Germany: The Early Years, 1800-1875" (Kocka), 92
Propositions, evaluation of, 131–134, 166–167
Protestant Ethic and the Spirit of Capitalism, The (Weber), 72, 131
"Psychiatrist Who Wouldn't Take No for an Answer, A" (Greenberg), 172–173

Quantification and knowledge claims, 119–120
Quasi-Experimentation: Design and Analysis Issues for Field Settings (Cook and Campbell), 122, 129

Racial violence and Marxist theory, 146
Rational action theory. *See* Rational choice theory
Rational choice theory, 44, 65, 83–84, 90–92, 110–113
and the Michigan model, 98
and proposition evaluation, 143–146
Rationality and claims to knowledge, 163, 166
Reality, nature of, 117, 153–154, 165–166
Registration laws, 25, 31, 34, 35, 38, 122, 126–127
Reliability, 9, 21–22
Reliability of data, 125–126
Religious violence and Marxist theory, 146
"Repertoires" of political action, 105–106
Research clusters in political science, 178–179
Responsible Electorate, The (Key), 97
Revolution, 66, 68, 69–72, 146
Riker, William, 47, 83, 112, 145–146
Riker, William and Peter Ordeshook, 50–51
Rival hypotheses, 13–14, 26, 62, 84–87, 124–131

Rogowski, Ronald, 135, 137, 146
Rose, Richard and Ian McAllister, 102–104, 113, 135, 137, 146
Ross, Marc Howard, 58, 60, 61–63, 83, 84

Schmitter, Philippe, 107–108, 109, 110, 113, 131
Science à la Mode (Rothman), 169–170
"Science as a Vocation" (Weber), 79
Selectivity bias, 127–128, 129–130
Self-interest, 45–50, 58, 88
"Selfish Voter Paradox and the Thrown-Away Vote Argument, The" (Meehl), 52
Shefter, Martin, 93–94, 138–139, 140, 141
Shively, W. Phillips, 99, 101
Social Democratic organization (Germany), 139, 140
"Socialism" (Weber), 73–74, 78, 131
Socialist party (Germany), 85
Social pressures and claims to knowledge, 164–167
Social status, 21–22, 24, 131
Statistical conclusion validity, 124, 130, 134–135, 142
Structural level of analysis, 39, 80, 83, 105
and class, 66–67
and economic issues, 64–65
and individual motivations, 110
and party systems, 106–107
and voting behavior, 28–33, 40–41
Structure of Scientific Revolutions, The (Kuhn), 151
Sweden, 108
Switzerland, 30, 31, 33, 108

Theory, 10–16, 117–118, 121, 180
and explanation, 43–45
and knowledge claims, 159–161
Theory of Political Coalitions, The (Riker), 47
Theses on Feuerbach (Marx), 64
Thick description, 59–60, 61, 75, 81, 92, 138, 141
Tilly, Charles, 105–106, 108, 109, 110, 113

INDEX

"Trade Unions and Political Machines: The Organization and Disorganization of the American Working Class in the Late Nineteenth Century" (Shefter), 93–94
Turnout, 50–52, 126–127, 178

Unions, 89–90, 93–94, 139

Validity, 9–10, 21–22. *See also* Construct validity of putative causes; External validity; Internal validity; Statistical conclusion validity
Van Der Eijk, C. and B. Niemoller, 101–102
Verba, Sidney and Norman Nie, 21–22
Verba, Sidney, Norman Nie, and Jae-on Kim, 29
Voters Begin to Choose: From Closed-Class to Open Elections in Britain (Rose and McAllister), 102
Voter turnout. *See* Turnout
Voting behavior, 24–25, 97, 178
  and age, 103, 136–137
  and class, 99, 135, 146
  and party identification, 95–104, 134–138
  See also Turnout

Walker, Jack, 90–91, 131
Weber, Max, 21, 81, 93, 101, 152, 181
  on capitalism, 84, 131
  on charismatic leadership, 86–87, 113
  on scientific knowledge, 80, 153, 176, 177
Weberian analysis, 15, 45, 121
Weisberg, Herbert, 97, 98–99
Western Europe, 30, 40–41, 107–110
West Germany, 31, 55. *See also* Germany
Who Votes? (Wolfinger and Rosenstone), 18–28, 27, 31, 32, 83
Why Americans Don't Vote (Piven and Cloward), 34–38
Why Men Rebel (Gurr), 83
Wolfinger, Raymond E. and Steven J. Rosenstone, 39, 43, 45, 63, 114, 121, 122
  and analysis of data, 76, 84, 125, 126, 128, 130, 141
  and Jackman, 33
  and Piven and Cloward, 35, 37
  and Powell, 29, 32
  and Riker and Ordeshook, 50
  on voting behavior, 31, 40, 54, 55, 59, 131, 178
"Working-Class Formation: Constructing Cases and Comparisons" (Katznelson), 92
Working-Class Formation: Nineteenth Century Patterns in Western Europe and the United States (Katznelson and Zolberg), 92

Zolberg, Aristide R., 92, 141
Zuckerman, Alan S. and Mark Irving Lichbach, 135, 146